EXPLORATIONS IN SOCIOLOGY
British Sociological Association conference volume series

* *from the same publishers*

Relating Intimacies

Power and Resistance

Edited by

Julie Seymour
Lecturer in Social Research
School of Comparative and Applied Social Sciences (CASS)
University of Hull

and

Paul Bagguley
Senior Lecturer in Sociology
Department of Sociology and Social Policy
University of Leeds

First published in Great Britain 1999 by
MACMILLAN PRESS LTD
Houndmills, Basingstoke, Hampshire RG21 6XS and London
Companies and representatives throughout the world

A catalogue record for this book is available from the British Library.

ISBN 0–333–74763–1 hardcover
ISBN 0–333–74764–X paperback

First published in the United States of America 1999 by
ST. MARTIN'S PRESS, INC.,
Scholarly and Reference Division,
175 Fifth Avenue, New York, N.Y. 10010

ISBN 0–312–22184–3

Library of Congress Cataloging-in-Publication Data
Relating intimacies : power and resistance / edited by Julie Seymour,
Paul Bagguley.
p. cm.
Includes bibliographical references and index.
ISBN 0–312–22184–3 (cloth)
1. Interpersonal relations—Great Britain. 2. Interpersonal
conflict—Great Britain. 3. Intimacy (Psychology) 4. Family—Great
Britain. 5. Marriage—Great Britain. 6. Same-sex marriage—Great
Britain. 7. Work and family—Great Britain. I. Bagguley, Paul.
II. Seymour, Julie.
HM132.R365 1999   99–18738
                                                                CIP

This book is printed on paper suitable for recycling and made from fully managed and sustained forest sources.

10   9   8   7   6   5   4   3   2   1
08   07   06   05   04   03   02   01   00   99

Printed and bound in Great Britain by
Antony Rowe Ltd, Chippenham, Wiltshire

Contents

List of Tables

List of Figures

Acknowledgements

Relating Intimacies comprises revised versions of papers originally presented at the British Sociological Association (BSA) Annual Conference, which was held at the University of York, 7–10 April 1997, on the theme 'Power/Resistance'. This volume is one of four produced from the papers given at the conference. The companion volumes are: *Consuming Cultures: Power and Resistance*, edited by Jeff Hearn and Sasha Roseneil; *Practising Identities: Power and Resistance*, edited by Sasha Roseneil and Julie Seymour; and *Transforming Politics: Power and Resistance*, edited by Paul Bagguley and Jeff Hearn.

The conference was one of the largest ever held by the BSA. Approximately 333 papers were presented, which made the task of selecting papers for publication particularly difficult. We would like to thank all the conference participants for their patience while we read the papers; inevitably there were many papers that we would have liked to have included but were unable to, in trying to make this and the other volumes into coherent collections. The contributors to this volume are particularly thanked for revising their papers so swiftly and efficiently in response to editorial comments and suggestions. We would also like to thank Valery Rose who carried out the copy-editing for Macmillan.

The theme of the conference – 'Power/Resistance' – is both a long-established theme within the discipline of sociology and one that has seen increased interest and re-evaluation in recent years. This sense of continuity and change was present throughout the conference. The four volumes bring together papers on major sub-themes that *emerged from* the conference, and as such it is probably fair to say that they give an indication and taste of some of the major preoccupations of sociology, particularly British sociology, in the late 1990s.

We are extremely grateful to the wonderfully good-humoured and patient staff at the BSA office both in Durham and at the conference itself – Nicky Gibson, Judith Mudd, Jean Punton (until November 1996), and especially Nicola Boyne. We also thank the Conference Office and the Department of Sociology at the University of York for their advice and hospitality, and the student helpers at the conference for their invaluable assistance. Special thanks are due to Sarah Irwin who was a member of the conference organizing committee in its early stages, prior to the demands of motherhood. Our thanks are also offered to our colleagues at the Universities of Leeds and Hull for their support and encouragement for the Yorkshire BSA Conference. Finally, the other two members of the organizing committee, Jeff Hearn and Sasha Roseneil, were a pleasure to work with, and the overall shape of the four volumes and the selections of the papers was decided collectively by all four of us.

JULIE SEYMOUR
PAUL BAGGULEY

Notes on the Contributors

Paul Bagguley is in the Department of Sociology and Social Policy at the University of Leeds. His main interests are in the areas of the sociology of protest, social movements, economic sociology and urban studies. He has carried out extensive research on unemployment and social protest, anti-poll tax protest and new social movements. His main publications include *From Protest to Acquiescence? Political Movements of the Unemployed* (1991), and he is co-author of *Restructuring: Place, Class and Gender* (1990). He has been a member of the editorial board of *Sociology*.

Pia Christensen is a Research Fellow in the School of Comparative and Applied Social Sciences (CASS) at the University of Hull. She is a social anthropologist with particular interests in childhood and is a founding member of the Centre for the Social Study of Childhood at CASS.

Catherine Donovan is a Senior Lecturer in the Department of Sociology in the School of Social and International Studies at the University of Sunderland. She has contributed to *The New Family?* (1999).

Gillian Dunne is a Research Fellow at the London School of Economics Gender Institute. She was formerly a Senior Research Associate in the Faculty of Social and Political Sciences at the University of Cambridge. She is currently researching different dimensions of gay fatherhood. Recent publications include *Lesbian Lifestyles: Women's Work and the Politics of Sexuality* (1997) and *Living 'Difference': Lesbian Perspectives on Work and Family Life* (editor, 1998).

Rosalind Edwards is a Reader in Social Policy at South Bank University. Her recent publications include *Feminist Dilemmas in Qualitative Research: Public Knowledge and Private Lives* (co-author, 1998).

Val Gillies is a Research Fellow at Oxford Brookes University, looking at the family lives of young people. She also has an interest in mothers in non-traditional relationships.

Brian Heaphy is a Research Fellow in the Social Sciences Research Centre at South Bank University. He has researched in the areas of non-heterosexual relationships, sexual identities and AIDS/HIV. He is currently completing (with Catherine Donovan and Jeffrey Weeks) a book based on the 'Families of Choice' research discussed in this volume.

Jenny Hockey is a Senior Lecturer in Health Studies in the School of Comparative and Applied Social Sciences (CASS) at the University of Hull. Her research interests include ageing, terminal care, bereavement and funeral management. She is co-editor of *Death, Gender and Ethnicity* (1997) and co-author of *Beyond the Body: Death and Social Identity* (1999).

Allison James is a Reader in Applied Anthropology in the School of Comparative and Applied Social Sciences (CASS) at the University of Hull. Her research includes the areas of medical anthropology and anthropological theory. She is a founding member of the Centre for the Social Study of Childhood at CASS and co-editor of *Theorising Childhood* (1998).

Steph Lawler is in the Department of Sociology and Social Policy at the University of Durham. Her research interests include: theories of selfhood and subjectivity with particular reference to gender and class, childhood as a social category, and mothering and the mother–daughter relationship. The work reported on in this volume will be published in *Mothering the Self: Mothers, Daughters, Subjectivities*.

Sara McNamee is a part-time lecturer in Sociology and Social Anthropology at the University of Hull. Her research interests include the sociology of childhood and youth, gender and leisure. She is a founder member of the Centre for the Social Study of Childhood at CASS.

Bren Neale is a Research Fellow in the Department of Sociology and Social Policy at the University of Leeds. She is a member of the Centre for Research on Family, Kinship and Childhood. She is co-author of *Family Fragments* (1998).

Jo Phoenix is a Lecturer in Criminology in the School of Social Science at Middlesex University. Her recent publications include *Making Sense of Prostitution* (1999). Her research interests include gender and crime, poverty, social justice and sexuality.

Jane Ribbens is a Senior Lecturer in Sociology and the Director of the Centre for Family and Household Research at Oxford Brookes University. She is co-editor of *Feminist Dilemmas in Qualitative Research: Public Knowledge and Private Lives* (1998) and author of *Mothers and their Children* (1994). Her research interests centre on family lives, especially parents and children, and theorising public and private.

Julie Seymour is a Lecturer in Social Research in the School of Comparative and Applied Social Sciences (CASS) at the University of Hull. Her current research interests are the distribution of resources in households and the associated negotiations between household members with a particular emphasis on gender; disability and social exclusion; and research methodology. She has contributed to *Men, Gender Divisions and Welfare* (1998) and *Gender, Power and the Household* (1999).

Carol Smart is a Professor of Sociology in the Department of Sociology and Social Policy at the University of Leeds. She has a long-standing interest in feminist approaches to the family, marriage and divorce. She is Director of the Centre for Research on Family, Kinship and Childhood. She is co-author of *Family Fragments* (1998).

Carole Smith is a Senior Lecturer in the Department of Social Policy and Social Work, University of Manchester. Her research interests and publications are particularly related to socio-legal aspects of the family and state intervention in children's lives. She is just finishing empirical research on adoption and direct control.

Matthew Waites is an ESRC-funded PhD student in the Faculty of Humanities and Social Science at South Bank University in London. He holds an MA in Sociology of Culture from the University of Essex. His PhD research explores past and present debates over 'age of consent' legislation in the UK, particularly in relation to changing understandings of citizenship for non-heterosexuals.

Jeffrey Weeks is a Professor of Sociology and Dean of Humanities and Social Science at South Bank University. His recent publications include *Invented Moralities: Sexual Values in an Age of Uncertainty* (1995).

1 Relating Intimacies: Power and Resistance

Julie Seymour and Paul Bagguley

Intimacy implies close familiarity, close in acquaintance or association, often pertaining to sexual relations.

This set of phrases serves less as a definition of the meaning of intimacy than as a start-point of enquiry into this topic. Does the closeness mentioned above refer to spatial proximity, affectiveness or kinship ties? Does the presence of one form of closeness automatically result in another of the forms? What rights and responsibilities are associated with different forms of closeness?

The term 'intimate relationship' can be used to describe a multitude of associations. Although, as shown above, in common parlance it is utilized as a substitute phrase for a sexual relationship, acknowledgement of a broader definition allows the term to also encompass non-sexual relationships such as those of parent and child, including step-parents, kinship networks, such as siblings or cross-generational linkages and adult friendships. Some of these relationships will be mutually created; many will be formed as a consequence of the actions of other, usually close, associates. This latter is particularly so in the case of children. The inclusive definition of intimate relationships hence allows sociologists to consider, within this topic: sexual relationships (both heterosexual and same-sex and looking at affective and material dimensions), aspects of parenthood (mother/father/step-parenthood) and inter-generational obligations. It also raises the issues of identity, citizenship, violence, moral panic and negotiation and, as a result, stresses the continuing necessity highlighted by C. Wright Mills (1973) to examine the linkages between private troubles and public issues.

The present-day formation of intimate relationships is presented by some authors as an exercise of active construction in a time of late

1

modernity (Stacey, 1990; Giddens, 1991, 1992; Plummer, 1992). Individuals are presented as consciously rejecting traditional models of association in favour of relationships whose form, boundaries and content are the subject of continued negotiation between participants. This applies in sexual, parental (Beck and Beck-Gernsheim, 1995) and kin (Finch, 1989) relationships. Such active construction is conceptualized most explicitly in Giddens' analysis of the 'pure relationship' ; one 'where a social relation is entered into for its own sake, for what can be derived by each person from a sustained association with another; and which is continued only in so far as it is thought by both parties to deliver enough satisfactions for each individual to stay within it' (1992: 58). The 'pure relationship' may seem at first most applicable to sexual, non-parental kin and friendship associations, but Giddens also extends this definition to incorporate the relationship between parent and child in as much as, in its contemporary form, it relies less on traditional social obligations and mutual expectations of assistance than was previously the case.

Concern as to the extent to which such models of fluid and flexible associations represent the reality of everyday intimate relationships has been expressed in three areas. Nearly a decade ago, Morgan (1991) was questioning the extent to which models of 'companionate marriage' were as much a product of professional discourse as a reflection of changing marital types. More recently, commentators have suggested that the emphasis on the egalitarian nature of the 'pure relationship' has diverted the focus of researchers from the (still unequal) material and structural conditions in which most intimate relationships take place (Dunne, 1997 and this volume; Seymour, 1999). As a result earlier work, particularly by feminists, examining the more mundane but equally important, issues of the gendered domestic division of labour and distribution of resources in households (Brannen and Wilson, 1987; Morris, 1990) has been, to a large extent, sidelined. Finally, recent publications which have empirically rather than theoretically examined intimate relationships (Bittman and Pixley, 1997; Jamieson, 1998) conclude that the 'pure relationship' remains in the realm of ideals rather than reality. These criticisms notwithstanding, there is evidence, as this volume shows, that individuals *are* involved to some extent in processes of creative construction with regard to their intimate relationships.

The shift in view suggested above from ideals to reality presages a change in focus from the form of intimate relationships to their content and nature. It is perhaps here that the theme of the 1997 BSA

Conference 'Power/Resistance' becomes most transparent. Foucault (1980) considered that power and resistance could be seen to operate at the micro-level of everyday interaction. A close examination of the processes occurring in intimate relationships therefore provides examples of the ways in which latent power both becomes visible and may be resisted. A key dimension here is the role played (or not played) by negotiations in such relationships: to what extent do they occur, between whom do they take place and how (and where) are they conducted? In the move from traditional associations to contextual commitments, the study of the processes of negotiation within intimate relationships will elucidate not only changing attitudes to familial obligations (Finch and Mason, 1993) but also the manifestation of dimensions of power and forms of resistance within the range of groupings this term encompasses.

A focus on negotiations is, Finch and Mason (1993) consider, a way in which social researchers can empirically examine the process of structuration at work: a site where agency and structure can be seen to interact with each other. The earlier discussion of the flexibility now considered to influence the formation and conduct of intimate relationships may have placed too much emphasis on the role of the individual(s) as creative agent(s). Social behaviour, even intimacy, does not happen in isolation and even 'private' relationships will be influenced by the structures and institutions present in the individual's social world. While Giddens (1992: 195), showing the influence of agency on structure, suggests that democratic behaviour in intimate relationships, particularly parental ones, has implications for democratic practice in the larger community, many authors focus on the influence of the historical, social, material and statutory context on the formation and operation of relationships (Smart, 1984; Porter and Weeks, 1990; Maclean and Groves, 1991). The person with whom a relationship can be formed, the nature and legal standing of that relationship, the associated rights and responsibilities that accompany its formation and the consequences of its demise are issues in which the individuals involved in an intimate relationship will find themselves aided and constrained by legislation, social censure, material goods, moral panics and, on occasion, researchers.

This volume contains recent writings in the area of intimate relationships developed from papers presented at the 1997 BSA conference on 'Power/Resistance'. The chapters include work both by established writers and researchers in the field and new voices. The book, which incorporates research on sexual, parental and kin relationships, is divided into three parts. The first deals with the formation of intimate relationships; the ways in which they are constructed and reconstructed to accommodate changes in the life-course. The second part considers the impact and influence of the state and legislation on intimate relationships. Finally, Part III considers a range of forms of relationships and, following the theme of the conference most closely, examines the manner in which power and resistance are made explicit in the everyday interactions of intimates.

In Part I, the research focus is on the ways in which individuals are constantly constructing and reconstructing their intimate relationships. The opening chapter, by Rosalind Edwards and Jane Ribbens with Val Gillies, explicitly addresses the issue of the ways in which the boundaries around relationships are formulated and maintained. In their chapter 'Shifting Boundaries and Power in the Research Process: The Example of Researching "Step-Families"' the authors show how biological and step-parents actively create and make sense of 'their' family and parenting; and how those outside the boundaries, including researchers, also become involved in this process. The chapter discusses both substantive and methodological dimensions of their research and shows how, as the study progressed, the two areas became increasingly intertwined. The authors show the complexity of relationships which make up the contemporary reconstituted 'family', and suggest ways in which gender and class contribute to the dynamics of boundary formation and maintenance.

The theme of family creation is continued in the second chapter in which Jeffrey Weeks, Brian Heaphy and Catherine Donovan report on their work on the 'Families of Choice' project. Focusing on non-heterosexual relationships, the chapter describes findings from interviews with 96 self-identified non-heterosexuals (half men, half women). The areas covered include partnership rights, issues of commitment and the construction of rituals to celebrate developments within the relationship. The accounts presented show how those interviewed understood their relationships as both similar to and different from heterosexual partnerships, and how the everyday natures of families of choice are created and negotiated.

The final chapter in Part I moves the focus of attention to a different form of intimate relationship, that between mother and child. Steph Lawler introduces the important argument that the position of one person in a relationship – in this case the mother – is predicated on the perceived social category of the 'significant other'. Hence she shows in her study how motherhood is formulated around social constructions of what it means to be a child. By focusing on 'needs talk' (the concept that children have needs which must be met, usually by the mother) she shows how the mother–child relationship has the potential to subjectify women. This occurs through the discourse of 'good mothering' where only those needs of the mother which are congruent with those of the child are considered appropriate for expression and action. Lawler demonstrates, however, using interview material from mothers, how women resist their potential invisibility in the relationship by redefining their children's needs to include the recognition of the separate needs of the mother. Her chapter thus uses 'needs talk' to illustrate the operation of both power and resistance.

The volume then moves onto Part II which focuses on 'Regulating Intimacy: the Role of State Legislation in Intimate Relationships'. The three chapters in this section examine the impact and influence of state intervention and legislation on the formation and conduct of relationships, and cover between them same-sex associations, fatherhood in post-separation or post-divorce families and parent–child relationships. The chapters by Waites and by Smith raise the issue of citizenship; in the former, sexual citizenship; in the latter, children as citizens with rights. Waites presents a historical account of the political and public development of the concept of the 'age of consent' and its application to heterosexual and gay relationships. He shows how lobbying around the age of consent moved between the latter part of the nineteenth century and the present day from the language of protection to the language of rights and equality. This leads Waites to question whether this indicates a more inclusive sexual citizenship where women and gay men are awarded the status of autonomous decision-makers. In his detailed account he also illustrates how the 1967 legislation decriminalizing homosexuality constrained as well as legalized male same-sex relationships over 21. As this volume was going to press the amendment to the Crime and Disorder Bill (1998), which would have equalized the age of consent for male homosexuals, was rejected by the House of Lords, although 'equalising' legislation is to be introduced in the 1998/1999 parliamentary sessions.

The second chapter in this section considers the role of recent legislation, particularly the Children Act 1989, on the construction of 'new' fatherhood following the breakdown of a marriage. Carol Smart and Bren Neale draw on material relating to the negotiations over children of 60 divorced and separated parents. They suggest that the recent legislation has contributed to the emergence of a new identity of post-divorce fatherhood, but question the extent to which it has altered the gendered relations of parenthood. As with Lawler's chapter on 'needs talk', these authors show how the identity of individuals can be reconstituted through their relationships; in this case the post-divorce woman may become constructed as the 'hostile mother'. Smart and Neale's chapter raises the issue of the balance between rights and responsibilities in intimate relationships, which is continued by Carole Smith in her examination of the role of the state in managing children's autonomy. In her chapter the social construction of childhood is once again acknowledged, as is the role of the juridical system to reflect and reinforce particular discourses of childhood. Smith shows how an increasing focus on the citizenship rights of children conflicts with, in the assumption of the juridical system, their needs for paternalistic protection and benign control. Using case studies, Smith describes how children are frequently considered to 'lack capacity' in decision-making around issues which involve their relationship with their parent(s). This construction is also extended to other adult–child relationships which may mimic the parental one such as *guardian ad litems*. Importantly, Smith highlights the use of the *parens patriae* jurisdiction of the High Court, which in England relates only to children and which, in essence, allows the court to make its own law. Smith describes how this has been used in a number of cases to override the views of the child if it is considered to be in the child's best interests. This chapter then extends the examination of the parent–child relationship to include that between the State and the child where the context is one of perceived paternal protection.

Part III of the book addresses most explicitly the topic of power and resistance in intimate relationships looking at inter-generational, same-sex, sibling and poncing relations. In Pia Christensen, Jenny Hockey and Allison James' chapter the gaze of the research is wider than in some of the previous studies, considering as it does intergenerational and community relations. The authors use an ethnographic study of an agricultural community to show the way in which social relations are interdependent, although often not recognized as such by those involved. They use the vignette of a central figure in the community to examine the relational, temporal and spatial dimensions of dependency which subsequently produce the individual's perceived independence. They show how, within various interdependent relationships, individuals develop strategies to manage the relations of power which are played out at both a familial and community level.

The following two chapters concentrate on same-sex relationships. Gill Dunne examines the divisions of labour of lesbian parents and, in their second chapter for this volume, Brian Heaphy, Catherine Donovan and Jeffrey Weeks consider 'Narratives of Power in Same-sex Couple Relationships'. The former chapter suggests that the lack of gendered scripts within lesbian relationships may lead to the construction of more egalitarian associations, particularly in relation to economic and domestic resources. Dunne shows how her study can therefore also highlight the workings of gender in heterosexual relationships and the extent to which heterosexuality can be regarded as an institution which impacts on the form and content of couple relationships. In Heaphy *et al.*'s chapter, the search for an egalitarian relationship between couples is again foregrounded with the associated negotiations between partners being explored. Forms of power within relationships, other than gender, are discussed including economic, emotional, ethnic and class-based inequalities. In a section which resonates with the earlier chapter on interdependency by Christensen *et al.*, the authors highlight the dimension of social capital as a source of power, particularly where it involves one partner who is well integrated within a community with a collective identity. To conclude, Heaphy *et al.* develop the idea of an emerging ethic of the possibilities of couple relationships which engages with gay and lesbian community knowledges and, in which, power is an issue which is explicitly considered and negotiated between partners.

The penultimate chapter in the volume, by Sara McNamee, looks at relations between siblings in the context of computer and video games. In this chapter the spatial dimension of power is privileged, as is the way that children use other individuals (mostly parents) as mediators in their negotiations. The primary focus of the work is on the influence of gender in sibling disagreements but dimensions of age, geographical location and physical size are also mentioned. McNamee discusses how the use of computers and video games as forms of leisure in the domestic sphere has led to the home, traditionally the site of female leisure, becoming contested space between male and female siblings.

The volume is completed with Jo Phoenix's chapter 'Prostitutes, Ponces and Poncing: Making Sense of Violence'. This looks at the way that women involved in prostitution make sense of poncing relationships: that is intimate relationships with men where the women are financially exploited often with the threat of violence. Phoenix argues that the behaviours of men who are intimates *and* ponces have to be understood via the symbolic meaning given to them by the prostitutes rather than as simply poncing behaviours *per se*. They may be interpreted as examples of love or business behaviour and this then has implications for the existence and type of resistance that the women may offer to such behaviours. Phoenix concludes her chapter, and suitably this volume, with the statement that resistance within intimate relationships cannot be considered until the form and process of the relationship, as it is understood by those in it, is made transparent.

The chapters in this volume, while considering a wide range of intimate relationships in a variety of contexts, present a number of common themes: the tension between the maintenance of self-identity and the involvement with a 'significant other'; the ways in which notions of citizenship are given expression through intimate relationships; the temporal changes in relationship balances and forms – legal, historical and throughout the life-course of the individual; the extent of active construction and ongoing negotiations which take place; and finally the extraordinary diversity of form and content in relationships which are given the same label. It is perhaps unsurprising then, given the last theme, that a one-line definition fails to sum up the salient features of an intimate relationship; this can be achieved only by listening to the narratives of those who are 'Relating Intimacies' to the researchers in this book.

REFERENCES

Beck, U. and Beck-Gernsheim, E. (1995) *The Normal Chaos of Love* (Cambridge: Polity Press).

Bittman, M. and Pixley, J. (1997) *The Double Life of the Family: Myth, Hope and Experience* (St Leonards, NSW: Allen & Unwin).

Brannen, J. and Wilson, G. (1987) *Give and Take in Families: Studies in Resource Distribution* (London: Allen & Unwin).

Dunne, G. (1997) *Lesbian Lifestyles: Women's Work and the Politics of Sexuality* (London: Macmillan).

Finch, J. (1989) *Family Obligations and Social Change* (Oxford: Polity Press).

Finch, J. and Mason, J. (1993) *Negotiating Family Responsibilities* (London: Routledge).

Foucault, M. (1980) *Power/Knowledge: Selected Interviews and Other Writings, 1972–1977*, edited by C. Gordon (Brighton: Harvester Press).

Giddens, A. (1991) *Modernity and Self-Identity* (Cambridge: Polity).

Giddens, A. (1992) *The Transformation of Intimacy: Sexuality, Love and Eroticism in Modern Societies* (Cambridge: Polity).

Jamieson, L. (1998) *Intimacy: Personal Relationships in Modern Societies* (Cambridge: Polity).

Maclean, M. and Groves, D. (eds) (1991) *Women's Issues in Social Policy* (London: Routledge).

Mills, C. W. (1973) *The Sociological Imagination* (Harmondsworth: Penguin).

Morgan, D. (1991) 'Ideologies of Marriage and Family Life', in D. Clark (ed.), *Marriage, Domestic Life and Social Change: Writings for Jacqueline Burgoyne* (London: Routledge) pp. 114–38.

Morris, L. (1990) *The Workings of the Household* (Oxford: Polity).

Plummer, K. (ed.) (1992) *Modern Homosexualities: Fragments of Lesbian and Gay Experience* (London: Routledge).

Porter, K. and Weeks, J. (1990) *Between the Acts: Lives of Homosexual Men, 1895–1967* (London: Routledge).

Seymour, J. (1999) 'Using Gendered Discourses in Negotiations: Couples and the Onset of Disablement in Marriage', in L. McKie, S. Bowlby and S. Gregory (eds) *Gender, Power and the Household* (London: Macmillan), pp. 76–95.

Smart, C. (1984) *The Ties that Bind* (London: Routledge & Kegan Paul).

Stacey, J. (1990) *Brave New Families* (New York: Basic Books).

Part I

Constructing and Reconstructing Intimate Relationships

2 Shifting Boundaries and Power in the Research Process: the Example of Researching 'Step-Families'

Rosalind Edwards and Jane Ribbens
with Val Gillies

INTRODUCTION

In this chapter we utilize the concept of boundaries as both a substantive and methodological issue, to look at aspects of power and resistance in the research process. Our substantive topic is parenting and step-parenting after divorce or separation. Our methodology is qualitative and intensive, concerned with listening on their own terms (as far as possible) to individuals' 'accounts of', or 'stories about', their understandings and experiences in the course of interactions with others.[1] We are particularly interested in the processes involved in how biological and step-parents actively create, understand and make sense of 'family' and parenting both within and between households, and within the enabling or constraining wider context of their lives.[2] Our fieldwork has involved interviews with resident parents, step-parents and non-resident parents, living in complex household arrangements that may also change significantly over time. To be a 'family' unit always implicitly involves issues about boundaries, for there needs to be some sense of what the unit refers to. In the particular complex and changeable circumstances of our interviewees' lives, the issue of household and family boundaries becomes crucial, being highly significant for our research focus of parenting within and between households.

Boundaries are also important in public and political debates about 'the family' [see Part II of this volume]. Institutions attempt to lay down particular notions of family relationships (as in the assumptions of ongoing caring, and requirement of financial, parental responsibility after separation contained in the Children Act, 1989 and Child Support Act, 1991) and to draw material and symbolic boundaries between different types of families (lone parent, nuclear, step, and so on), such as in statistical presentations of household types. Voluntary sector pressure groups, notably here the National Stepfamily Association, can also have a stake in establishing the existence and boundaries of particular family forms. Even within the generic term 'step-family', 'finer' categorizations are constructed, based on criteria such as biological and/or step-parents' marital status and children's residence and access patterns. For example, Batchelor *et al.* (1994) identify 16 forms of step-family derived from a classification of who in the step-family couple has birth children and which of these children reside with them. As researchers we also draw boundaries around our area of interest and define the characteristics of those who 'fall inside' our research topic. As we discuss below, deciding what and who could or should be included or excluded in our particular sample raised fundamental substantive and methodological issues concerning the topic of our research and the nature of in-depth data analysis; it was not a simple task.

On the other side of institutional and/or research boundaries, however, amongst family members themselves there can be resistance both to legal and policy prescriptions of family relationships and responsibilities, and to categorizations as particular sorts of family. This can also be linked to a resistance or willingness to participate in research. In other words, as we will discuss, our potential interviewees had their own ideas around what or who could or should form our sample. Moreover, as the fieldwork progressed, we found ourselves increasingly aware of the relevance of the concept of 'boundaries', both as revealed in the interviews with those who took part in our research and in the research process itself.

In this research context, issues of access are complex and involve negotiations and resistances around boundaries of many different types. Our 'snowball' method involved contacting one member of a 'step-cluster' – usually the biological or step-mother (a gender issue we return to later). We then sought to interview others in the cluster – usually the biological and step-fathers. This process raised questions around the dynamics of power and resistance amongst members of step-clusters. Such negotiations of access boundaries – or refusals to negotiate at all – are shaped by issues around gender, race/ethnicity, social class and culture, as well as researchers' own social networks and participants' views of family boundaries. They are, however, not just processes to be confined to methodological discussions. Importantly, matters are further complicated by the fact that it is these very individual and collective negotiations of material and symbolic boundaries, and the dynamics of power and resistance, within and across households, that we wish to explore as the substantive focus of our research. Thus, an issue we have had to grapple with is that the intellectual boundary between methodology and topic broke down and became ambiguous for us.

Such ambiguities between substantive topic and the process of research are issues for all social research, although researchers may avoid confronting and exploring them. These issues, however, are revealed with particular clarity in research addressing individuals' private and personal relationships and understandings of family life (Edwards and Ribbens, 1998). This is perhaps especially so in a context of fluid and changing family forms and households. The symbiotic nature of methodology and topic thus has implications for other family researchers.

We now clarify what we mean by the concept of 'boundaries', as this term can have quite different emphases and implications for researchers from different disciplines and professions. We then move on to explore and consider how a 'boundaries analysis' of the processes of defining and reaching our sample of step-clusters points up particular aspects of power and resistance within, between and around families and households.

CONCEPTUALIZING BOUNDARIES

The notion of boundaries has been explicitly used in therapeutically orientated discussions of family life by writers and professionals who use the approach broadly described as family systems theory. This sort of analysis of the boundaries of family systems (with individuals within a family being 'sub-systems') is concerned with three separate main processes: (i) internal dynamics within 'the system'; (ii) how 'the system' maintains its boundaries in relation to the outside world; and (iii) the inputs, outputs or exchanges that take place between 'the system' and its environment. Features considered as issues around which family boundaries are maintained, adapted or break down include: physical residence, kinship terminology, interdependencies and values shared or contested through interactions between family members, and shared or contested histories and rituals over time. Many of the academic articles and books written about step-families are located within a systemic framework (for example, Schulman, 1981; Visher and Visher, 1988; Robinson, 1991). Overall, within a systems boundaries analysis, the emphasis is on the various 'positive and negative' 'feedback loops' involved in 'the system' and its relationship with the outside world. However, as Morgan (1985: 144) concludes, those applying a systems boundaries analysis rarely pay attention to the nature of the 'environment' within which the 'family system' is contained. Relationships and exchanges within the system are often regarded as the outcome of individual and psychological factors, rather than focusing on an analysis of resource distribution as reflecting wider social norms and structures such as gender relations (Brannen and Wilson, 1987).

Boundaries have also received close attention within anthropology, as symbolic social entities, even if signified concretely via demarcation of physical space and geographical areas, or speech, dress and skin colour. The emphasis here is on the ways in which people may work with differing understandings of individual and collective identities, such as through ideas about what constitutes 'people like me' and 'us' as distinct from 'others' who are not like 'me' or 'us'. Attention is paid to the ways in which certain criteria can be brought into play to demarcate such social boundaries. An anthropologically informed analysis of boundaries has not, as far as we know, been specifically used to examine step-parenting. Nevertheless, we can learn from its application to the study of the processes by which ethnic groups maintain boundaries in relation to each other (Barth, 1969; Wallman, 1978). This application draws our attention to the fact that boundaries have two sides to them, and that changes on one side of a boundary may lead to changes on the other. Of course, authority and power are not equally distributed and some individuals and groups attempt to, or are able to, impose their definitions and understandings on others, who may resist or accede. Nevertheless, people on one side of a boundary may experience it differently from people on the other side, and people on each side may have different sets of meanings by which they understand the nature of the boundary, and these may change according to context. For example, those from minority ethnic groups may perceive racial/ethnic boundaries as oppressive and constraining, such that they wish to challenge or resist them. At the same time, however, in some contexts they may experience these boundaries as empowering and desirable, such that they wish to embrace and maintain them. Indeed, Wallman (1978) suggests that, as such, the interfaces of boundaries are likely to signal issues of confusion, ambiguity and danger in social life.

Within family sociology there has also been some attention to boundaries, latterly largely in order to deconstruct them. 'The family' as a paradigmatically 'private' and bounded sphere in relation to the 'public' sphere of paid work, politics and so on, has received some critical feminist attention (see Edwards, 1993 for review). Others (such as Bernardes, 1987; Gubrium and Holstein, 1990) have been concerned to reveal the social construction of discourses of 'the family' that treat it as a distinct and concrete entity with an 'inside' surrounded by an 'outside' (as in systems theory). Nevertheless, while insights can be gained from deconstructing boundaries around the 'private sphere' and 'family' as social objects, these notions do not just occur within professional and academic writings, but also can relate to individuals' and groups' interpretations, understandings and everyday concrete experiences (David *et al.*, 1993; Edwards, 1993; Ribbens, 1994). Indeed, it is women's deep-rooted association with the private sphere, family life, domesticity and childrearing that has been pointed to by feminists as the source, or one of the sources, of women's oppression (for example, Pascall, 1986; Walby, 1990). However, there is also recognition that this situation is double-edged. On the one hand it may place women in a powerless position in a wider and institutionalized sense, *vis-à-vis* men. On the other hand, in their daily actions within family life, women do have some power, particularly with regard to rearing children, albeit informal, contingent and constrained (Elshtain, 1981; New and David, 1985; Ribbens, 1994). Black feminists have also challenged the portrayal of 'the family' as universally oppressive to women, arguing that, for Black women, it is a source of support and resistance against racism (for example, hooks, 1982).

Also from a sociological perspective, Morgan (1985) makes a useful distinction between three types of boundaries around families. Firstly, there are administrative and social policy boundaries, which we have already referred to in our introduction, and which form a wider context for our research and our interviewees' lives. Secondly, there are personal and affectual boundaries, in terms of people's own understandings and constructions – the topic of our research. Thirdly, there are theoretical boundaries, constructed in research and analysis – the research process we have indicated as having collapsed into the substance of Morgan's second boundary in our study.

Our own approach here is to meld both anthropological and sociological insights around boundaries. This allows for individuals as members of collectivities constructing and experiencing clear family boundaries at times but fudging or rejecting them at others, within enabling or constraining contexts. It lets us appreciate that motives and experiences may be understood in quite different ways by different parties to a situation, at individual, collective and institutional levels. Furthermore, it enables us to recognize that our research decisions and approaches are integral to our topic of study, how biological and step-parents bring up children within and across households.

BOUNDARY ISSUES FOR STEP-PARENTING

While step-families have existed for centuries, in contemporary industrialized societies such households are now predominantly created following the separation or divorce of parents rather than a parent's death (Haskey, 1994). So far, however, there has been little direct research attention paid to the changes that occur after divorce or separation, as children acquire a new potential 'carer' or 'parent' when one or both of their biological parents commits herself or himself to a new spouse or resident partner. In the overwhelming majority of step-families the resident children are the biological offspring of the mother, living with a 'step-father'.

Within step-families the structure and boundaries of family forms that children may experience can be complicated. One or both parents may have children from one or more previous relationships, as well as from their current relationship; children may regularly or irregularly come and go in the household for short or long periods. For example, our own study sample (discussed further below, and see Table 2.1) includes family household situations ranging through:

- shared or co-parenting (half-weekly with each biological parent) of children from the mother's previous relationship;
- shared parenting of the father's children and with the mother's resident children having regular contact with the non-resident father;
- resident children of the previously widowed father and resident children from the mother's previous relationship having regular contact with the non-resident father;

- resident children from the mother's previous relationship with a range of high, some or no contact with the non-resident father and with children from the couple's current relationship;
- children from the mother's previous relationship with some or no visiting from children from the father's previous relationship/s;
- children from the father's previous relationship with some contact with the non-resident mother and children from the couple's current relationship; and
- children from the mother's previous relationship with no contact with the biological father, with or without children from the current relationship.

Thus 'family' boundaries can both demarcate and cross-cut these situations. It is not clear, in systems terms, who is 'inside' and who is 'outside' 'the family', and family members themselves may wish to pose this in different ways in different contexts.

The development of ever 'finer' professionally or research-derived typologies in order to describe step-family formations is not just a matter of technical adequacy. It relates to a desire to create order and impose boundaries in a situation where there is confusion about how to describe the complexity and intricacies of many children's living arrangements and where there are powerful emotions around the imagery and ideals associated with being 'a family'. Some sociologists, such as Stacey (1990) and Giddens (1991), see the overall diversity of family forms, of which step-families represent a part, as indicative of individuals reflexively dismantling the ascribed boundaries of 'traditional' family forms and creating new fluid gender and kinship relations. Yet what changes in family make-up and lifestyles mean for parenting, and for continuities or discontinuities of kin and social networks, remains to be fully explored. Little is known about people's own understandings and experiences of their parenting in step-families. We lack understanding of how parents and their current spouses or partners seek to care for their children (either with or without the involvement of previous spouses/partners) and work out their 'family' relationships.

Most academic research has been clinical and/or concentrated on measuring children's upbringing and development in step-families (for example, Clingempeel and Segal, 1986; Kiernan, 1992). It is implicitly based on a 'social problem' perspective, constructed within the administrative/policy boundary around families and incorporated in the theoretical position adopted in much research (including a systems approach). In contrast to the social problem perspective, our own research is concerned with people's own understandings and concrete experiences of working out their parenting and 'family' relationships within step-clusters. Over a decade ago, Burgoyne and Clark's (1984) influential study noted the normative vacuum in society concerning the 'rules' (and, in our terms here, including the boundaries) governing step-family relationships. More recently, in exploring kin obligations and support in families, Finch and Mason (1993) have argued that not only are there 'rules' but also normative guidelines about general family relationships. These guidelines are more subtly concerned with how to work out what to do than with specifying what should be done. This would signal that the vacuum, in both step-family practice and research on step-families, concerns the processes surrounding such normative guidelines. Step-parenting appears to be left in a quandary. People tend to be at a loss to know how to define the step-parenting relationship (Nemenyi, 1992). There is a persistence of negative stereotypes of step-parents' relationships to their children, which may be drawn on by parents, step-parents and step-children themselves (Hughes, 1991; Nemenyi, 1992). Step-mothers may face particular difficulties (Hughes, 1991; Moxnes, 1992), but there is also the increasingly anomalous position of men in relation to parenting, whether as resident, non-resident or step-fathers (Kruck, 1991; Bawin-Legros, 1992). Yet another issue is that of the step-family 'couple' relationship as separate from parenting, and with which childrearing may be in conflict (Stacey, 1990; Duncombe and Marsden, 1993).

We now move on to consider how, before we set out to empirically explore these issues and dilemmas in step-parenting, we had to create a variety of methodological boundaries in constructing our substantive topic.

THE BOUNDARIES OF OUR RESEARCH

Our intensive study, as we have said, is concerned with the processes underlying continuities or discontinuities of parenting after divorce or separation. We consider these within the wider contexts of kin and social relationships as well as those of social and institutional norms and policies. We are interested in what it is that people bring to and evoke in undertaking, or resisting, negotiations around childrearing within and across households, and which may shape and have an effect upon any negotiations or resistances, in terms of images or resources. These include: images of 'family', notions of moral obligations, parenting identities, images of children's needs, kin and social network perceptions, support and sanctions, links with quasi-formal and statutory organizations and agencies, legal agreements, material circumstances, and so on.

Our main sample concerns 23 step-clusters (comprising interviews with 46 individuals), with heterogeneous socio-structural characteristics and household structures. In each cluster we have sought, but not always obtained, interviews with the resident or co- parent (usually the biological mother), the step-parent (usually the social father) and non-resident or co-parent (usually the biological father).[3]

We have experienced a range of boundaries within the research process, in terms of definitions and access, that have required exercises or negotiations of power in relationships and posed resistances, both amongst ourselves as a research team and between us and our potential interviewees. These, as we have said, in themselves have provided us with important insights into our topic of investigation. We now begin to detail these through a consideration of the boundary between us as researchers and family members as research subjects, initially examining how we, as researchers, constructed this boundary and how the boundary looks from our side of it.

DEFINING BOUNDARIES FROM THE RESEARCHERS' SIDE

Before attempting to contact potential interviewees we had to draw boundaries around our area of interest and define the characteristics of what and who would form our sample. We had agreed that we wanted our sample to be 'heterogeneous' in order to explore a diversity of social circumstances. But just how encompassing could our sample be in a situation where our research had a particular focus (negotiating parenting and childrearing) and we had practical and analytical limitations on the number of step-clusters we could include in an in-depth study? Resolving these boundaries was not merely a technical matter, but would have major implications for our research conclusions about the nature of parenting and step-parenting after divorce or separation. Two of us have worked together quite amicably over the years (Jane and Ros) but the issue of defining our sample sometimes found us at loggerheads as to where we should draw the boundaries, and revealed dilemmas over the nature of in-depth social research.[4]

One of the first issues we confronted – addressed without tension – was sexuality. Should we draw a heterosexual boundary or include gay and lesbian step-couples? The deciding issue for us was our interest in if, and how far, members of a step-family may work towards 'passing' as a traditional nuclear family (as found by Burgoyne and Clark, 1984), and the implications for negotiations or resistances around childrearing within and across households. While heterosexual step-couples can attempt to draw on and represent themselves within the boundary of traditional conceptions of 'the family', such a boundary cannot be crossed by gay and lesbian families and households. We thus decided not to include the latter in our study. However, we were aware of ongoing work examining gay and lesbian families in one of our institutions [see Chapter 3 by Weeks *et al.* and Chapter 10 by Heaphy *et al.* in this volume] and discussed with these researchers where we could overlap in our collection of data to make possible cross-project comparisons at a later date.

Another initial issue – also addressed without tension – was the boundaries of what constituted 'parenting' and 'childrearing' for the purposes of our research. Being a parent (and being the child of your parent/s) does not end at a particular age or stage, but 'childrearing' can be more circumscribed. We are interested in negotiations, agreements, acceptances and resistances around parenting in terms of the practical, physical and emotional aspects of caring for and about children. We also wish to explore concepts of authority and responsibility in childrearing, as well as the variety of practical and material resources drawn upon in parenting children and which can have symbolic and emotional content. We decided against drawing a fixed boundary in terms of an upper age limit for children of the separated or divorced parents within our step-clusters. Instead we used a notion of these children being of an age and situation that required (the slightly woolly working notion of) 'substantial input' in their daily lives.

This boundary of 'substantial childrearing input' also led on to other issues, in terms of the household forms we should include in our research. Here tensions did arise between us. Should we require the 'step-parent' to actually be living on a permanent basis with the biological resident or co-parent? Should we include situations where a biological parent was 'absent' because he/she had died, rather than separated or divorced and no other previous relationships were involved in the cluster? Such questions arose in the context of our focus on negotiations or resistances within (as well as across) house-holds. Our decisions thus held implications for the type of accounts or stories about these matters that we would hear. After much discussion, we made an initial (but later reconsidered) decision not to include households where the biological parent's partner was not living permanently with her or him. This had potential implications for including African–Caribbean interviewees, where 'live-out', 'visiting' or 'outside' relationships have been identified as a feature of family/household structures (see Song and Edwards, 1997).

However, we stretched this boundary to include a 'step-couple' who were in the process of moving into a home together. We also included two step-couples where the only children involved were the previously widowed mothers'. This allowed us to explore negotiations and resistances with memories and images of the 'absent' parent only, and to make comparisons with other situations where this occurred alongside there also being a living 'absent' parent of other resident children of the other partner in the same step-cluster.

Another initial decision concerning the heterogeneity of our sample focused around ethnicity and pointed up issues around whether, even if we 'listened' to interviewees' accounts or stories, we could 'hear' them. Did we risk misunderstanding and misrepresenting the perspectives of some minority ethnic groups if we included them in our research? This dilemma produced a discussion about whether we could ever presume full knowledge and appreciation of meaning even where we shared social characteristics with our interviewees. In turn, this raised issues about the nature of data as constructed in interviews between interviewee and interviewer, and the interplay between imposing research agendas and 'grounded' concerns in analysis of interviewees' accounts and stories. We went ahead and included minority ethnic groups, including efforts to interview a Bangladeshi step-cluster with an interpreter (see Edwards, 1998 on working with interpreters) – although, as we discuss below, this is not to say that minority ethnic step-clusters were just waiting to be interviewed!

Definitional issues around describing our sample became relevant again once we had accessed and interviewed them, in terms of how to set about describing to our research audiences the research sample that resulted. At this point our sample consists of specific individuals who we have been able to interview. The sample ends up being whatever it has evolved into through the concrete processes of the research. We experienced a considerable tension between describing interviewees as individuals, or attempting some sort of description of the step-clusters involved, and what their boundaries are. We thus struggled with how to pin down and define some of the complexities of their living arrangements.

We wanted to retain a sense of categorization around individuals (for example, simply, as a non-resident father; or, more complexly, as a mother with resident children from a previous relationship who is also the mother of children from a current relationship as well as a part-time step-mother to her partner's children from a previous relationship). But we also wanted to address the more collective notion of placing these individual parenting situations in the context of the step-cluster, as attempted by the typologies already developed mapping the diversity of step-family forms. The table we have devised to represent this has become quite complex (see Table 2.1).

There are also equivalent problems around how we define the social class of our sample – in terms of individual attributes, such as education and occupation, or the collective household attributes, such as housing tenure and income level – as well as the gendered implications of standard measures of social class (see Morgan, 1996 for a discussion). Burgoyne and Clark (1984: 42–3) discuss similar difficulties in assessing the social class of their step-family sample. Such issues are controversial enough in relation to 'conventional' nuclear family households, but they proliferate in considering the social class of parents, step-parents and the various children in step-clusters.

Moreover, in the same way as administrative and social policy boundaries around families may not accord with people's own personal and affectual boundaries (to return to Morgan's 1985 distinction), neither may these research world familial categorizations – as we discuss below. We have imposed them, however, partly in an attempt to order the complexity of aspects of the everyday family lives we are investigating, and partly because research audiences expect to be able to obtain some sort of overall descriptive profile of our sample.

These and other questions around the definitional boundaries of our sample were not always resolved purely on the basis of intellectual arguments about the implications for our research focus, although arguments about what was 'good' for the research provided the moral 'trump card' in our disputes. Other means of resolution included unspoken, 'I'll give on this if you give on that', or, 'you gave on this so I'll give on that' settlements. At other times, though, one of us would refuse to negotiate and imposed a wider or narrower definitional boundary (perhaps a 'middle way' was not possible, or perhaps one of us merely wanted to make the point that she had some 'ownership' over, or 'authority' within, the research). The other then gave way in order to allow us to 'get on' with

Table 2.1   Household characteristics of step-family couples

Primary couple	Sets of children involved	Levels of contact with other parent
June/Alan	Aa, C	4
Gina/Tom	Aa	4
Lyn/Chris	Aa, Ba	4, 1
Jackie/Richard	Aa, Bc	4, 2
Tina/Jo	Aa, C	4
Karen/Paul	Aa, C	2/3
Kate/Rob	Aa, C	3
Lisa/Mark	Ac, Aa, C	3, 2
Sarah/Dave	Aa × 2, Bd, D	2, 3, 3
Attia/Rashid	Aa, C	1
Gill/Tony	Aa, C	2
Louise/Neil	Aa, C	2
Trevor/Dawn	Aa, Bb × 3, E	4, 2, 2, 3
Catherine/Simon	Aa, C	4
Sheena/Paul	Aa, C	3
Sally/Michael	Aa	4
Elizabeth/Jonathan	Ba, C	4
Kim/Ben	Aa	2
Lorna/Pete	Aa, C, D	3
Sue/John	Aa, Bc, E	5, 1
Jessica/Bob	Aa, Ba	3, 5
Margaret/James	Aa	1
Frank/Mary	Aa, Bc	3, 1

Key: *Sets of children involved*:
  A – Woman's from previous relationship: (a) resident/shared care;
  (b) non-resident; (c) adult.
  B – Man's from a previous relationship: (a) resident/shared care;
  (b) non-resident; (c) adult.
  C – Couple have child/ren together.
  D – Ex-partner has children in a new relationship with contact with the
  primary-couple children.
  E – Ex-partner has step-children in a new relationship with contact with
  primary-couple children.

Levels of contact with other parent:
  5 – Shared care; 4 – High contact; 3 – Some contact; 2 – No contact; 1 – Dead.

the research. Sometimes a 'definite' decision was renegotiated as we progressed with our interviewing, came to have a 'feel' for the issues, and realized exploring a particular 'defined out' situation might have relevance (for example, 'live-out' step-father relationships). However, this reassessment could come too late (too little time, too much data). All these processes can be similarly identified within the accounts and stories of our step-cluster interviewees, although the moral legitimating images drawn on are obviously different from our own.

Importantly, however, working out or fudging definitions on the research side of the 'step-family' boundary did not mean that the decisions we reached were what shaped our sample alone. Our boundaries could remain firm and we could exercise power through resistance where we had agreed (even if reluctantly) to define a certain group 'out' of our research. For example, the definitional boundary of 'substantial input' into children's daily lives led to disappointment for some potential interviewees with whom we were put in contact, or contacted, whose children had 'grown up'. A few attempted to negotiate telling retrospective stories or pointed out continuing implications for their lives, but we resisted their efforts at inclusion. Similarly, we refused an enthusiastic contact who was no longer part of a step-family but a lone mother, her relationship having broken down, but who wanted to tell her story. In contrast, we were in a powerless position and subject to others' boundaries when we approached people who 'fell inside' our definitional boundaries but who refused to take part in our research. Similarly, having agreed to take part themselves, interviewees could resist our requests to 'snowball' out to particular members of the step-cluster, or a person 'snowballed to' would refuse to be interviewed when approached. In itself this threw some light on power, negotiation and resistance within step-clusters, as did lack of resistance to, and concurrence with, our definitions and methods. Each of these latter situations is shaped by issues around gender, race/ethnicity, social class, culture and social networks – both our potential interviewees' and our own. We thus now move on to consider how far (potential) interviewees negotiated and resisted or facilitated our attempts at setting our research boundaries.

PUTTING THE RESEARCH BOUNDARIES INTO ACTION

Having armed ourselves with agreed criteria of how to set the boundaries of our research area, we then set out to cross the divide between researcher and researched worlds, and attempted to put our definitions into practice. At this point we sought to minimize the boundary between researchers and researched, but in Wallman's (1978) terms, this proved to be a moment of ambiguity and danger.

In seeking to access potential interviewees we were aware that the boundaries drawn around different types of families at the administrative/policy and theoretical/research levels were not necessarily in accord with boundaries drawn at the level of people's personal and affectual understandings and constructions. At an intellectual level, following the work of people such as Gubrium and Holstein (1990), we see 'family' language and categorizations as socially constructed. This language has fluid and dynamic meanings, but also has powerful and concrete implications for people's lives. On a personal level it was not until we began work on the funding proposal for our research that two of us consciously realized, in each case, 'our family' was 'a step-family'.

Thus, in contacting potential main sample interviewees (see below on our methods), and initially in our interviews with those who agreed to take part, we sought to avoid using the words 'step-family' and even 'family' to describe their circumstances. We did not want to impose a definition of their relationships with each other. We found this extremely difficult, struggling to find an alternative language! We ended up saying we wanted to talk to: 'women and men who are living with a husband, wife or partner (whether married or not), who have at least one child from a previous relationship living with them, at least for most of the time, and where there may or may not be children from their own relationship living with them'.

Indeed, all but two of our step-couple interviewees made it clear that the word 'step-family' in particular did not constitute part of their every-day thinking or vocabulary about their 'family' lives. While they sometimes recognized that they can be 'technically' defined as step-families, and often acknowledged that step-families are 'different' from 'other' families, they rejected its relevance for their lives on a variety of grounds. These grounds included: 'technically' not fitting their own definition of the word, suspicion of labels, negative connotations attached to the word and its inability to describe the closeness of the relationships involved or, in contrast, its implication of greater involvement than was felt appropriate (see Ribbens and Edwards with Gillies, 1996). The two cases of acceptance of the label 'step-family' seemed to be linked to these women's desire not to be incorporated into traditional notions of 'the family' (although others with similar concerns did not take this particular course to differentiate themselves). We have yet to disentangle the complex and subtle ways in which people do understand their relationships to each other and, within this understanding, the ways they seek to make sense of bringing up children.

Resistance to, or lack of association with, the word 'step-family' amongst the majority of those who did agree to be interviewed, to some extent, may be related to our method of approaching potential inter-viewees. Previous qualitative studies have either relied on clinical/therapy self-presented cases, or have experienced real problems in gath-ering a sample. Burgoyne and Clark (1984), for example, had great difficulty in reaching their target sample of 40 step-couples (originally intended to examine only step-mothers, but ultimately changed to include step-fathers for practical and 'having a feel for it' theoretical reasons). Amongst other avenues they tried re-marriage registrations, primary schools, general practitioners, putting up posters at their university, and even chasing up a step-mother who featured in a local newspaper story. (See also Masson *et al.*, 1993, for their difficulties.)

We did not want to seek contact entirely through formal organiza-tions in the first instance, fearing that we would be regarded as falling inside, or incorporated within, the agenda boundary of the particular agency. Rather, we decided largely to approach people through our, and their, informal social networks and to 'snowball' out from there. The significance for family research of approaching interviewees through trusted intermediaries was first discussed by Bott (1957; and see also Standing, 1998 for a recent example), although it appears not to be an issue recognized by all family researchers.

However, we have also attempted some approaches through more formal organizations in order to see whether or not this might shape the accounts or stories we hear. For example, we contacted the National Stepfamily Association in order to reach people who had defined themselves as 'step-families' in a public manner, but, interestingly, none of the people accessed in this way were actually in step-families (and included the enthusiastic lone mother mentioned earlier). Approaches through schools have been as unsuccessful as they were for Burgoyne and Clark (1984). Formal access routes have provided us with some step-clusters though, including clusters reached through a general practitioner, a Church of England minister, and an Asian women's voluntary agency.

Working through our informal networks raised and involved many issues in terms of who we came to interview, which we address further below. At this point it is worth considering how this route also revealed the sort of resistances around the definitional and language boundaries to which we have already referred.

RESISTANCE AND FACILITATION

Resisting inclusion within the boundary of our research interest (even with our avoidance of the word 'step-family'), or not wishing to think about themselves in this way, was one of the reasons we were given by some of those contacted who refused to take part in our research. For example, a friend of one of us who approached his brother, living in a step-family, on our behalf, reported that his brother and partner did not wish to be interviewed because they did not want to think of themselves as anything other than a 'normal' family. Similarly, a direct approach to an acquaintance by one of us elicited a refusal, after a period of thought, on the grounds that she had been divorced many years ago, had been through some hard times, and did not want to bring them all back to mind. Another direct approach to a resident mother in a step-family (mediated by another friend) prompted a denial that she had any children from a previous relationship (although the mediating friend swears she does!).

Another significant reason for refusal to take part in our research concerned people's own uneasiness about relationships within the step-family itself at the time of contact (and perhaps implicit in some of the refusals discussed above). Not wishing to 'rock the boat', or the relationship with their partner being 'shaky', was referred to by several of the people we unsuccessfully approached to take part.[5]

Two of those defining themselves out of our research on definitional grounds were Black, and the inclusion of Black stepclusters in our sample has been a particular difficulty for us. As a research team we may have agreed the inclusion of minority ethnic groups in our sample but they have not reciprocated such inclusion. Previous experiences had alerted us to difficulties – the exercise of power through resistance – in attempting to successfully contact Black (mainly African–Caribbean) women, from a White institutional base and as White people, in order to interview them about their family lives (Edwards, 1996). They had led us to the conclusion that approaches through Black women's social networks were most likely to bring 'positive' outcomes (from a researcher's perspective). However, in this instance, even using informal approaches through intermediaries, we have been notably unsuccessful in including Black people (although one of the people whose children had 'grown up' and was enthusiastic was, in her terms, a member of a Black step-family). Two of us, for example, spoke to women students of African–Caribbean origin who seemed prepared to help approach several (non-student) people for us (including some cases in which there was a 'visiting' rather than resident step-parent involved). One student later e-mailed that she had not been able to get anyone to agree, and a reply asking for further information about their reasons for refusal has not elicited a response. The other Black student had also met with refusals and attributed this to people not wanting to be interviewed by a White person. Other avenues have proved equally unsuccessful, including refusals on the grounds of being 'too busy' to be interviewed – a legitimization employed across ethnic groups.

Thus, our interviewed step-clusters are predominantly White (although encompassing people of Irish and Italian origin), containing only one African–Caribbean step-couple and two African–Caribbean/ White step-couple relationships (where racial boundaries have already been 'breached'), in addition to the Bangladeshi step-couple mentioned previously.

We had quite limited access to Black people through our own informal social networks, and so it was one of the 'gaps' we made concerted efforts to rectify (albeit with minimal success). We gave considerable thought to the composition of our networks when we embarked on this method of access; their strengths and lacunae. (Within all of this, as well, we were mindful of balancing newly and more established households, and younger and older people, within our sample.) Another 'gap' in all our networks comprises financially very affluent or 'upper-class' people (a comment on academic pay scales?). The difficulties of even beginning to reach 'elite' groups you are not part of, who can draw firm, even authoritative boundaries around themselves and their social worlds, have been noted by others (for example, Cassell, 1988; Punch, 1986; Neal, 1995) – though not in relation to studying their family lives. Our efforts here, including contacting private schools and a National Childbirth Trust teacher in an affluent area, have failed. Thus we have not even been able to get close enough to affluent or upper-class groups in order to get a sense of why they may resist scrutinization of their step-family lives, so totally closed is the boundary.

In other social class respects, however, between the three of us, our personal backgrounds have proved wider. Here we decided to 'play to' each of our strengths. One of us (Jane) is living with a partner (and as part of a 'grown up' step-family) who has clear working-class networks, which proved very fruitful for her allocated portion of interviews. She also considered opportunities through her own more conventional 'middle of the road' middle-class contacts. Step-families, however, appeared to be 'hidden' within this latter social group, in that we or our intermediaries did not immediately register them amongst such acquaintances. This could, of course, be what such step-families wanted (as in our discussion of refusals on the basis of 'normality' and 'not wanting to think about it' above). Another of us (Val) has a working-class background herself and mixed class networks between herself and her partner. These networks mediated with and provided interviewees, but included many 'in-cluster' 'snowballing' refusals. The other (Ros) has middle-class networks, overwhelmingly 'liberal' left-leaning, and mostly professionals (including, through her partner, a step-father). These provided her with more interviewees and introductions to others than she could cope with. She also had some access to younger working-class people through one of her daughters. The status of two of us (Jane and Ros) as mothers, developing or having developed contacts through our children, has also been important, and perhaps proved a barrier for the other researcher (Val). Perhaps family and friends, for a while at least, felt that our only interest in them was who they could put us in contact with! Another area of strength in our social networks is our academic contacts. We have not utilized these to any great extent, however, feeling that we had enough middle-class professional voices amongst our sample. Apart from our efforts to recruit through Black students, the only instance of utilizing this path has been one of us approaching (successfully) an academic whom she knew to be a resident step-mother in a step-cluster containing a non-resident mother – a situation previously unrepresented in our sample.

Thus our discussion of refusals and agreements to participate in our research highlights the conflation of our topic of study – negotiations, power and resistances within and across households in step-clusters – with how we reach (or not) interviewees. It is also notable that we have often referred to approaching 'step-families' through women, either as intermediaries or as part of a step-couple. We now turn to examine how our 'snowballing' method is integral to negotiations around boundaries in step-clusters, and the importance of gender and class within this.

GENDER ISSUES IN FAMILY BOUNDARIES

Our research has once again highlighted issues about the significance (if precariousness) of women's positioning as mediators. This is both in terms of managing the boundary with us as researchers in the public sphere, and in terms of mediating relationships within their family situations – in this case the process of negotiating our access to other potential interviewees within their networks. There are exceptions to this, both at the point of first access to a step-cluster and in the snow-balling process, but these turn out very largely to be modifications or exceptions that confirm the rule.

The fact that we overwhelmingly approached and negotiated with women as the first 'point of entry' into our step-clusters might be argued to be a function of our own gender – we are women and there-fore we know more/feel more comfortable with approaching women. However, we found ourselves negotiating with women even where we had a male partner or friend as an intermediary. Moreover, the women we approached accepted this role as 'point of entry' into their family lives and relationships. There is plenty of research evidence, consistently over the past decade, showing that, within western soci-eties at least, it is principally women who hold responsibility across the family–public world boundaries for linking and co-ordinating chil-dren's and partners' needs with services and agencies' provisions and requirements (for example, Graham, 1984, 1993; Balbo, 1987; Smith, 1987; Reay, 1995; Ribbens, 1994). They also mediate kin and friend-ship relations on behalf of their partner and children within the boundary of the private sphere (for example, Cotterill, 1994; Ribbens, 1994), and took on this role in our research in mediating our access to others within their step-clusters. While this situation can be regarded as a function of their powerless position and constraining association with family life and the affectual/emotional aspects of the social world, at the same time it also potentially vests power in their hands.

There were some modifications to this 'women as mediators' scenario. Two occurred where we already knew the non-resident father in a cluster and contacted him directly with the knowledge of the resident mother. It is interesting to note that we did not think to seek the step-parent's (largely step-fathers) permission for, or agree-ment to, our contacting a non-resident parent (largely fathers). What is more, resident parents (largely mothers) also did not seek their current partner's views on this, whether agreeing or refusing the request. In another case, where contact with a non-resident father was mentioned first to the step-father (although it was put in terms of wanting to ask his wife about contacting her ex-husband), he immedi-ately seemed quite uncertain about this and suggested his wife be phoned direct. Another, lesser, modification occurred at the point of first access to a step-cluster, where both mother and step-father were known to one of us (Jane), who initially mentioned the research to the step-father when he was round at her house one day. He was immediately receptive to the idea and confident his partner would also be amenable, but then suggested Jane contacted her directly. Since then it has been the mother who has made all the arrangements with Jane for the interviews (a point we return to below).

However, two interesting exceptions – yet proving the rule at a different level – occurred when one of us (Ros) contacted a Church of England vicar, serving an affluent suburban parish, as part of our efforts to contact more 'conventional' middle-class families (and with the added factor of being practising Christians). After 'sounding out' suitable people, the vicar indicated to Ros that he had consulted with the men (both step-fathers) and passed on their telephone numbers to her. Thus, the negotiation and point of entry was initially with the men in these step-families. In both these men's accounts they referred to themselves quite explicitly as 'head of the household'. Mediation across the family–public world boundary, in the case of research, was their responsibility. However, this is not to say that this was the situation for other interactions with services/agencies or kin and friendship relations. In one of these cases the step-father, Frank, had attempted to take on a head of household role and negotiate with, or rather confront, his wife's ex-husband about this non-resident father's meagre (in Frank's eyes) financial support of his children. The result was much discomfort, not only in overt conflict between the non-resident fathers and step-fathers, but also threatened conflict between Frank and his wife and her children. This fed into Frank's lack of perception of himself as holding a 'fathering' relationship to the children and his rejection of the description 'step-family' as implying too much intimacy. Frank had to back down from his attempts to impose greater financial responsibility on the non-resident father, and leave cross-household negotiations to his wife once again. Again, the initial point of entry for us as researchers and the uneasy negotiations/resistances and exercises of power within the step-cluster is indicative of the breakdown between our methodology and topic. It is further reflected in the fact that Frank's wife refused Ros' request to snowball out to her ex-husband either through herself or by Ros contacting him directly.

The women in our sample could thus exercise power and authority (the latter being vested in being knowledgeable about the situation) in acting or refusing to act as intermediary to other members of their step-cluster on our behalf. Refusing to mediate could be based on variable considerations, including some form of fear of the ex-partner, a desire for the ex-partner's story not to be heard, and/or a wish to maintain a sense of the step-family as a complete and bounded family unit in itself. In this respect our research endeavour to explore negotiations across family and household boundaries could be at odds with our interviewees' endeavours to maintain clear-cut boundaries between households. Women's intermediary role in our research thus reflects the situation whereby it is largely women, within step-families generally as well as our sample, who are resident mothers and who have ex-partners who are non-resident fathers, and it largely appears to be their responsibility (rather than step-fathers) to conduct most aspects of any continuing relationship around childrearing. However, the gender effect could also be seen to be occurring in the one step-cluster that included a resident step-mother, resident father and non-resident mother. Here, also, it was the resident woman, albeit the step-mother, who negotiated our access to the other two interviewees. This she did by first obtaining their separate agreements to taking part in the research, and then passing their work telephone numbers to Jane (who was to do the interviews) so that Jane could make direct contact with them. In this process, then, she directly facilitated our access but then seemed to 'step back' from the further arrangements.

Equally though, the resident mothers could be unsure of their ex-partners' willingness to take part in the research, but could either allow us to contact the men directly or could offer to attempt to 'persuade' their ex-partner themselves and get back to us. (We leave aside cases where non-resident parents' whereabouts were not known, and/or there was no contact with them at all, or they were deceased.) Both strategies could prove successful or meet with resistance. Either way, at this point we might become aware of the significance of women again in these processes as we found ourselves in negotiation with, or encountering resistance from, the non-resident father's new wife or partner (see Ribbens and Edwards, 1999).

Women's simultaneous placing as powerful and powerless in their position as mediators is also evident in the attempts at snowballing from them to their partners. In several cases where we interviewed step-fathers, we had no contact with them prior to turning up to interview them; all the arrangements were made through the women. For example, Ros' interview with one 'step-father'[6] was organized through his partner, Kim (a younger resident mother approached through Ros' daughter). Kim had been unsure whether he would want to take part in the research, asked him herself, told Ros he had agreed and arranged a time for the interview. Kim then rang Ros to cancel that interview as he was 'very busy', and went back and forwards between him and the phone to arrange a new time. This can be perceived as Kim being 'used' as a form of secretary by her partner, or alternatively as Kim exercising some control over her partner's involvement in the research. Certainly Kim's story of her relationship with her partner is one of her deciding the boundaries of his involvement in bringing up her daughter, or taking on any 'fathering' role (while his account is one of 'taking things slowly and letting them evolve'). Either way, it is notable that in no cases did men ever make arrangements on behalf of women; we always negotiated their interviews with the women themselves. And once again, the playing out of our 'snowballing' research process is related to, and reveals, the topic we are investigating.

SOME REFLECTIONS ON CLASS CULTURE IN OUR RESEARCH

Issues of particular forms of class culture, cross-cut with gender, are also woven into all these and other 'snowballing' scenarios. Access to the men in step-clusters, as non-resident fathers and, to a slightly lesser extent, as step-fathers, was particularly curtailed amongst the White working-class members of our sample.[7] Thus we have quite a few 'step-clusters' that consist of interviews with the resident mother only. These resistances to our research process were, as we have argued throughout this chapter, integrally linked to the negotiation of material and symbolic boundaries, and dynamics of power and resistance, within the step-clusters themselves. Resistances amongst the men (and particularly the non-resident fathers) in our White working-class clusters often reflected uneasy or distant relationships within the step-cluster, as well as women's responsibility for 'family life'. Such uneasy relationships could and did occur amongst our White middle-class families, but only resulted in one case of refusal to take part in the research, which took the form of constant evasion, by a step-father (as opposed to non-resident fathers). (See Ribbens and Edwards, 1999, for further discussion and examples of such class issues in accessing our step-clusters.)

In particular, no resistances occurred in our access to any step-cluster members among the 'liberal' left-leaning White middle-class clusters in our sample, even where there were difficulties in relationships between step-parents and children, or between both or either member of a step-couple and the non-resident parent. Not only were no barriers posed or refusals encountered, but there was positive encouragement to contact everyone concerned. Many commented on what an important topic the research was addressing, and how important it was to gain different perspectives on the subject. In these 'liberal' middle-class clusters, there appears to be a general surface acceptance of everybody's point of view being different, and being open in offering your experiences for others to learn from. Across these step-clusters there was a stress on getting along together, in terms of being 'civilized' and 'mature' (words particularly used by several of the men) in how you handle your and your partner's ex-relationships. Yet such stances can be in conflict with individual feelings and there can be seething resentments under the surface apparent in individual interviews. Thus the expressed commitment to having everyone's version heard can be more related to being seen to be fair in making sure you encourage stories that differ from your own to be heard – a rhetoric for public (including researcher) consumption – rather than always being a *modus operandi* within the step-cluster itself.

Interviewees' views on the importance of our research topic may also relate to our earlier discussion of boundary issues for step-parenting. Our reading of the literature signalled that there might be a vacuum in both step-family practice and research concerning the normative guidelines involved. Several of the more conventional White middle-class interviewees referred to having consulted advice books about living in a step-family (many of which are written from a family systems/therapeutic perspective), while some of our White 'liberal' middle-class interviewees expressed the hope that our research might come up with guidelines for conducting step-cluster relationships. The desire to consult self-help books and to have guidelines to refer to in conducting relationships is likely to be the case for people who are unsure about how to act (see Ribbens, 1993, regarding mothers and childrearing manuals). It may be that it is middle-class people who feel that they are attempting something 'new' by seeking to develop looser household/family boundaries. As a result, they may feel more at a loss as to how to define relationships and work out what to do in the step-cluster situation. They thus see a value in taking part in research that purports to throw light on, and produce knowledge about, the topic. In contrast, working-class people, particularly men, with more defined ideas about their family and household boundaries, may not see any need to consult books or contribute to the production of knowledge on the topic through taking part in research. Indeed, in refusing to participate in the research, one working-class step-father described the whole enterprise as 'stupid'.

Furthermore, it was through reflection on these issues that we saw the class-based assumptions underlying our research methodology. Our research had been devised and carried out in terms and processes that resonated strongly with the understandings of our 'liberal' middle-class group of interviewees. These values are also mirrored in the legislation concerning divorce and access arrangements, which enshrines the principle of joint parenthood in a climate of mutual trust and collaboration (Neale and Smart, 1995). We thus, in effect, have a closed circle between legal and policy assumptions, our own research assumptions, and the assumptions of a particular (White 'liberal' middle-class) group within the research sample as a whole (see Ribbens and Edwards, 1999). This is a salutary demonstration of the importance of researchers systematically exploring and critically reflecting upon their methodology and its links with their topic.

CONCLUSIONS

There are other boundaries within the research process that we could also examine for their substantive insights. We could consider boundaries that occur within the interviews themselves, most clearly exemplified by our one Bangladeshi step-family, who seemed to have been persuaded and cajoled into taking part in the research by the interpreter, who had also facilitated our access. Having agreed to do the interview, however, this couple clearly wanted to maintain a considerable boundary between themselves and the interviewer. With interviewees who are more directly part of our own networks, there are other issues about how we deal with the boundary between being a researcher and being a friend. This boundary has undoubtedly raised ethical issues at times in the tension between wanting to intervene as a friend while wanting to respect the anonymity of information imparted during a research interview. Other issues arise in connection with the dynamics of relationships between individuals interviewed from particular clusters, who may have their own boundaries and alliances between themselves, and may seek to draw us, as researchers, into the same dynamics (see also Song, 1998, on this issue). Issues of confidentiality also require us at times to assert very strong boundaries, since people from within a cluster may feel they have a right, or agreement, to know what has been said by others close to them.

We have explored here in some detail, then, only a few of the themes where we can see a close connection between the substance of the topic on the one hand, and interactions within the research process itself on the other.[8] Yet it was only as we came towards the end of the fieldwork that we began to explore the relevance of the concept of boundary, and it was only as we started to explore the relevance of boundaries and power in substance and in process that we became aware of how far the boundary between research process and research 'product' had itself dissolved. It was at this point that we began systematically to explore the substantive insights to be gained from the research process as such. We have yet to come across such an explicit discussion of the relationship between topic and methodology in qualitative family research. While such issues may be especially central for negotiations, power and resistances within step-clusters, we are convinced that they also have deep implications for our ability to use research to understand contemporary family life more widely. We have yet to see quite how far all these preliminary issues are echoed within the main analysis of our interviews, but this particular vein will only be mined if researchers look for it systematically.

NOTES

1.   These social research terms may be used interchangeably in referring to in-depth qualitative data solicited from interviewees, but they do have different stresses. 'Accounts' refers to interviewees' drawing on particular sorts of vocabularies and images in recalling and describing experiences or events in order to justify, excuse or legitimate ('account for') their social situation and actions. 'Stories' (or narratives) refers more to interviewees' organising their understanding and retelling of their lives in terms of a series of key events, influences and decisions. (See Coffey and Atkinson, 1996, for further discussion.)

2.   This two-year research project is funded by the Economic and Social Research Council under grant no. R000236288.

3.   From this main sample we have selected three case-study clusters, which involves reinterviewing the 'step-couple' and also talking with up to six people from their social networks whom they identify as significant (whether positively or negatively) and including interviews with their children where possible.

4.   The third member of the team (Val) made tentative interventions into these disputes at times, but the research was not originally her 'child' (to stretch a point, she has 'come in' as a 'step-parent'). She is

also in a less powerful position academically and institutionally, so 'taking sides' with one or other of the project's 'parents' has particular implications.

5. If people who do not regard their step-family lives as 'successful', or feel unable to present us with an 'positive' account, define themselves out of our research, this obviously could have implications for the sorts of stories we hear and from which we draw conclusions. However, we have not just heard positive accounts from our actual interviewees – although the sorts of difficulties being experienced by those who resisted inclusion in our research may be different; we do not know.

6. A term he rejected as implying a fatherly relationship with his partner's daughter that he felt he did not have, although he was fond of, and committed to, her.

7. Other researchers have pointed to the general difficulty of accessing and actually interviewing men about intimate and relational issues (for example, Brannen, 1988; Duncombe and Marsden, 1993).

8. Birch (1998) describes how she became aware of a 'mirror image' between her substantive topic of research, concerned with practices of story-telling within alternative therapy groups, and the story of her own research experience and process. She also describes how this theme only became apparent once she was a considerable way into the research process itself.

REFERENCES

Balbo, L. (1987) 'Crazy Quilts: the Welfare State Debate from a Woman's Point of View', in A. S. Sassoon (ed.), *Women and the State: The Shifting Boundaries of Public and Private* (London: Hutchinson).

Barth, F. (ed.) (1969) *Ethnic Groups and Boundaries* (London: Allen & Unwin).

Batchelor, J., Dimmock, B. and Smith, D. (1994) *Understanding Stepfamilies: What Can Be Learned from Callers to the STEPFAMILY Telephone Counselling Service* (London: STEPFAMILY Publications).

Bawin-Legros, B. (1992) 'From Marriage to Remarriage: Ruptures and Continuities in Parenting', in U. Bjornberg (ed.), *European Parents in the 1990s* (New Brunswick: Transaction).

Bernardes, J. (1987) '"Doing Things with Words": Sociology and "Family Policy" Debates', *Sociological Review*, 35(4), pp. 679–702.

Birch, M. (1998) 'Re/constructing Research Narratives: Self and Sociological Identity in Alternative Settings', in J. Ribbens and R. Edwards (eds), *Feminist Dilemmas in Qualitative Research: Public Knowledge and Private Lives* (London: Sage).

Bott, E. (1957) *Family and Social Networks* (London: Tavistock).

Brannen, J. (1988) 'The Study of Sensitive Subjects', *Sociological Review*, 38(3), pp. 552–63.

Brannen, J. and Wilson, G. (1987) *Give and Take in Families: Studies in Resource Distribution* (London: Allen & Unwin).

Burgoyne, J. and Clark, D. (1984) *Making a Go of It* (Hemel Hempstead: Harvester/Wheatsheaf).

Cassell, J. (1988) 'The Relationship of Observer to Observed when Studying Up', in R. G. Burgess (ed.), *Studies in Qualitative Methodology*, vol. 1: *Conducting Qualitative Research* (Greenwich, CF: JAI Press).

Clingempeel, W. and Segal, J. (1986) 'Step-parent–Stepchild Relationships and the Psychological Adjustment of Children', *Child Development*, 57(2), pp. 474–84.

Coffey, A. and Atkinson, P. (1996) *Making Sense of Qualitative Data: Complementary Research Strategies* (London: Sage).

Cotterill, P. (1994) *Friendly Relations? Mothers and their Daughters in Law* (London: Taylor & Francis).

David, M., Edwards, R., Hughes, M. and Ribbens, J. (1993) *Mothers and Education: Inside Out? Exploring Family-Education Policy and Experience* (London: Macmillan).

Duncombe, J. and Marsden, D. (1993) 'Love and Intimacy', *Sociology*, 27(2), pp. 221–42.

Edwards, R. (1993) *Mature Women Students: Separating or Connecting Family and Education* (London: Sage).

Edwards, R. (1996) 'White Woman Researcher – Black Women Subjects', *Feminism and Psychology*, 6(2), pp. 169–75.

Edwards, R. (1998) 'A Critical Examination of the Use of Interpreters in the Qualitative Research Process', *Journal of Ethnic and Migration Studies*, 24(1), pp. 197–208.

Edwards, R. and Ribbens, J. (1998) 'Living on the Edges: Public Knowledge, Private Lives, Personal Experience', in J. Ribbens and R. Edwards (eds), *Feminist Dilemmas in Qualitative Research: Public Knowledge and Private Lives* (London: Sage).

Elshtain, J. B. (1981) *Public Man, Private Woman* (Princeton, NJ: Princeton University Press).

Finch, J. and Mason, J. (1993) *Negotiating Family Responsibilities* (London: Tavistock/Routledge).

Giddens, A. (1991) *Modernity and Self-Identity* (Cambridge: Polity Press).

Graham, H. (1984) *Women, Health and the Family* (Brighton: Harvester).

Graham, H. (1993) *Hardship and Health in Women's Lives* (Hemel Hempstead: Harvester/Wheatsheaf).

Gubrium, J. and Holstein, J. (1990) *What is Family?* (Mountain View, CA: Mayfield).

hooks, b. (1982) *Ain't I a Woman? Black Women and Feminism* (London: Pluto).

Haskey, J. (1994) 'Stepfamilies and Stepchildren', *Population Trends*, 76 (London: HMSO).

Hughes, C. (1991) *Stepparents: Wicked or Wonderful?* (Aldershot: Avebury).

Kiernan, K. (1992) 'The Impact of Family Disruption in Childhood on Transactions made in Young Adult Life', *Population Studies*, 46 (London: HMSO).

Kruck, E. E. (1991) 'Discontinuity Between Pre- and Post-divorce Father–Child Relationships', *Journal of Divorce and Remarriage*, 16, pp. 195–227.

Masson, J., Norbury, D. and Chatterton, S. G. (1983) *Mine, Yours or Ours* (London: HMSO).

Morgan, D. H. J. (1985) *The Family, Politics and Social Theory* (London: Routledge & Kegan Paul).

Morgan, D. H. J. (1996) *Family Connections: An Introduction to Family Studies* (Cambridge: Polity).

Moxnes, K. (1992) 'Changes in Family Patterns – Changes in Parenting?', in U. Bjornberg (ed.), *European Parents in the 1990s* (New Brunswick: Transaction).

Neal, S. (1995) 'Researching Powerful People from a Feminist and Anti-Racist Perspective: a Note on Gender, Collusion and Marginality', *British Educational Research Journal*, 21(4), pp. 517–31.

Neale, B. and Smart, C. (1995) 'Negotiating Parenthood: a Framework for Research', and 'The Family and Social Change: Some Problems of Analysis and Intervention', *Research Working Paper 13*, GAPU, University of Leeds.

Nemenyi, M. (1992) 'The Social Representation of Stepfamilies', in U. Bjornberg (ed.), *European Parents in the 1990s* (New Brunswick: Transaction).

New, C. and David, M. (1985) *For the Children's Sake: Making Childcare More Than Women's Business* (Harmondsworth: Penguin).

Pascall, G. (1986) *Social Policy: A Feminist Analysis* (London: Tavistock).

Punch, M. (1986) *The Politics and Ethics of Fieldwork* (Beverley Hills, CA: Sage).

Reay, D. (1995) 'A Silent Majority? Mothers in Parental Involvement', *Women's Studies International Forum*, 18(3), pp. 337–48.

Ribbens, J. (1993) 'Standing by the School Gate – the Boundaries of Maternal Authority?', in M. David, R. Edwards, M. Hughes and J. Ribbens (eds), *Mothers and Education: Inside Out? Exploring Family-Education Policy and Experience* (London: Macmillan).

Ribbens, J. (1994) *Mothers and their Children: A Feminist Sociology of Childrearing* (London: Sage).

Ribbens, J. and Edwards, R. (1999) 'Breaking Out from our Circles of Assumptions: Contingent Categories in Researching "Step-families"', in S. Ali, K. Coate and W. wa Goro (eds), *Belonging: Contemporary Feminist Writings on Global Change* (London: UCL Press).

Ribbens, J. and Edwards, R. with Gillies, V. (1996) 'Research Report: Parenting and Step-parenting after Divorce/Separation: Issues and Negotiations', *Changing Britain*, 5, pp. 4–6.

Robinson, M. (1991) *Family Transformation through Divorce and Remarriage: A Systematic Approach* (London: Routledge).

Schulman, G. (1981) 'Divorce, Single Parenthood and Stepfamilies: Structural Implications of these Transactions', *International Journal of Family Therapy*, 3(2), pp. 87–112.

Smith, D. E. (1987) *The Everyday World as Problematic: A Feminist Sociology* (Boston, MA: North Eastern University).

Song, M. (1998) 'Hearing Competing Voices: Sibling Research', in J. Ribbens and R. Edwards (eds), *Feminist Dilemmas in Qualitative Research: Public Knowledge and Private Lives* (London: Sage).

Song, M. and Edwards, R. (1997) 'Comment: Raising Questions around Perspectives on Black Lone Motherhood', *Journal of Social Policy*, 26(2), pp. 233–44.

Stacey, J. (1990) *Brave New Families* (New York: Basic Books).

Standing, K. (1998) 'Writing the Voices of the Less Powerful: Research on Lone Mothers', in J. Ribbens and R. Edwards (eds), *Feminist Dilemmas in Qualitative Research: Public Knowledge and Private Lives* (London: Sage).

Visher, E. B. and Visher, J. S. (1988) *Old Loyalties, New Ties* (New York: Brunner-Mazel).

Walby, S. (1990) *Theorising Patriarchy* (Cambridge: Polity).

Wallman, S. (1978) 'The Boundaries of "Race": Processes of Ethnicity in England', *Man*, 13(2), pp. 200–17.

3 Partnership Rites: Commitment and Ritual in Non-Heterosexual Relationships

Jeffrey Weeks, Brian Heaphy and Catherine Donovan

HAPPY FAMILIES?

Headlines do not always mislead. They can sometimes tell some new truths, or at least tell stories in new and revealing ways. Consider one from the *London Evening Standard* (26 March 1997): 'Happy Families, 1997'. Over a cheerful picture of a pleasant-looking couple sitting on the grass, 'with their dog Zeb', the article discusses 'the modern face of parenting in London'. The couple are clearly deeply committed, 'partners of 22 years', and fairly affluent, living in a large house in a comfortable, quiet suburb of North London. One is a university lecturer, the other a theology student – clearly ideal parents. The only jarring note is the sub-head: 'These two men are gay and see nothing wrong with being foster parents.'

The immediate context for the story was an *exposé* a couple of days before, by the same newspaper, relating that a young adolescent had been placed for fostering with another gay couple, apparently against the wishes of the natural (and heterosexual) mother. After a few hours of embarrassing headlines in the early editions of the *Evening Standard*, the final edition was able to report that the local authority had backed down, and removed the child. But if the immediate explanation for this minor media flurry is unexceptional, particularly with the approach of a general election (1 May 1997), residually at least preoccupied with ethics and cultural values, and concern especially for the welfare and future of young people, the wider context is a profound, if uneven and certainly incomplete shift in concepts of relationships, intimacy, parenting and family.

Attitudes to homosexuality are, as they have been for over a hundred years, key markers of such shifts, and the *Evening Standard* story is one of hundreds that have appeared in the past decade or so: on lesbian parenting, self-insemination, surrogacy, 'pretend families', 'gay marriage' and the like. From the sober social democratic legislative changes in Scandinavia (see Bech, 1997) and elsewhere, which have allowed the registration of lesbian and gay partnerships, to the more flamboyant legal action in Hawaii, which has sought the legalization of non-heterosexual marriage, the question of lesbian and gay partnership rights, and attendant issues relating to parenting, adoption, marriage and family, are clearly on the agenda (see for example Weston, 1991; Saffron, 1994). Even in Britain – despite, or perhaps because of, the fact that this is a country which has been slower than most other advanced democracies to recognize and enshrine any concept of rights – partnership rights now form a key part of the political agenda of the gay lobbying group Stonewall. The press, sometimes hysterically, sometimes with detached puzzlement, have both reflected and shaped popular reactions to these developments.

We have argued elsewhere that this concern with partnerships rights can be seen as an aspect of a wider reshaping of non-heterosexual patterns of relationships, and the emergence of what we describe as 'families of choice': flexible but often strong and supportive networks of friends, lovers and even members of families of origin which provide the framework for the development of mutual care, responsibility and commitment for many lesbians and gays (Weeks *et al.*, 1999). The key terms used by members of such elective networks are 'choice' and 'created'. Many lesbians and gays have a strong sense that opportunities now exist on a greater scale than ever before for the construction of relationships that have some at least of the qualities attributed (in ideology at least) to the traditional family: continuity over time, mutual support, a focus for identity and for loving and caring relationships. This is not to say the historical families have always, if ever, been like this, nor that such supportive networks of marginalized non-heterosexuals, female and male, did not exist in earlier periods (see Weeks and Porler, 1998). What we would argue, however, is that families of choice can be seen as indices of something new: positive and creative responses to social and cultural change, to 'detraditionalization', which are genuine 'experiments in living' (Giddens, 1992, 1994). The regular, though not invariable, deployment of the language of family, which suggests continuity, should not be allowed to obscure the emergence of an important change in the social geography of intimate life. Within this evolving broad framework of relationships, same-sex partnerships (usually, but not invariably, couple relationships) both propel a new claim to rights, and reveal evolving patterns and rituals, through which commitment and trust are affirmed and confirmed.

The emergence of what could be termed a relationship paradigm in the discourse of lesbians and gays represents an important, though usually unnoticed, shift in non-heterosexual cultural politics. From the late 1960s the basic effect (if not the original inspiration) of the lesbian and gay movement was the assertion of identity and community: an affirmation of a positive sense of self and of the collective means of realizing this (see Weeks, 1995). This implicitly involved a challenge to heterosexual hegemony, but in practice the main activist effort was concentrated on the development of a politics of identity that asserted the validity of difference. This emphasis is still very strongly present, but over the past decade or so a different nuance has also become apparent: an emphasis that does not displace a politics of life chances but also concentrates more on what could be called life quality issues, in which questions of relationships, and their place in the wider society, come more to the fore. This can be related to what Giddens (1994) describes as a shift from emancipatory politics to 'life politics' in conditions of high modernity, or what Plummer (1995), using a quite different language, but with similar implications, describes as new sexual stories circulating in and through developing interpretive communities, raising questions about 'intimate citizenship'. On a political level this has led to a greater concentration on the legitimization of forms of lesbian and gay relationships (cf. Sullivan, 1995, 1997), but this is just one aspect of a reshaping of the practices of everyday life amongst the non-heterosexual population.

Until recently the empirical study of these changes has been limited, especially in Britain (Weeks *et al.*, 1996). What follows is based on the findings of a research project designed to redress this absence.[1] Entitled 'Families of Choice: The Structure and Meaning of Non-Heterosexual Relationships', it was funded by the Economic and Social Research Council as part of its research programme on Population and Household Change. The research was conducted in 1995 and 1996, and involved in-depth semi-structured interviews with 96 self-identified non-heterosexuals (lesbians, gays, bisexuals, queers – the self-descriptions varied), half of whom were women, half men. We are not claiming that these interviews are statistically representative of all non-heterosexuals – a notoriously elusive goal at the best of times.

Rather, we would emphasize three points. First, we suggest the emergent patterns revealed can be seen as indicative of the type of life experiments that are both common, and perhaps inevitable, in the late modern world. Secondly, they are important evidence for the development of new narratives or stories through which everyday experience is being reordered and new meanings emerge. Thirdly, they are revealing of the processes through which non-institutionalized patterns of sexual and emotional interaction are being negotiated in a world of rapid cultural change (see Heaphy *et al.*, 1998 for a fuller discussion). The sections that follow will explore three aspects of non-heterosexual partnerships: attitudes to legal partnership, which suggest apparently contradictory but in fact coexisting discourses of difference from and similarity with heterosexual patterns; the creation of spaces for life experiments and the working-out of commitment; and finally, the rituals developed within relationships – the construction of partnership rites themselves.

PARTNERSHIP RIGHTS

Two discourses intertwine in the stories of non-heterosexual people: one which affirms difference, which roots lesbian and gay relationship patterns in a distinctive history; and another which asserts a claim to equivalence, equality and ultimately similarity. These come out strongly when questions about the legal recognition of partnerships, lesbian and gay marriage and parenting are broached. On the one hand there is a passionate affirmation of difference:

> ... to me the whole basis of lesbian and gay relationships is different from heterosexual relationships. ... I don't know whether it's good or bad, but I mean, that's a fact. It is blatantly different. And trying to tailor heterosexual laws and understanding towards gay relationships is bound to fail.   (M012)

I do not, as a black lesbian, want to be seen as the same as a heterosexual couple. I do not want to marry my lover, nor do I want to do anything that even remotely looks like that. I don't want to make a commitment publicly. I'm quite content with the fact that I can make a commitment privately, and that's just as important. I don't think that lesbians and gays are the same as heterosexuals, therefore deserve the same rights. I think everyone should have rights, but I don't think they should only have those rights because they happen to be married to another man or married to another woman. (F02)

On the other hand, as these quotes suggest, there is an equally forceful assertion of similarity, at least in the claim to rights:

I feel that people should have equal rights whatever, and it all comes ... under equal opportunities. Equal opportunities doesn't exist, particularly for gay and lesbian people ... . I believe that people should have them. ... I think it really doesn't matter what race you are, or what sexuality you are so long as you can provide a supportive and healthy environment to someone else. (F13)

The contradiction is more apparent than real, however. Overwhelmingly, our informants feel that being lesbian and gay opens opportunities for more equal and fulfilling relationships than are available to most heterosexuals. This echoes wider historical studies which have indicated that the twentieth century has seen a significant shift in the traditional pattern of homosexual interactions for men and women, with traditional patterns of intergenerational or cross-class relationships being displaced by an egalitarian model (see, for example, Dunne, 1997 and Chapter 9 by Dunne in this volume). There are also significant sociological accounts, of course, which indicate that this is increasingly true for relations between men and women, largely as a result of the changing role of women and the 'transformation of intimacy' (Giddens, 1992; Beck and Beck-Gernsheim, 1995; but see Jamieson, 1998). The interesting feature, however, is that many lesbians and gay men have consciously shaped their relationships in opposition to assumed heterosexual models, and especially the power imbalance they are seen as shaped by:

[in heterosexual relationships] there is an essential power imbalance that there are certain roles, which are backed up by economics and backed up by sanctions. And also ... men and women are socialized differently in terms of what ... heterosexual relationships are. (F34)

A number of women, particularly, see their lesbianism as empowering them to move beyond heterosexuality, offering opportunities for cooperation and egalitarian relationships that do not require marriage (Dunne, 1997). For many women the idea of marriage is itself loaded:

as far as I'm concerned, marriage or partnership rights, or whatever you want to call it, is about ownership – and I do not want to own another person. I don't want that at all. I'll be responsible for my own relationship but I will not own someone. And I think it's very strange that there are women who think that this is a good thing. Because marriage has never been in women's interests – ever. And I don't quite see how doing it with another woman or two men doing it with each other, is going to make anything any different.   (F02)

Less strongly, but making a similar point, a gay man who is not averse to some sort of legalization of same-sex partnerships remarks: 'I think that marriage is not a word that I would like – because it is still wrapped up in the heterosexual bigotry' (M04).

The assumption, amongst men as well as women, is that 'it's much easier to have equal relations if you're the same sex' (M31), because this equalizes the terms of the intimate involvement. As one of our lesbian interviewees says: 'The understanding between two women is bound to be on a completely different wavelength' (F33). This means, for example, that the division of labour in the household is seen to be a matter for discussion and agreement, not taken for granted, because of 'being able to negotiate, being on an equal level to be able to negotiate in the first place' (M04); 'Everything has to be discussed, everything is negotiable' (F29; cf. Tanner, 1978; Blumstein and Schwartz, 1983; McWhirter and Mattison, 1984; Dunne, 1997).

Equality is seen as integral to intimacy:

I think there is ... less a kind of sense of possession, or property, in same sex relationships, and more emphasis on ... emotional bonding ... . that's not quite what I mean, but they're less ritualized really. ... I think that kind of creates a necessity for ... same sex relationships to kind of find their own identity.   (M39)

Egalitarian relations do not, of course, automatically develop. They have to be constantly worked at in the face of inequalities of income, the hazards of daily commitment, the time-consuming pressures of emotional labour, and all the differences and power imbalances which mark everyday life. Typically heterosexual everyday involvements like sharing income or joint ownership of a home may be not only practically difficult but politically rejected by many lesbians and gays, as this little exchange illustrates:

Q: Did you ever have joint bank accounts?
A: No. No. That was too heterosexual.   (M05)

Whatever the practical difficulties, however, there is a strong emphasis amongst lesbians and gays on the importance of building intimate couple involvement: 'being in a relationship helps to affirm one as a person and we all need that' (M44); 'I love the continuity. ... I like the sex. I like doing some things jointly. ... A sense that you are loveable' (F06). The opportunity to participate in a democratic, egalitarian relationship is becoming a central non-heterosexual goal. The ideal echoes closely to Giddens' (1992: 58) definition of the 'pure relationship':

> ... a situation where a social relation is entered into for its own sake, for what can be derived by each person from a sustained association with another; and which is continued only in so far as it is thought by both parties to deliver enough satisfaction for each individual to stay within it.

Dunne, in her study of lesbian relationships (1997: 200ff.) makes a useful distinction between the 'intimate strangers' of heterosexual marriage, and the 'intimate friendships' that characterize many lesbian relationships. Relationships conforming to such a model of egalitarian friendship and commitment have become the desired norm for many non-heterosexuals.

Despite this there is an ambivalence about formalizing such relationships in legal partnerships or same-sex marriages, should they be available:

> I think if we were fighting for equal rights for lesbians and gay men, and we got those rights, then that [partnership rights] would automatically follow. What I don't agree with is the fact that ... it's like taking a short cut to equal rights, and it's not going to give equal rights to everyone – it's only going to give equal rights to people who are in long-term relationships. And that doesn't seem fair to me. ... And what bothers me about it that it's kind of like, we want to be seen as the same as heterosexuals, therefore ... it has to be legal on paper what we're doing.   (F02)

Many, like this gay man, want:

> minimal interference by the state in the way people live their lives.
> ... I think that people should be able to make a contract between
> them saying exactly what their relationship is. ... I also think that it
> is no good trying to apply laws that apply to heterosexual couples to
> homosexual couples.   (M44)

On the other hand, there is strong hostility to what is widely seen as a
discriminatory and homophobic legal system, and it is in this context
that some sort of formal framework of partnership rights is seen as
(often reluctantly) necessary:

> I suppose the things I object to about marriage, in the legal sense,
> are the social security and tax implications which always seem to
> end up one person less equal than the other. ... I would like social
> security reform to be in the direction of everybody having an
> independent income, regardless of marital or cohabitation status or
> gender. And I think that is the way to go with heterosexual couples,
> so that lesbian and gay couples aren't any worse off ... it shouldn't
> be on a marriage model, it should be more on a sort of legal con-
> tract model – and there should be varying kinds of legal contract
> for what people want.   (F29)

> I think we should be equal in the eyes of the law. I think we should
> have ... well, equal age of consent and also equal rights around tax
> and the sort of benefits that straight people get for being married
> and having children. And I think if people want to get married they
> should be allowed to – but I wouldn't.   (F36)

> Yes, it is a good idea. Particularly if they allow you to register as
> multiple couples.   (F30)

Parenting issues bring a sense of inequality particularly to the fore. It
is noticeable that most of the existing European legislation on same-
sex partnerships explicitly excludes rights to adoption (for example,
see Bech, 1997): non-heterosexual parenting rights remain a taboo, no
doubt because they evoke deeply embedded fears concerning the
'corruption' of children. Not surprisingly, many lesbians and gays are
particularly concerned with legal access to parenting rights. In this
extract a man involved in caring for his (biological) daughter with his
male partner remarks that when he first heard arguments for partner-

ship registration and marriage: 'I just thought there were so many more important things that we ought to be addressing and dealing with that it irritated the shit out of [me]'. But:

> ... if our relationship could be registered, and the fact that we are co-parents could be registered, then ... when B. [their daughter] was younger it would have made me feel more secure. As it was I had a certain amount of paranoia ... about social workers barging into your life and deciding that this is not proper, and taking the child away ... there was a fair amount of paranoia on my part. So I suppose if those rights existed, then it would remove some of the paranoia, but part of me is just suspicious that it's trying to be normal and trying to be 'Look, we're as good as heterosexuals'. And I don't actually care. It's got to the point in my life where I don't give a stuff.   (M17)

Another major issue that pointed to the value of legal partnerships concerns property. Same-sex couples face recurrent problems about access to pensions, mortgages, spousal rights and so on. But the most emotive issues of all are around illness and bereavement:

> You should have a right to have a say in each other's health care. If your partner was hospitalised you should have the same rights as any other partner would have ... we should all be able to have a say in what happens, say with funeral things. I mean, S ... 's funeral was horrific. His parents completely took it over; his boyfriend was hardly mentioned or ... spoken to, and it was a very Christian burial. It was hideous. Absolutely nothing to do with his life – the preacher didn't know a thing about him and just stood reading from a piece of paper. And because his parents preferred his female friends, they had a bigger say in what happened than his partner did. And you just think, 'No way ... .'   (F14/15)

MAKING IT WORK

For many respondents, then, the question of partnership recognition and lesbian and gay marriage is essentially a pragmatic question: ensuring legal rights and protection, without surrendering what is seen as the real core of non-heterosexual partnerships – the possibilities of more democratic relationships, and the possibility of creating something different:

I couldn't say that, for instance, I would never want to celebrate my relationship with someone. And you know, that might go for ... for a relationship with someone who's not a sexual partner, but you know, we have to create those things for this ourselves. They don't exist currently.   (F01)

The legal framework might be necessary, but it is not sufficient:

I don't have a problem with working within the law to change it to establish those kinds of rights. ... [But] actually the law doesn't make a great deal of difference, it's not really terribly relevant. It's about what people do at their own level, how they organize, how they establish their own rights and their own space at a local level, whatever level that is ... so I suppose I perceive the real battle to be taking place in a more kind of hidden way in terms of local organisation, local empowerment, local action. I think those are the things which matter in the long term.   (M34)

In creating spaces for life experiments – or spaces through experimentation – there is a constant awareness of the outside world. Stigma in various forms, despite all changes that have taken place, is always a potential experience of lesbians and gays, however 'respectable' the relationship:

... because it's monogamous, because we live together in a stable unit with a child, it sometimes feels in that sense that it's like [a marriage]. But I only have to walk out into the street to know that it's not. ... [T]here's one neighbour next door that just won't speak to us. She spoke to us before we had the baby, and now she won't speak to us. So, you know, when it, when it feels like that, I only have to walk out the door, and I know it's not [like a marriage].

(F36)

The presence of children tends to accentuate the social pressure, dictating sometimes careful strategies of avoidance. As the male co-parents mentioned above observed, it is possible to come out as parents in small circles; coming out as gay parents at her school is quite another matter, not least because of the likely embarrassment to their daughter: 'it's like the difference between being out personally and the fact that you're out as a family. I think we're out as individuals, but the family isn't' (M17/18).

Similarly, two lesbian parents, when asked what they most feared about being openly homosexual, replied it was 'the crap' their daughter would get:

> *S:* I think with adolescence she's going to have a lot of problems of her own without. ... It's more a concern, you know, for her than for ourselves really, isn't it?
>
> *J.* Mm. We're already aware that she has to be secretive.
>
> (F04/05)

Recognition, and respect, is therefore a crucial goal. Attitudes of friends are crucial, and it is here that the family of choice provides the essential emotional and moral support, especially if relations with the family of origin are difficult or non-existent. But responses from families of origin remain important in confirming recognition of the reality of the relationship:

> *R:* Our anniversary is important.
>
> *S:* Our anniversary, it's important for us, and we get a card from my mum and dad. We do get cards. ... We always did off your mum and dad. We do now off my mum and dad. Well, we have done now for the past four years.
>
> (M06/ 07)

Both these forms of external influence, negative and positive, can bind: one in opposition to a hostile world, the other in sustaining the relationship as a living, creative force. But in the end, what matters are the dynamics of the relationships themselves. Several American studies have attempted to investigate what might be called the 'natural careers' of lesbian and gay couples. Harry and DeVall (1978) suggest the absence of predictable patterns is because of the lack of institutional expectations. Others, however, have attempted typologies. Laner (1977) divides homosexual couples into 'parallel' and 'interactional' types, the former suggesting independent lives, while the latter share a single world. Bell and Weinberg (1978) divide their male partnerships into 'closed couples' and 'open couples', while Silverstein (1981) offers 'excitement seekers' and 'home builders'. Tanner's (1978) study of lesbian couples suggested three prototypes: the traditional-complementary', the 'caretaking', and the 'negotiated-egalitarian'. McWhirter and Mattison (1984), in their study of 156 male couples, present the most extensive typology, with a six-stage model of relationship careers, 'from blending' and 'nesting' to 'releasing' and 'renewing'.

Although each of these models no doubt exists, we would argue both that no single model can capture the complexity and fluidity of lesbian and gay patterns, and that a democratic–egalitarian norm in fact suggests diversity of life choices within a common framework. We would therefore tend to agree with Blumstein and Schwartz (1983) that the most enduring relationships are those like hetero-sexual ones which are most committed in a variety of ways, but in the end this is a tautology. The critical point is that each of the forms of commitment has to be negotiated afresh, and though these negotia-tions may follow relatively well-defined pathways, the end-result is not predetermined. The will and wish to go on is the most vital component:

> It's very fluid – and like we were saying about being monogamous or not – we're neither. There's no point in making a commitment to something that you don't know you can be committed to. And there's a lot of changes in the boundaries of our relationship and I'd much rather keep it as something fluid than commit to one thing and not be able to keep that commitment.   (F14/15)

Bauman (1993: 98) has argued that there are two characteristic strategies for dealing with the perceived flux of modern relationships, what he calls 'fixing' and 'floating'. Fixing takes place when the potential openness of what Giddens (1992) calls 'confluent love' is set firmly in place by the demands of duty. Floating occurs when the labour of constant negotiation on the terms of a relationship leads to people cutting their losses, and starting all over again. This is often, of course, the case in non-heterosexual as well as heterosexual relationships:

> ... a lot of lesbians and gay men split up more often than hetero-sexuals because they're not necessarily conventionally married, and they don't have to go through all the hassle, so it is easier to split up, I think, in some cases.   (F44)

This is not, however, the only pathway. Many work through the vicissitudes of their relationship, constantly remaking it, trying to 'make a go of it' by affirming their long-term commitment.

Inevitably, given the absence of an institutional framework, there is a recognition of a certain contingency in lesbian and gay relationships, but many see this as a positive rather than negative factor:

> I think it's an advantage for lesbian relationships that there isn't a kind of whole structure built around them, like marriage or whatever, because it allows you to be freer within the relationship to build the relationship that you want. And that's why I don't want public recognition in the way of any kind of ceremony or anything like that for lesbian relationships. (F06/07)

But a recognition that relationships do not last for ever does not mean they cannot be worked at 'as if' they will last:

> ... we've never, ever said that – you know – till death us do part. But we do plan ... while the relationship is going well, we will be planning long-term. Because you can't keep planning short-term and expect long-term things to sort themselves out. (F06/07)

Commitment based on mutual trust is seen as the key to sustaining a relationship (cf. Weeks, 1995), and this is not dependent on any institutional backing:

> Why do I need a licence to commit myself to somebody? The very idea is really quite abhorrent. (F43)

> ... we were very insistent when we had our meeting of thankfulness that this was not a form of marriage and it was not creating a relationship or commitment because the commitment had been there for nine years. (M44)

The commitment takes many forms, from sexuality to domestic involvement, and there appears to be no common pattern. Sexual attraction may be the first step towards mutual involvement, but it is not necessarily the decisive factor. When asked if his relationship was primarily sexual, one gay man replied:

No. I would say it's very much more a friendship ... we don't have a tempestuous relationship at all. I think we have a very stable relationship. Sex is obviously part of it, but ... I wouldn't say our relationship was based on sex.   (M12)

A lesbian similarly put sex in its place:

[Intimacy] is about closeness really. And there's different degrees of it. It's about trust ... friendship, right through to sexuality. It's about being close and trusting.   (F40/41)

Living together may be an essential for many partners, but something to be avoided by others. Commitment broadly for our respondents means two basic things: a willingness to work at difficulties, which implies a constant process of mutual negotiation; and a responsibility to care, and 'emotional labour' (cf. Johnson, 1990; Marcus, 1992).

Mason (1996) has made an important analytical distinction between 'sentient activity' and 'active sensibility' which is highly relevant in understanding these dynamics in same-sex partnerships. Sentient activity stands for the various ways in which the skills of being attentive to others develop. It is highly gendered in our culture, but it is skilled activity learned in the various interactions of everyday life. That, however, does not tell us why these skilled activities are deployed in some circumstances and not others. To understand this, Mason (1996: 31) argues, we have to see sentient activity in combination with active sensibility, the activity of feeling a responsibility for someone else, or offering a commitment to someone else, taking responsibilities on board as something which is your own.

Finch and Mason (1993) earlier imply active sensibility as a way of explaining the complex processes by which responsibilities for kin are negotiated in the contemporary world, rather than seen as necessary obligations. They suggest that although ties to family of origin remain highly significant, they cannot be assumed, and are as much a product of 'working out' as of blood. The authors prefer to use the concepts of 'developing commitments' and of a sense of responsibility that is worked out over time, so that while kin relationships remain distinctive, the extent to which they differ from other relationships, particularly friendships, is blurred. Commitments, they suggest, are likely to feel particularly strong precisely because they are developed in negotiation with specific others. This is clearly of great significance in relationship to non-traditional commitments.

It is striking that many of our respondents avoid the language of obligation, which they see as being about duty, something imposed from outside. Duty is 'Like some kind of moral code that people use to put on you. ... I don't think I need that kind of external thing put on me' (F04/F05). These terms were compared unfavourably with the concepts of responsibility and mutual care and commitment:

> Responsibility is something I decide to do and I keep to; obligation is when I feel I have to. (F01)

> ... duty is something that is imposed on you ... if you feel responsible for someone ... then you do that because you feel you want to, not because somebody else feels you ought to. (M44)

> I have a duty to care for my mother. And I feel I have a duty of care to C., but only because that's what we've chosen. (M03)

EPIPHANIES: RITUALIZING COMMITMENT

If commitment, mutual responsibility and care are the defining characteristics of partnerships, then many feel these need to be confirmed in demonstrable ways:

> ... there are things in this life that only happen once, that are about celebrating you being here, and celebrating the changes as they happen. ... You know, if you were in a group – one of the groups, a Native American group – you might have a tribal kind of particular dance that you do, or if you were Jewish, you'd have a Bar Mitzvah. It seems important to create those. (M19)

In his self-help book for lesbians and gay men, Uhrig (1984) suggests that many are looking for four things in their relationships: affirmation, celebration, symbolization, and something that goes beyond traditional ways of doing things. In practice, Driggs and Finn (1991) argue, this often takes place through two processes: the creation of couple traditions, and the creation of couple rituals as symbolic ways of affirming bonds and deepening attachments.

Our own research suggests that these two processes are usually merged: rituals become part of the traditions of a relationship, though not unproblematically. Partners seek ways of confirming their involvement, but are often reluctant to do anything that seems too 'heterosexual'. So many find ways of celebrating with irony, or play with traditional modes, balancing ambivalence with an underlying seriousness.

Anniversaries can be particularly important: celebrations of first meeting, first sex, when partners moved in together or made a commitment (cf. Johnson, 1990; Marcus, 1992):

G: … . we have two [anniversaries]. The first night we met, or the weekend you moved in. Which was a bank holiday.

M: The weekend I moved in is usually celebrated, isn't it?

G: Yes, that's usually the one we …

M: You usually turn up with a huge bunch of flowers – and tell me not to! And then you come through the …

G: If you can't tell me the date of our anniversary, then … !

M: You tell me not to, you shit!   (M 17/18)

Similarly, partners may celebrate St Valentine's Day, with flowers or gifts. Others, however, are made of sterner stuff: 'I'm very anti-Valentine's day because I've always thought it was heterosexual' (F22). For some people, anything can be an excuse for celebration: '… anything we can think of, we celebrate' (F33); 'Birthdays, Christmas, New Year, St Patrick's Night, and Eurovision Song Contest night' (M04). Birthdays may be particularly important, especially if there are painful memories of family rejection:

Especially birthdays, because I think that a lot of my friends are people who don't have close relationships with their families and who don't see their families so when birthdays come round it's really important.   (F03)

Traditional 'family' feast days and holidays can be a particular trial for many partners, making for tensions between a sense of obligation to family of origin and current commitments (compare Tanner, 1978):

… we did celebrate Christmas together as a family … that was quite difficult. Well, I found it a bit difficult because my mum and dad saw it as a rejection of them ... after Christmas she did actually say ... 'Yes, you've got your family now.' (F05)

Lesbian and gay events, however, such as Pride [the annual parade and carnival which commemorates the start of the gay liberation movement], do offer alternative foci for family celebration:

I'd never ever seen S ... so animated as she was there ... I thought she was going to take all of her clothes off. (F05)

Perhaps what is chosen as a focus for celebration is less important than the fact that many people do feel the need for a symbolic cementing of the relationship. 'Some people exchange rings. We bought ourselves rings ... because that was our way of saying "this is our commitment".' (M06/07)

For others that symbolism arouses faint horror:

Exchange of rings ... it's just something I've never believed in. ... I just don't think I would need to go through an exchange of rings, I just don't believe in it. (F13)

Or playful rejection:

S: ... we're completely against marriage.
J: ... I gave you your nose ring.
S: ... I gave you an eyebrow piercing. It had nothing to do with the relationship, but. You know – it's the nearest we've got.
(F14/15)

But the question of formal commitment ceremonies arouses much greater controversy, evoking as it does similarities to marriage: 'I'd like to do some kind of marital type ceremony, but I don't want it to be legal' (M19). For some they offer the forum for an important public statement:

Partly, I think, it's political. Partly I think it is about visibility and about saying publicly that our relationships are – some of us might say better – but are certainly no less worthy of celebration and public acknowledgement than heterosexual relationships.
(F21)

For the religious it may also be an important way of affirming commitment:

> ... we're not lovers any more, and we have separate sex lives, but he's the most important person in the world to me ... we had a Quaker meeting to celebrate our relationship, not to get married, not to create the relationship, but to celebrate nine years as it then was. ... [I]t was a Thanksgiving. A 'meeting for thankfulness' .... it was not creating a relationship or commitment because the commitment had been there for nine years. What we were doing is giving thanks to God for what we had. ... So it was a celebration, it wasn't even a recommitment, but after the event, I realised it was a watershed for me. I was totally committed to him after that.
>
> (M44)

The ultimate problem, for the non-religious, is finding the right balance between play and seriousness:

> I suppose what was really important for me was getting the balance right between it being a pastiche (which is what it was, clearly) and it being deadly serious. And that was, at the end of the day, that was what I was most happy about, that we got that right. People weren't quite sure – you know, 'Are you just taking the piss?' 'Is this unbearably serious?', I mean, 'What's this about?' And you know, that balance was quite difficult to find. I mean, fortunately the people with us were great, and it was a huge send-up but also extraordinarily moving, and I think that was most important for me, really, that we could, you know, be taking the form of something but sending it up, and being incredibly serious about it. ... It was kind of making a commitment to be true to each other, but also to be reasonable about our differences.   (M34)

The growth of a self-help literature (for example, Driggs and Finn, 1991; Uhrig, 1984) suggests the developing importance for many lesbians and gays of finding ways of publicly as well as privately affirming commitment, without necessarily following traditional heterosexual modes. Early in the 1980s, in a study of gay male couples, McWhirter and Mattison (1984) commented on the absence of set rules and of ways of formalizing relationships. In the late 1990s it is clear that this situation is rapidly changing, for better or worse, for richer or poorer.

CONCLUSION

Blasius (1994) has recently discussed the ways in which lesbians and gays have constituted themselves in and through erotic practices, and the kinds of relationships formed around sexuality. The result is the emergence of 'erotic friendships' which both differentiate lesbians and gays from traditional heterosexual patterns, and establish valid and fulfilling ways of life. In this chapter we have examined some of these developing practices of everyday life around three axes: the play of difference and equality; forms of commitment and trust; and the ritualization of partnership. There are many other aspects we could have explored, the most publicly salient of which relate to parenting. Our point, however, is not to offer an exhaustive account of lesbian and gay life. Rather we want to put forward a conclusive argument: that despite the frequent lamentation about the decline of the family, many people are creatively shaping ways of life which provide support and succour through what we describe as 'families of choice'. In and alongside these, erotic partnerships are creatively exploring ways of living and loving together which, far from pretending to be heterosexual, signal ways of being which are no less valid for being different. These developments pose many questions for sociology and social policy which have until recently barely been explored. We would argue that until we understand these changes in non-heterosexual life we are unlikely to comprehend fully, if at all, the changing sociology and social geography of late modern culture.

NOTE

1. This chapter is based on research conducted for a project funded by the Economic and Social Research Council, entitled 'Families of Choice: The Structure and Meanings of Non-Heterosexual Relationships' (reference no. L315253030). The research took place between 1995 and 1996, as part of the ESRC's research programme on Population and Household Change, and was based in the School of Education, Politics and Social Science, South Bank University, London. The director of the project was Jeffrey Weeks, with Catherine Donovan and Brian Heaphy as the research fellows. The core of the research involved in-depth interviews with 48 men and 48 women who broadly identified as non-heterosexual. All the first-person quotations in this chapter come from these interviews. All female interviews are denoted by an 'F', the male interviews by an 'M', each followed by a number. The numbers reflect the order in which the interviews took place.

REFERENCES

Bauman, Z. (1993) *Postmodern Ethics* (Oxford: Blackwell).

Beck, U. and Beck-Gernsheim, E. (1995) *The Normal Chaos of Love* (Cambridge: Polity).

Bech, H. (1997) *When Men Meet: Homosexuality and Modernity* (Cambridge: Polity).

Bell, A. P. and Weinberg, M. S. (1978) *Homosexualities: A Study of Diversity among Men and Women* (London: Mitchell Beazley).

Blasius, M. (1994) *Gay and Lesbian Politics: Sexuality and the Emergence of a New Ethic* (Philadelphia, PA: Temple University Press).

Blumstein, P. and Schwartz, P. (1983) *American Couples* (New York: William Morrow).

Driggs, J. H. and Finn, S. E. (1991) *Intimacy Between Men: How to Find and Keep Gay Love Relationships* (London: Plume).

Dunne, G. (1997) *Lesbian Lifestyles: Women's Work and the Politics of Sexuality* (London: Macmillan).

Finch, J. and Mason, J. (1993) *Negotiating Family Responsibilities* (London: Routledge).

Giddens, A. (1992) *The Transformation of Intimacy* (Cambridge: Polity).

Giddens, A. (1994) *Beyond Left and Right: The Future of Radical Politics* (Cambridge: Polity).

Harry, J. and DeVall, W. B. (1978) *The Social Organization of Gay Males* (New York: Praeger).

Heaphy, B., Donovan, C. and Weeks, J. (1998) ' "That's like my life": Researching Stories of Non-Heterosexual Relationships', in *Sexualities* 1(4), 453–70.

Jamieson, L. (1998) *Intimacy: Personal Relationships in Modern Societies* (Cambridge: Polity).

Johnson, S. E. (1990) *Staying Power: Long-Term Lesbian Couples* (FL: Naiad Press).

Laner, M. R. (1977) 'Permanent Partner Priorities: Gay and Straight', *Journal of Homosexuality*, 3(1), pp. 21–40.

Marcus, E. (1992) *The Male Couples' Guide: Finding a Man, Making a Home, Building a Life* (New York: Harper Perennial).

McWhirter, D. and Mattison, A. M. (1984) *The Male Couple: How Relationships Develop* (Englewood Cliffs, NJ: Prentice-Hall).

Mason, J. (1996) 'Gender, Care and Sensibility in Family and Kin Relationships', in J. Holland and L. Adkins (eds), *Sex, Sensibility and the Gendered Body* (London: Macmillan).

Plummer, K. (1995) *Telling Sexual Stories: Power, Change, and Social Worlds* (London: Routledge).

Saffron, L. (1994) *Alternative Beginnings* (London: Cassell).

Silverstein, C. (1981) *Man to Man: Gay Couples in America* (New York: Morrow).

Sullivan, A. (1995) *Virtually Normal: An Argument about Homosexuality* (London: Picador).

Sullivan, A. (ed.) (1997) *Same-Sex Marriage: Pro and Con – A Reader* (New York: Vintage Books).

Tanner, D. M. (1978) *The Lesbian Couple* (Lexington, MA: Lexington Books).

Uhrig, L. J. (1984) *The Two of Us: Affirming, Celebrating and Symbolising Lesbian and Gay Relationships* (Boston, MA: Alyson Publications).

Weeks, J. (1995) *Invented Moralities: Sexual Values in an Age of Uncertainty* (Cambridge: Polity).

Weeks, J., Donovan, C. and Heaphy, B. (1996) 'Families of Choice: Patterns of Non-Heterosexual Relationships – A Literature Review', Social Science Research Papers No. 2, South Bank University.

Weeks, J., Donovan, C. and Heaphy, B. (1999) 'Everyday Experiments: Narratives of Non-Heterosexual Relationships', in E. Silva and C. Smart (eds), *The 'New Family'?* (London: Sage).

Weeks, J. and Porter, K. (1998) *Between the Acts: Lives of Homosexual Men, 1885–1967* (London: Rivers Oram Press).

Weston, K. (1991) *Families We Choose* (New York: Columbia University Press).

4 Children Need but Mothers Only Want: the Power of 'Needs Talk' in the Constitution of Childhood

Steph Lawler

Need is also a political instrument, meticulously prepared, calculated and used.

(Michel Foucault, 1979: 26)

INTRODUCTION

Childhood, according to Stainton Rogers and Stainton Rogers (1992), is 'knowledged into being'. In other words, and claims for the 'naturalness' of childhood notwithstanding, the temporal period bracketed off as 'childhood' is a social creation, whose inhabitants are marked as 'other' to the world of adults (Prout and James, 1990; Hockey and James, 1993; Jenks, 1996). This social creation is forged on the basis of the knowledges which surround childhood and which produce the 'truths' by which childhood is 'known' (Walkerdine, 1990; Rose, 1991; Stainton Rogers and Stainton Rogers, 1992). These knowledges, which claim to be describing a pre-existing category of 'childhood', can be seen as *producing* this category. They generate schemata of understanding through which the individuals marked as 'children' come to be known and understood.

Although they have the status of objective 'fact', truths around childhood are founded on the basis of specific social and political preoccupations and concerns (Walkerdine and Lucey, 1989; Walkerdine, 1990). Yet their status as 'facts' makes them particularly intractable. Knowledges around childhood are not normally presented as *theories,* open to contestation, but as *truths*. They become the only way to speak about childhood and children. This is the case in the majority of both 'popular' and 'expert' accounts of childhood,[1] where these 'truths' become incorporated, more or less wholesale, into the account, often presupposing the category they seek to explain. The categories 'child' and 'childhood', in other words, frequently remain unexamined and untheorized. As Chris Jenks puts it:

> It is as if the basic ontological questions, 'What is a child?' and 'How is the child possible as such?' were, so to speak, answered in advance of the theorizing and then summarily dismissed.
>
> (Jenks, 1996: 4)

This chapter is concerned with one specific axis around which childhood is constituted — that is, with conceptualizations of children's 'needs'. It will examine the ways in which 'needs talk' comes to define and produce the category 'child'. 'Need' is an important underpinning to conceptualizations of the child's nature: indeed, childhood may be said to be 'knowledged' on the basis of needs which are ascribed to the child (Woodhead, 1990).[2] I am specifically concerned here, however, with the impact of 'needs talk', not on children themselves, but on their mothers. My argument here is that 'motherhood' as a social category is formed on the basis of a *prior* social category – that of childhood. Hence, motherhood is constituted on the basis of, and as response to, 'truths' about the 'nature' of the child. As this chapter will show, this leaves mothers with extremely limited space within which to assert needs-claims of their own. However, the chapter is also concerned with the ways in which women as mothers may *resist* the demands of needs talk through using the very formulations which, potentially, position them as little more than the meeters of children's needs. Hence, this chapter is about needs talk both as the operation of power and as the operation of resistance.

THE POLITICS OF NEED INTERPRETATION

Nancy Fraser (1989) argues that talk about 'needs' inevitably implies a relationality: '*A* needs *x* in order to *y*'. However, she argues, this structure occludes the complexity of needs talk: exactly how should needs be met, in what form, and by whom? These questions underlie discussion of needs, and it is this 'thick' analysis of needs which forms the basis of Fraser's analysis of need interpretation. Fraser argues that conventional accounts of needs have tended to focus on the *satisfaction* of need. Hence these accounts obscure a number of important questions. Fraser herself identifies four main problems arising from a focus on 'need satisfaction', rather than 'need interpretation':

> Firstly, [theories which focus only on need satisfaction] take the interpretation of people's needs as simply given and unproblematic; ... Secondly, they assume that it doesn't matter who interprets the needs in question and from what perspective and in the light of what interests; ... Third, they take for granted that the socially authorized forms of public discourse available for interpreting people's needs are adequate and fair; ... Fourth, such theories ... neglect such important political questions as, Where in society, in what institutions, are authoritative need interpretations developed? and What sorts of social relations are in force among the inter-locutors or co-interpretors?   (Fraser, 1989: 164)

In relation to children's needs, Fraser's analysis provides a lever with which to go beyond what she calls 'thin' descriptions of need, to 'thicker' descriptions – the knowledges and 'truths' which underpin need statements. Her analysis draws important attention to the ways in which categories of 'need' arise out of political preoccupations and the ways in which what counts as 'need' is forged on the basis of specific, expert or 'authoritative' knowledges.

The constellation of knowledges which define children's needs in contemporary Euroamerican societies are, overwhelmingly, those of what have come to be known as the 'psy professions' – medicine, psychiatry, psychology, psychotherapy and so on (Ingleby, 1986; Rose, 1991), and it is within the knowledges generated by these disciplines that descriptions of children's needs become most explicit. The Royal College of Psychiatrists, for example, defines the following as the most important needs of children:

> physical care and protection;
> affection and approval;
> stimulation and teaching;
> discipline and control which are consistent and age-appropriate;
> opportunity and encouragement gradually to acquire autonomy.
>   (Quoted in Adcock, 1990: 16)

This list is similar to the four basic needs outlined by Mia Kellmer-Pringle: for love and security, for new experiences, for praise and recognition, and for responsibility (Kellmer-Pringle, 1980). One problem with both lists is that they tell us very little; in Fraser's terms the needs are too 'thin'. For example: what is 'age-appropriate' discipline? (and, indeed, what counts as 'discipline'?), how should children be encouraged/given the opportunity to 'gradually acquire autonomy'? And who should provide for these needs? An almost endless list of questions could be proliferated.

Another problem, though, is that children's 'needs' are assumed to derive from some intrinsic quality of children themselves, rather than from the social and cultural context in which adults formulate statements about children's 'nature'.[3] Indeed, the child's 'nature' may be seen as being constituted in terms of its 'neediness'. Although these lists of needs are presented as deriving from some quality or characteristic which inheres within the child her/himself, they reflect specific social concerns and social beliefs about the nature of not only children, but also the adults into which they will grow and the society in which they live. For example, and as Woodhead (1990) points out, 'autonomy' is a characteristic highly valued in Euroamerican cultures, but one which may have little meaning or value in other cultures.[4] By making autonomy into an inherent 'need' of the child, this social and historical specificity is obscured through processes of naturalization.

Yet 'needs talk' carries tremendous authority. This authority inheres in three principal features of needs statements. First, statements and knowledges about children's needs originate, in the main, from the authoritative 'psy professions'. 'Needs talk' therefore carries the authority conferred by the disciplinary bases within which it is formulated. It assumes the status of 'truth' through its apparent basis in scientific discovery.[5]

Secondly, and as Martin Woodhead (1990) points out, the very formulation *'needs'* invokes a moral/ethical compulsion; 'needs' has an authority which alternative formulations (such as 'wants' or 'desires') would lack. 'Wants' can be met, or not. 'Needs' *must* be met, or (the implication is) dire consequences will result. Who can argue against a *need*? Hence, once children are defined in terms of 'needs', then, by extension, something must be done to meet those needs. Thirdly, the term 'needs' invokes implications of a more objective reality than alternative formulations. As Woodhead puts it:

Framing professional judgements in terms of 'children's needs' serves to direct attention away from the particular adult value-position from which they are made. Projected on to children themselves, they acquire spurious objectivity. In this way, cultural prescriptions for childhood are presented as if they were intrinsic qualities of children's own psychological make-up.

(Woodhead, 1990: 72)

The constitution of childhood in terms of an inherent and universal set of 'needs' is an embedded feature of Euroamerican 'psy' knowledges in the post-war period and underwrites most popular and academic discussion of concerns around children and their parents. In an explicit form it can be found in work as apparently diverse as that of the British psychoanalyst Donald Winnicott[6] (writing in the 1950s and 1960s) and the North American philosopher Sara Ruddick (writing in the 1980s). For example, Winnicott argues that:

The essential needs of the under-fives belong to the individuals concerned, and the basic principles do not change. This truth is applicable to human beings of the past, present and future, anywhere in the world and in any culture.   (Winnicott, 1964: 184)

Ruddick, in her work on 'maternal thinking' (Ruddick, 1993a and b; 1990) outlines a basic, universal category of maternal work which exists in relation to a fixed and universal set of children's 'needs'. She supports her argument in favour of universalism of children's needs by arguing that not to universalize childhood (and what she sees as its 'complexity') is racist. Yet not all cultures or historical eras have recognized childhood needs in the ways envisaged by contemporary Euroamericans. In these circumstances are children's 'true' needs going unrecognized and unmet? Making Euroamerican conceptualizations of childhood the basis for *all* childhoods can be read as a form of cultural imperialism, in which only 'we' know the 'truth' (Woodhead, 1990).

'Needs talk' around children's needs, then, is not the transparent, apolitical talk it might represent itself as being. Rather, it is political, theory-laden talk which obscures the political and social preoccupations which underwrite its production through its claims to be describing something inherent within the child's 'nature'. It is also powerful talk, as the next section will show.

THE POWER OF 'NEEDS TALK'

[W]hen the model of 'mothering' itself escapes questioning we, as feminists, have abdicated the infinitely complicated task of seeking the means towards the institution of new norms.
(Adams, 1983: 51)

'Truths' about childhood and its needs are, as I have indicated, over-whelmingly produced by the 'psy' professions: yet it would be mistaken to see these truths as contained within this area. Rather, they 'escape' from their specialist enclaves (to use Fraser's (1989) terminology) to form part of the theory and practice of professionals such as health visitors, social workers and teachers, to inform the writing of laws,[7] and so on. The knowledges and truths produced within 'psy' professions tend to 'leak' into mechanisms of the state such as social services, education and the law; they are also more directly available through child-care advice manuals (Ehrenreich and English, 1979; Urwin, 1985; Marshall, 1991) and they are also reproduced in popular representations (Kaplan, 1992; Walters, 1992) and in newspaper and magazine articles. Hence these knowledges extend their domain and, by virtue of their frequent repetition in a range of different social sites, contribute to notions of 'common sense' about childhood and maternity.

Indeed, these knowledges become part of the fabric of everyday life. As Nikolas Rose (1996) argues, 'psy' disciplines have been characterized by their 'generosity':

'psy' has been happy, indeed eager, to 'give itself away' – to lend its vocabularies, explanations and types of judgement to other professional groups and to implant them within its clients.
(Rose, 1996: 139)

And the knowledge about 'human nature' produced by 'psy' goes even further afield, interpellating us through forums such as 'the radio call-in, the weekly magazine column' (Rose, 1991: 208) to such an extent, Rose claims, that 'It has become impossible to conceive of person-hood, to experience one's own or another's personhood, or to govern oneself or others without "psy" ' (1996: 139).

Mothers could hardly escape the regulatory gaze of the 'psy' experts. Through the institutional procedures of child welfare, social services, education, and the law, welfare state societies monitor children's needs and interests. Within these procedures it is the mother/child dyad which is the primary focus of the regulatory gaze of state agencies, and hence the defining feature of good (enough) mothering is how adequately mothers meets children's needs. To ensure that they do, mothers are routinely handed out charts which show their baby's 'normal' development; their children's progress is routinely monitored by child health clinics and schools; and they are always at risk of *post-hoc* judgements. If their children turn out 'badly', their mothering comes under more intense scrutiny in order to determine 'what went wrong'.[8]

Whatever the exact constituents of children's needs are held to be, it is mothers who are positioned as the primary meeters of these needs. This formulation looks obvious: children have needs; it is generally mothers who care for children; therefore, mothers meet children's needs. But to take the formulation at face value is not only to preclude any investigation of exactly how children's needs or 'neediness' come to be constituted; it is also to fail to interrogate the ways in which knowledges around childhood produce a 'natural' link between the nature of children and the normative behaviour of mothers. As Anne-Marie Ambert puts it, children become 'maternalized' through this linkage:

> This linkage between what we conceive to be the nature of childhood and that of parenting is based less on the natural unavoidability of parents for children's survival and well-being, as on society's structure and socioeconomic requisites, which not only place children in the context of family, but 'parentalize' them, and, I will add, 'maternalize' them. Thus, when one sees children, one 'sees' parents. When one sees children who have problems, one looks for parents, especially mothers.   (Ambert, 1994: 530)

Certainly, fathers, too, receive social attention in relation to children's needs, but this attention tends to be focused on *absent* fathers (Dennis, 1993; Dennis and Erdos, 1993; Halsey, 1993). Very often, in both 'popular' and academic forums, it is as if the physical presence or absence of the father is the determinant of how children (particularly boys) turn out. Fathers, in this context, represent a bulwark against social disorder largely by just being there. Mothers' presence in the home, however, is not sufficient: they are also responsible for the 'sensitivity', 'fine-tuning' and responsiveness which children are held to 'need' (Ainsworth *et al.*, 1971; Ainsworth and Bell, 1974; Kellmer-Pringle, 1980, 1987; NSPCC, 1989).[9]

Some feminist authors in this area have problematized the linkage between children's needs and mothering through proposing 'shared parenting' between mothers and fathers (Dinnerstein, 1976; Chodorow, 1978). However, what has largely remained unquestioned and untheorized is what mothering itself *means* (Adams, 1983).[10] This leads to a situation in which 'mothering', as functional meeting of a child's needs, remains intact. As Walkerdine and Lucey put it, 'the notion ... stands that, in principle, "anyone can mother", but that "mothering" must be done by *someone*' (Walkerdine and Lucey, 1989: 20; their emphasis). To a large extent this is because little attention has been focused, in discussions of motherhood, on the social constitution of the category 'child' and of children's 'needs'. While these social phenomena remain untheorized, there are few ways to radically question the concept of 'mothering' as a function to meet the child's needs, or to examine the ways in which mothers are governed through subjection to an authoritative set of truths which purport to speak the nature and the needs of the child.

My argument, then, is that mothers are subject to a form of power which works through producing knowledges about 'the child'. This power works primarily not through overt coercion, but through advice and encouragement; it is a form of power which works productively, creating subjects (the categories 'child' and 'mother', for example), creating meaning, naming and inducing forms of pleasure. Discourses surrounding childhood are not necessarily imposed on mothers 'from above'. Women as mothers may make heavy investments in them, participating in these discourses and gaining a sense of themselves as 'good mothers' from them (Urwin, 1985). This does not mean, though, that power is not at work. Certainly there is pleasure (and social approval) to be gained from such a positioning, but it would be mistaken to see power and pleasure as necessarily antithetical. If subjection to 'psy' knowledges is seen as 'freedom' rather than a subjection to the workings of power, this is because of a conventional view of power as denying and repressing, forbidding pleasure rather than inducing pleasure, obscuring the truth rather than producing the 'truths' by which contemporary Euroamericans conduct their lives. The question is whether this is the only or the best way to envisage power or whether such a view of power might itself work to obscure the ways in which power works productively within the subject. As Michel Foucault puts it:

If power were never anything but repressive, if it never did anything but to say no, do you really think one would be brought to obey it? What makes power hold good, what makes it accepted, is simply the fact that it doesn't only weigh on us as a force that says no, but that it traverses and produces things, it induces pleasure, forms knowledge, produces discourses. It needs to be considered as a productive network which runs through the whole social body, much more than as a negative instance whose function is repression.

(Foucault, 1980: 119)

As Foucault (1979) argues, power and knowledge are inevitably implicated with each other; the extension of one involves the extension of the other. It is in discourse that power and knowledge are conjoined; discourses define and delimit what can be said and thought on the basis of what is 'known', what counts as 'true', in any specific social and historical formation. They are, as Edward Said (1991: 10) puts it, 'epistemological enforcers'. Knowledges and 'truths' about the nature and the needs of the child are the means by which not only the category 'child', but also the category 'mother', are given meaning, as mothers are constituted in terms of their functional requirement to meet children's needs. In this context mothers can be seen to be subjectified within 'psy' discourse in the dual sense identified by Foucault:

There are two meanings of the word *subject:* subject to someone else by control and dependence, and tied to his [*sic*] own identity by a conscience or self-knowledge. Both meanings suggest a form of power which subjugates and makes subject to.

(Foucault, 1982: 212)

Mothers become *subjected* to the rules and norms engendered by knowledges about the nature and the needs of children. But also they become tied to the identity 'mother' through these relations of power and knowledge; they become (maternal) *subjects*. In subjecting themselves to the norms of 'good mothering', they occupy the category 'good mother'. In this sense 'psy' knowledges about the child and mother form part of the relationship of the self to itself – what Foucault has called a 'technology of the self' (Foucault, 1988). They form a matrix of truths through which mothers are induced to act on themselves and regulate themselves. In the next sections of the chapter I will outline some of the costs to mothers of their subjection to discourses around motherhood.

MOTHERING AND CHILDREN'S NEEDS

> *What was it we needed?*
> *Not much. Perhaps only the mothers and fathers with which we*
> *started. Perhaps to own and not to disown us. Mothers to love us,*
> *and put themselves out on our behalf. And smile as they did so.*
> (Fay Weldon, 1989, *Female Friends*)

Motherhood, as I have already argued, is socially constituted in terms of a *response* to children's needs. The 'sensitivity' or 'responsiveness' mothers are supposed to display is a functional requirement engendered by the child's 'needs'. As Woollett and Phoenix put it:

> [C]onceptualizations of motherhood and of good mothers merely reflect ideas about children. What children are considered to need for development is generalized to define good mothering.
> (Woollett and Phoenix, 1991: 40)

Within such a schema of understanding, women as mothers become invisible outside of their capacity to meet these needs. Although mothers may be afforded an individuality in that they are sometimes held to 'uniquely' understand their child (Winnicott, 1964; Kellmer-Pringle, 1980), their subjectivity *as* mothers is effectively effaced by that of the child. In these circumstances any 'needs claims' made by mothers on their own behalf would seem bound to fall flat. As Elly Singer argues, within much child psychology (and particularly that built on some form of 'attachment theory'):

> [T]he mother should figure as a secure base from which the child (and the husband) can explore the 'strange' and 'dangerous' outside world. In order for the child to feel safe, the mother has to be devoid of needs of her own.
> (Singer, 1992: 147)

But how do mothers become constituted as having no (legitimate) needs of their own? In the next part of the chapter I want to identify two movements which simultaneously invoke and efface maternal 'needs claims'. As I will go on to argue, 'good mothers' are constituted as having needs congruent with those of the child. In contrast, the potential needs claims of 'bad mothers' may be rewritten as manifestations of want, rather than need.

CONGRUENT NEEDS

One type of construction of maternal 'needs' is that they are the same as those of the child. This construction is implicit or explicit in much child-care advice; it achieves an emphasis on child-centredness which comes close to proposing that child-centredness is, for the mother, the same as self-centredness or self-fulfilment. I will take just two examples from many. Winnicott's 'ordinary devoted mother' (Winnicott, 1964) has a 'need' to behave in exactly the way that is good for the baby. There is a perfect match between what 'good enough' mothers 'naturally' want, and what infants need:

> The mother's bond with the baby is very powerful at the beginning and we must do all we can to enable her to be preoccupied with her baby at this, the natural time.
> Now it so happens that it is not only the mother that this experience is good for; the baby undoubtedly needs exactly this kind of thing too.   (1964: 26)

Winnicott constructs a 'good enough' mother whose desires and pleasures exactly coincide with the needs of the infant. More recently, Penelope Leach advises that:

> ... taking the baby's point of view does not mean neglecting your, her parents' viewpoint. Your interests and hers are identical. You are all on the same side, the side that wants to be happy, to have fun. If you make happiness for her, she will make happiness for you. If she is unhappy, you will find yourselves unhappy as well, however much you want or intend to keep your feelings separate from hers.   (Leach, 1988: 8)

As Hariette Marshall (1991) comments, Leach's argument is 'ingenious' in that it encourages mothers to give up aspects of their lives (particularly any aspects other than those as wife and mother[11]) without resentment. Indeed, as Urwin (1985: 193) notes, this argument that the baby's and the mother's needs are identical only works by 'totally discounting the needs of the mother as an independent person altogether'. This type of account contributes to a normalizing process in which 'normal' (or 'good-enough' or 'sensitive') mothers are constructed as without any needs or desires of their own. Their 'interests' are valid only in so far as they coincide with those of the child – an extremely restricted sphere.

There is a second, though rather more subtle, way in which an identity of interests between mother and child is asserted. This assertion rests on the prior assertion that 'good mothers' are those who have received 'good mothering', since, 'If we were mothered well by our parents [*sic*], we have a head start on those whose intellect is the same but whose childhood experiences were less happy' (Jolly, 1986: 1).

Here the work of mothering becomes a quasi-natural extension of childhood. It emerges unproblematically out of the self engendered by the mother's own mother. Of course, if we were not 'mothered properly' (and judging by the literature on mother–daughter relationships, most of us were not!) then there is a tremendous incentive to redouble our efforts to make up for this disadvantage which is a disadvantage, not only to mothers themselves, but to their children. Interestingly, Jolly (1986) suggests that women should not rely on their own mothers for child-care advice: these older women lack the expertise which will assist 'new' mothers in their mothering. This expertise belongs properly to the medical and 'psy' professions. So, while mothers can pass on the *personality traits* associated with 'good' mothering, this by-passes consciousness and knowledge; it is a psychological, rather than an epistemological, inheritance which is passed on. 'Good mothering' becomes a feature of the 'self' which is neither 'rational' nor conscious. But, ironically, it can also be engendered through an attention to 'psy' knowledges.

In either case, all is harmony here: the only power implied is that which the mother holds over the child (Walkerdine and Lucey, 1989). And presumably the mother can make this power go away by 'understanding' the child's true nature. She must repress her own authority, and her own claims to subjectivity separate from those which serve the interests of the child.

CHILDREN'S NEEDS VERSUS MOTHERS' DESIRES

The second movement in the effacing of maternal needs claims which I want to explore here consists in the denial of those needs *as* needs. I have argued that 'good' or 'normal' mothers are constituted in many sites as having no needs beyond those which are 'functional' for the child. Their desires, too, are written out of most discussions of childhood, beyond the (biologically or socially impelled) desire to have children (Warnock, 1985). However, this desire is appropriate only in married, heterosexual women ('normal' mothers), in whom it is often translated into a 'need' (Stanworth, 1987). In women who fall outside of this category of 'normality', though, the reverse process occurs. These mothers seem to have plenty of desires; what they do not have are (legitimate) 'needs'.

To illustrate my argument here, I want to refer to a story which preoccupied the British press in March 1991. This story concerned a woman who had become pregnant through the use of artificial insemination by donor (AID). She had received the AID through the British Pregnancy Advisory Service. What made her story into one which attracted so much attention, not only from the media but from MPs, church leaders, counsellors and psychotherapists, were two facts: she was unmarried, and she was described as a 'virgin'.

The main focus of the representation of this story in the press was the clear unsuitability of such a woman for motherhood. What I want to focus on here is the way in which 'children's needs' were used as a means of effacing any potential needs claims which might have been made on the woman's behalf.

There is considerable consensus in the nature of the press coverage of this story. Every national newspaper presented the story in more or less negative terms, and used more or less the same quotations from the same group of people, with only a few exceptions. The emphasis on the needs of the (potential) child within these accounts is an example of the psychological discourse of children's needs escaping from their specialized arenas (Fraser, 1989). Psychologists were in a minority among the persons quoted (although they appeared more frequently in 'broadsheet' newspapers), but the emphasis on children's needs originated from this specialism, and presents a particularly intractable argument.

Throughout the national press coverage a polarity was produced which set children's needs against maternal desires. For example:

Opponents believe women who want to exclude men are being perverse and will harm the emotional and psychological well-being of their children.   (Carr, 1991: 7)

A spokesman [for Barnardo's] said: 'The *needs* of the child are of paramount importance and must come before the *preferences* of parents'.   (Chaytor, 1991: 7; emphasis mine)

We do not carry out assisted conception for single women except when they are in a stable relationship of, say, a year or more. I know this upsets women's rights organizations, but I do not plan any changes. We have a clinical ethical committee which ... decided that *the prime concern is for the baby – not the women –* and that it was not right deliberately to create children, in addition to those produced accidentally, in an environment that might not be ideal'.

(Peter Brinsden, medical director of Bourne Hall, which pioneered *in vitro* fertilization, quoted in Doyle, 1991: 17; emphasis mine)

One newspaper story in particular (Milhill, 1991) encapsulates well both the opposition which was set up between the interests of the woman and the foetus and the movement from maternal 'needs' to maternal 'wants'. This story appeared in *the Guardian* under the headline 'Child's needs before mother's desires.' After a general introduction, and a discussion of the ethics of offering AID to single women, the story moves on to children's needs, quoting Dame Mary Donaldson (chairwoman of the Interim Licensing Authority):

I am old-fashioned enough to believe that a child *needs* two parents. In these cases it seems that the *needs* of the women are being seen as paramount.   (Quoted in Milhill, 1991: 2; emphasis mine)

Later in the story these needs become translated into 'wants' in the following quotation from John Habgood, the Archbishop of York:

A child *wanted* because the parent [*sic*] *wants* someone to love, *wanted* as an act of defiance, *wanted,* in extreme cases, as a kind of accessory, has to carry too much of the emotional burden of its parent's *needs*. It can be the victim of dangerous selfishness.
(Milhill, 1991: 2; emphasis mine)

Although Habgood introduces the concept of 'needs', it is clearly not the 'need' for a child to which he is referring, but broader emotional 'needs' which the child, once born, will have to meet. The illegitimacy of these 'needs' in mothers is signified by Habgood's contention that these needs represent a 'burden' on the child, and one which will make the child into a 'victim'. It is also clear that the 'parents' referred to here are not any parents; they are obviously not fathers (since it is not men becoming pregnant!) and neither are they married, heterosexual mothers, who are presumably free of these desires.

There is, then, a narrative closure of the women's potential needs claims, congruent with the story's headline. Within this story and, indeed, throughout the press coverage, a hierarchy is set up between the (imagined) child and the woman. Within this hierarchy the child is attributed a set of needs which are the absolute priority, while any possible needs of the woman are pathologized.[12]

This story illustrates one way in which the mother's potential needs claims can be discounted and rendered illegitimate. The construction of children as having 'needs' while (bad) mothers only have 'desires' means that any claims made by the woman as mother on her own behalf can be rendered as no more than 'dangerous selfishness'. The story is significant because of its context within other stories of motherhood, which use the same themes – stories in which women who express and act on what can be formulated as their own desires become pathologized as 'bad mothers' (Walkerdine and Lucey, 1989; Singer, 1992).

(RE)DEFINING NEED

In this part of the chapter I want to move on to consider the ways in which mothers themselves may use 'needs talk' to position themselves in relation to their children. As I have suggested, childhood 'needs talk' leaves mothers with an extremely limited space in which to assert 'needs claims' of their own. Yet this does not mean that there is *no* space. As I will outline here, women may be able to use the very discourses around children's needs, which position them as little more than the passive nurturer of the child's 'self', to assert their own subjectivities.

The data here are taken from interviews I conducted with 14 White women living in the northwest of England during 1992 and 1993.[13] The focus of the research was an exploration of issues of self and subjectivity in the mother-daughter relationship. I was concerned, *inter alia*, with looking at the ways in which the women positioned themselves *vis-à-vis* their children's needs. I carried out repeated, semi-structured interviews with the women, and one group discussion in which six of the women participated. All of the women were either in heterosexual relationships or lived without a partner. Seven of the women defined themselves as middle-class but from working-class birth families; three as working-class from working-class birth families and four as middle-class from middle-class birth families. All were English, Welsh or Scots.[14] At the time of the interviews the women were aged between 38 and 55; their daughters ranged in age from 10 to 29.

All of the women defined motherhood in terms of meeting children's needs and, in particular, in terms of meeting children's emotional needs. This was the measure by which they defined good and bad mothering. The following, fairly typical, quotations are examples of answers to my question 'What does it mean to mother someone?'

LYNNE:[15]   Erm to care for, to nurture. ...... I suppose to be available for them as well in the sense that ...... you're there to fulfil their needs.

RACHEL: Well, I suppose just to provide them with an environment in which they can grow up, really. Physically keep them healthy, and emotionally ...... secure. So they can grow up as sort of un- ...... undamaged as possible, and then live their own lives.

KATE: To take care of them, to look after them ...... both in terms of their physical and emotional needs, I guess. Being able to provide support when it's required.

Good mothers, according to the women's accounts, give children what they need (principally unconditional love, attention, freedom), while bad mothers gave their children either too much or too little of these things (invoking the twin 'others' of mothering – excess and lack).

It was children's needs, then, which structured the women's relationships with their children. They actively participated in these discourses, gaining a sense of themselves as 'good mothers', knowledgeable about the 'right' ways in which to bring up their children. This does not mean, however, that there was no cost to them of engaging in these discourses. All of the women considered there were sacrifices involved in being a mother. Middle-class women, in particular, frequently spoke of their lives as almost dictated by their children's demands and many of these women spoke of mothering (and especially mothering babies and young children) as involving a 'loss of self' (see Lawler, 1999, 2000).

All of the women drew, to a greater or lesser degree, on knowledges generated by the 'psy' professions. However, it is important to note in passing that not all of them stood in the same relationship to these knowledges. Most of the middle-class women had been trained in the 'caring professions' and therefore possessed an easy familiarity with the discourses around childhood selves and children's needs. Many of their jobs involved scrutinizing and monitoring mothers who are more readily deemed 'other', and whose mothering is deemed 'wrong': mothers who are working-class and/or Black, single mothers and/or lesbian mothers (Walkerdine and Lucey, 1989; Phoenix and Woollett, 1991). Working-class women were the *objects* of this kind of scrutiny.

The women's investment in meeting their children's needs left them with very little space within which they could articulate any needs claims or desires of their own. However, all of the women did find means of subverting this situation. One way in which they did so was by drawing on the very language of needs which might make them little more than the passive respondents to their children's active demands. In other words, they engaged in a process of defining their children's needs so that they (at least at times) coincided with their own. This looks like a form of the 'congruence of needs' model which I mentioned earlier, but with the crucial difference that, rather than their needs being subsumed under those of their children, their children *needed* to recognize the (separate) needs of the mother. For example:

KATE: I think [to be a good mother] you've got to have endless sup-
plies of love and concern about the needs of the other person,
but at the same time you've got to be able t) set boundaries so
that you're not totally washed out by it all. You've got to be
able to provide yourself with time and some kind of nurturing
from someone else, or perhaps from the child, even, erm, so
that you can get refreshed. I think you can be a very bad
mother if you put so much into it that you're left drained
yourself and left with nothing. It's a matter of, erm, setting
limits, I suppose, both in time and space.

SL: How do you set those boundaries?

KATE: Erm [*long pause*] partly to do with organization. You know,
deciding, I'm going to have so much time off or whatever a
week, and getting someone else to take care of the children.
And getting the children to understand that you have rights
as well, and that sometimes you need half an hour of peace
and quiet to read or whatever. It doesn't always work, but
it's worth a try.

Or, as another woman put it:

HAZEL: [Children] need nurturing. I think at times, certainly when
they're very young, you have to be completely unselfish.
Their needs have to come first. I mean that's it, you know,

they just do. ... I think you have to be honest. I think a
mother has to be real with the children. I think it's point-
less for her to pretend to be something she's not.

SL: Why d'you think it is so important to be real?

HAZEL: How do they learn to be themselves, if you don't act like
that? I mean it's no good, erm – a woman who doesn't go
out to work and stays at home, when she wants to be out at
work, is gonna be frustrated, pissed off, unfulfilled, unhappy,
and the kids aren't gonna get any good out of her.

Finally:

LYNNE: When I don't come up with the ironed shirt, or the cake, or
whatever it is I'm supposed to come up with as this perfect
mother, I just say, 'Well, failed again!' ... You know, they
have to learn that I have limitations and not expect everybody else to be perfect. ... But I think it makes them into
better people. Recognition of the parent's need, I think,
makes them into more understanding people, so I don't
feel guilty about it

In these extracts, maternal needs claims are framed in terms of their
benefits to children. Not all women 'married' their own and their children's needs in this way but most did. Thus, these women are able to
make 'needs claims' of their own by invoking the 'needs claims' of
children. They are able *both* to occupy the category 'good mother'
(through meeting their children's needs) *and* to resist some of its
demands (through redefining those needs).

Discourses are always shifting and unstable, and one element of their
instability lies in their 'reversibility'. 'Identical formulas' can be used for
'contrary objectives' (Foucault, 1990: 100). In invoking children's needs
as a vehicle for their own needs claims, these women might be seen as
reversing the discourses which define their position as 'mothers' and as
carving out a space (however limited) in which they can be 'subjects'.

CONCLUDING REMARKS

'Needs talk' is more than just representation: it is about 'acts and
interventions' (Fraser, 1989) in people's lives. In this chapter I have

presented the argument that conceptualizations of children's needs are social phenomena, deriving from specific sociopolitical pre-occupations and forged within specific social and political settings. However, their existence as social phenomena is obscured by their representation as 'natural', that is, as deriving from characteristics which inhere within the child her/himself. As I have argued, this formulation leads to mothers being positioned not only as the meeters of children's needs, but in such a way that any claims to 'need' which they might make on their own behalf – and indeed any expression of a subjectivity outside of the category 'mother' – can be pathologized. That women find ways of manipulating these discourses is testimony to their unwillingness to be wholly positioned in this way.

I do not want to suggest that maternal 'needs claims' are any more 'real' or valid than needs claims made on behalf of (and by) children. Rather, I am arguing that needs talk is *political* talk which reflects specific political positioning. Since the category 'mother' is constituted on the basis of the prior category 'child', a radical problematizing of motherhood must involve a deconstruction and problematization of childhood and its 'needs'

ACKNOWLEDGEMENTS

My thanks to all of the women who participated in the interviews. I also thank Julie Seymour for editorial comments, and participants at the 1997 BSA conference for helpful feedback on an earlier version of this paper.

NOTES

1. Including some sociological accounts – see, for example, Giddens, 1991.
2. 'Need' is also often held to be easily and straightforwardly 'read off' from understandings of what the child's 'nature' is. For example, Penelope Leach, in her child-care book *Baby and Child* says that the book is 'designed to tell mothers . . . how their babies develop, and *therefore* what they need' (Leach, 1988: 18; emphasis mine).
3. While children themselves may participate in 'needs talk', formulations of childhood and knowledges around childhood and its needs do not originate with them.
4. Or, indeed, for many groups within Euroamerican cultures – see Walkerdine and Lucey, 1989.

5. Certainly, the 'truths' of 'psy' do not go uncontested. For example, the apparently liberal stress on the need for 'autonomy' in the child is sometimes supplanted by claims that children need 'discipline'. However, this distinction may be overdrawn. It is when children are considered not to have had their needs for love and security met in early childhood that they are frequently held to become the 'out-of-control' children who 'need' discipline. This theme has remained remarkably consistent from Winnicott to the present day. See Winnicott, 1950b; Kellmer-Pringle, 1980, 1987; Pilkington, 1994. Hence the 'normal' and the 'delinquent' child may be two sides of the same coin.

6. Winnicott's work remains remarkably influential, even if implicitly so. His concept of the 'good enough mother' still has currency, and has been taken up by many later theorists (see, for example, Bettelheim, 1987; Adcock and White, 1990) While this concept looks like a generous and empowering one which suggests that to be 'good enough' is no great effort, Winnicott's portrait of the 'good enough mother' is one of a woman whose whole life is bound up with the needs of her child (though, for Winnicott, this is not an achievement, since it is 'natural'; it is wholly congruent with being a woman). Indeed, through this concept, Winnicott formulates a perfect match between the needs of the infant and the needs of the mother. Moreover, Sayers (1986), for example, suggests that Winnicott believed that very few mothers were not 'good enough', but he argued that many of 'those who care for children' (presumably he means mothers) are 'neurotic or near-insane' (Winnicott, 1950a: 24). Neurosis and near-insanity are emphatically not in the psychic make-up of Winnicott's 'good enough mother'.

7. For example, the 1989 Children Act follows the child-centredness of much 'psy' discourse in a number of ways: it replaces the notion of parental 'rights' with that of parental 'responsibilities'; it reiterates the primacy of the 'best interests of the child'; and it refers to children's (physical, emotional and educational) 'needs'. Interestingly, however, it does not seek to define what the child's 'best interests' are: this creates a gap into which must come the evaluations of 'psy' professionals. This piece of legislation could be seen as one example of what Smart (1989) calls the 'symbiotic relationship' between law and 'psy'.

8. One recent example in Britain is what has come to be known as 'The Bulger case', in which two 10-year-old boys, Robert Thompson and Jon Venables, murdered the two-year old James Bulger. In the case, tremendous 'expert' and media scrutiny was focused on Thompson and Venables' mothers, and also the absence of their fathers (see, e.g., Neustatter and Hunt, 1993; Pilkington, 1994; Sereny, 1995; Morrison, 1997. For an excellent analysis of this scrutiny, see Young, 1996).

9. Although many commentators now refer to 'parents', it is important to note that 'mothering' is a gendered activity. As Walkerdine and Lucey (1989) point out, it is no accident that the characteristics which children are held to 'need' from their care-givers are characteristics which are socially 'marked' as feminine. Woollett and Phoenix (1991) point out that, within developmental psychology, lack of 'sensitivity' is interpreted differently depending on whether it is found in mothers or in fathers:

Insensitivity in mothers would be viewed as pathological and as having a negative impact on children's development. In fathers, however, the same behaviour is often seen as beneficial, providing children with a context in which they can learn about unpredictability and learn to express themselves directly.

(Woollett and Phoenix, 1991: 35)

In my own research I found that most of the women considered that fathers could also 'mother' children. Many also claimed that their male partners did as much 'mothering' as they themselves did. However, the 'mothering' done by men consisted, almost always, of practical tasks. It was the emotional care and support mothers themselves gave (and which, in general, fathers did not give) which most women defined as what *really* counted as 'mothering'; see Lawler (2000).

10.   Important exceptions here include Urwin, 1985; Walkerdine and Lucey, 1989; Phoenix and Woollett, 1991. Christine Everingham (1994) problematizes the concept of 'needs' as an essential quality of the child, but seems to reinstate them in the form of 'the child's perspective'. Everingham contends that mothers and their children constitute children's needs 'intersubjectively'. However, this obscures the ways in which some definitions of need carry the status of 'truths' while others do not.

Hill-Collins' (1991) work on African-American motherhood and, in particular, her reference to 'othermothers' who assist birth mothers in child-care, does, however, fundamentally disrupt mainstream Euroamerican models of motherhood. Hill-Collins draws attention to the ways in which Black women's mothering often consists of a necessary toughness, as they prepare their children for a world structured by racism. See also Jordan, 1985.

11.   The simultaneous roles of 'wife and mother' are, of course, a potential source of tension. I found in the course of my research that some women had to 'mother' their male partners, and demands from men and children may be competing. However, this is not usually considered in child-care advice or in psychological texts. Where it is considered, it is in the context of some pathology in the woman.

12.   This powerful contrast is an important feature of discourses of 'foetal personhood', in which the potential child is afforded a subjectivity, while that of the pregnant woman is wholly effaced (Petchesky, 1986; Stanworth, 1987; Franklin, 1991).

13.   This research was funded by an ESRC postgraduate studentship. For a full account of the methodology see Lawler, 2000.

14.   The women were asked to self-define both class and ethnicity. Their self-definition of class was congruent with classifications used in the Registrar General's Standard Occupational Classification (SOC), when class was measured in terms of their current or last employment.

15.   All names are pseudonyms. The following are used to mark quotations from the interviews: three dots (...) indicates material has been edited; six dots (......) indicates a pause.

REFERENCES

Adams, P. (1983) 'Mothering', *m/f,* 8, pp. 40–52.

Adcock, M. (1990) 'Assessing Parenting: The Context', in M. Adcock and R. White, (eds), *Good-Enough Parenting: A Framework for Assessment* (London: British Agencies for Adoption and Fostering).

Adcock, M. and White, R. (eds) (1990) *Good-Enough Parenting: A Framework for Assessment* (London: British Agencies for Adoption and Fostering).

Ainsworth, M. and Bell, S. (1974) 'Mother–Infant Interactions and the Development of Competence', in K. Connolly and J. Bruner (eds), *The Growth of Competence* (London: Academic Press).

Ainsworth, M., Bell, S. and Stayton, D. (1971) 'Individual Differences in Strange-situation Behaviour in One-year-olds', in H. R. Schaffer (ed.), *The Origins of Human Social Relations* (London: Academic Press).

Ambert, A. M. (1994) 'An International Perspective on Parenting: Social Change and Social Constructs', *Journal of Marriage and the Family,* no. 56, pp. 529–43.

Bettelheim, B. (1987) *A Good Enough Parent: The Guide to Bringing Up Your Child* (London: Thames & Hudson).

Carr, A. (1991) 'No Woman Should Be Able to Have her Baby the Way You Would Buy a Tin of Beans', *Today,* 11 March.

Chaytor, R. (1991) 'The Virgin Mother', *Daily Mirror,* 11 March.

Chodorow, N. J. (1978) *The Reproduction of Mothering: Psychoanalysis and the Sociology of Gender* (London: University of California Press).

Dennis, N. (1993) *Rising Crime and the Dismembered Family* (London: IEA Health and Welfare Unit).

Dennis, N. and Erdos, G. (1993) *Families without Fatherhood* (London: IEA Health and Welfare Unit).

Dinnerstein, D. (1976) *The Mermaid and the Minotaur* (New York: Harper).

Doyle, C. (1991) 'When Does a Gift Become a Folly?', *Daily Telegraph,* 12 March.

Ehrenreich, B. and English, D. (1979) *For Her Own Good: 150 Years of the Experts' Advice to Women* (London: Pluto).

Everingham, C. (1994) *Motherhood and Modernity: An Investigation into the Rational Dimension of Mothering* (Buckingham: Open University Press).

Foucault, M. (1979) *Discipline and Punish: The Birth of the Prison,* trans. A. M. Sheridan (Harmondsworth: Penguin).

Foucault, M. (1980) *Power/Knowledge,* ed. C. Gordon, trans. C. Gordon, L. Marshall, J. Mepham and K. Soper (Hemel Hempstead: Harvester/ Wheatsheaf).

Foucault, M. (1982) 'The Subject and Power', in H. Dreyfus and P. Rabinow (eds), *Michel Foucault: Beyond Structuralism and Hermeneutics* (Chicago, IL: Chicago University Press).

Foucault, M. (1988) 'Technologies of the Self', in L. H. Martin, H. Gutman and P. H. Hutton (eds), *Technologies of the Self: A Seminar with Michel Foucault* (London: Tavistock).

Foucault, M. (1990) *The History of Sexuality,* vol. I: *An Introduction,* trans. R. Hurley (London: Penguin).

Franklin, S. (1991) 'Fetal Fascinations: New Dimensions to the Medical–Scientific Construction of Fetal Personhood', in S. Franklin, C. Lury and J. Stacey (eds), *Off-Centre: Feminism and Cultural Studies* (London: Harper Collins).

Fraser, N. (1989) *Unruly Practices: Power, Discourse and Gender in Contemporary Social Theory* (Cambridge: Polity).

Giddens, A. (1991) *Modernity and Self-Identity: Self and Society in the Late Modern Age* (Cambridge: Polity).

Halsey, A. H. (1993) 'Foreword', in N. Dennis and G. Erdos (eds), *Families without Fatherhood* (London: IEA Health and Welfare Unit).

Hill-Collins, P. (1991) *Black Feminist Thought: Knowledge, Consciousness and the Politics of Empowerment* (London: Routledge).

Hockey, J. and James, A. (1993) *Growing Up and Growing Old: Ageing and Dependency in the Life Course* (London: Sage).

Ingleby, D. (1986) 'Development in Social Context', in M. Richards and P. Light (eds), *Children of Social Worlds* (Cambridge: Polity).

Jenks, C. (1996) *Childhood* (London: Routledge).

Jolly, H. (1986) *Hugh Jolly Book of Child Care: The Complete Guide for Today's Parents* (London: Unwin).

Jordan, J. (1985) *On Call: Political Essays* (Boston, MA: South End Press).

Kaplan, E. A. (1992) *Motherhood and Representation: The Mother in Popular Culture and Melodrama* (London: Routledge).

Kellmer-Pringle, M. (1980) *The Needs of Children* (London: Hutchinson).

Kellmer-Pringle, M. (1987) *Putting Children First: A Volume in Honour of Mia Kellmer Pringle*, ed. I. Vallender and K. Fogelman (Lewes: Falmer Press).

Lawler, S. (1999) ' "A real giving up of self": Children's Needs and Material Subjectivities in Narratives of Middle-Class Motherhood', in K. Atkinson and S. Oerton (eds), *Feminisms on Edge* (Cardiff: Cardiff Academic Press).

Lawler, S. (2000) *Mothering the Self: Mothers, Daughters, Subjectivities* (London: Routledge).

Leach, P. (1988) *Baby and Child: From Birth to Age Five* (Harmondsworth: Penguin).

Marshall, H. (1991) 'The Social Construction of Motherhood: an Analysis of Childcare and Parenting Manuals', in A. Phoenix, A. Wollett and E. Lloyd (eds), *Motherhood: Meaning, Practices and Ideologies* (London: Sage).

Milhill, C. (1991) 'Child's Needs Before Mother's Desires', *Guardian*, 12 March.

Morrison, B. (1997) *As If* (London: Granta).

NSPCC (1989) *Putting Children First* (London: NSPCC).

Neustatter, A. and Hunt, L. (1993) 'Young Criminals are "Sad Rather Than Bad" ', *Independent*, 25 November.

Petchesky, R. (1986) *Abortion and Woman's Choice: The State, Sexuality and Reproduction* (London: Verso).

Phoenix, A. and Woollett, A. (1991) 'Motherhood: Social Construction, Politics and Psychology', in A. Phoenix, A. Woollett and E. Lloyd (eds), *Motherhood: Meanings, Practices and Ideologies* (London: Sage).

Pilkington, E. (1994) 'Killing the Age of Innocence', *Guardian*, 30 May.

Prout, A. and James, A. (1990) 'A New Paradigm for the Sociology of Childhood? Provenance, Promise and Problems', in A. James and A. Prout (eds), *Constructing and Reconstructing Childhood* (London: Falmer Press).

Rose, N. (1991) *Governing the Soul: The Shaping of the Private Self* (London: Routledge).

Rose, N. (1996) 'Identity, Genealogy, History', in S. Hall and P. du Gay (eds), *Questions of Cultural Identity* (London: Sage).

Ruddick, S. (1983a) 'Maternal Thinking', in J. Treblicot (ed.), *Mothering: Essays in Feminist Theory* (Savage, MD: Rowman & Littlefield).

Ruddick, S. (1983b) 'Preservative Love and Military Destruction: Some Reflections on Mothering and Peace', in J. Treblicot (ed.), *Mothering: Essays in Feminist Theory* (Savage, MD: Rowman & Littlefield).

Ruddick, S. (1990) *Maternal Thinking: Towards a Politics of Peace* (London: Women's Press).

Said, E. (1991) 'Michel Foucault, 1926–1984', in J. Arac (ed.), *After Foucault: Humanistic Knowledges, Postmodern Challenges* (New Brunswick, NJ: Rutgers University Press).

Sayers, J. (1986) *Sexual Contradictions: Psychology, Psychoanalysis and Feminism* (London: Tavistock).

Sereny, G. (1995) *The Case of Mary Bell* (London: Pimlico).

Singer, E. (1992) *Child Care and the Psychology of Development*, trans. A. Porcelijn (London: Routledge).

Smart, C. (1989) *Feminism and the Power of Law* (London: Routledge).

Stainton Rogers, R. and Stainton Rogers, W. (1992) *Stories of Childhood: Shifting Agendas of Child Concern* (Hemel Hempstead: Harvester/Wheatsheaf).

Stanworth, M. (1987) 'The Deconstruction of Motherhood', in M. Stanworth (ed.), *Reproductive Technologies: Gender, Motherhood and Medicine* (Cambridge: Polity Press).

Urwin, C. (1985) 'Constructing Motherhood: the Persuasion of Normal Development', in C. Steedman, C. Urwin and V. Walkerdine (eds), *Language, Gender and Childhood* (London: Routledge & Kegan Paul).

Walkerdine, V. (1990) *Schoolgirl Fictions* (London: Verso).

Walkerdine, V. and Lucey, H. (1989) *Democracy in the Kitchen: Regulating Mothers and Socialising Daughters* (London: Virago).

Walters, S. (1992) *Lives Together, Worlds Apart: Mothers and Daughters in Popular Culture* (Berkeley, CA: University of California Press).

Warnock, M. (1985) *A Question of Life: The Warnock Report on Human Fertilisation and Embryology* (Oxford: Blackwell).

Weldon, F. (1989) *Female Friends* (London: Pan).

Winnicott, D. W. (1950a) 'Growth and Development in Immaturity', in D. W. Winnicott (ed.), *The Family and Individual Development* (London: Tavistock).

Winnicott, D. W. (1950b) 'Some Thoughts on the Meaning of the Word Democracy', in D. W. Winnicott (ed.), *The Family and Individual Development* (London: Tavistock).

Winnicott, D. W. (1964) *The Child, the Family and the Outside World* (Harmondsworth: Penguin).

Woodhead, M. (1990) 'Psychology and the Cultural Construction of Children's Needs', in A. James and A. Prout (eds), *Constructing and Reconstructing Childhood* (London: Falmer Press).

Woollett, A. and Phoenix, A. (1991) 'Psychological Views of Mothering', in A. Phoenix, A. Woollett and E. Lloyd (eds), *Motherhood: Meanings, Practices and Ideologies* (London: Sage).

Young, A. (1996) *Imagining Crime* (London: Sage).

Part II

Regulating Intimacy: the Role of State Legislation in Intimate Relationships

5 The Age of Consent and Sexual Citizenship in the United Kingdom: a History

Matthew Waites

INTRODUCTION

What is an 'age of consent', and how does it contribute to defining and regulating sexual life? Contemporary public debates, such as those surrounding attempts to lower the male homosexual 'age of consent' during 1998–9, often ignore even the recent history of this shifting concept. This chapter explores changing understandings of the 'age of consent' in the United Kingdom from a historical perspective. It discusses several periods when political debates and changes to the law have restructured definitions of the 'age of consent', and explores the forms of power and resistance which have shaped the law and social attitudes. It then moves on to explore how the meaning of the age of consent is currently being contested, and signals how the concept might be rethought in the light of developments in social and political theory, particularly in relation to changing understandings of 'citizenship'. The chapter concludes by examining whether recent developments support claims that sexuality is becoming more democratically negotiated. It argues that the evidence is complex and contradictory, demanding an analysis which is sensitive to gendered attitudes, a complex legal context and the variety of forms of sexual behaviour. Nevertheless, changing understandings of the relationship between sexuality, consent and citizenship are apparent.

THE MEANING OF SEXUAL CITIZENSHIP

To map the changing meaning of an age of consent, this chapter employs the notoriously contested concept of 'citizenship'. Citizenship describes the membership of political communities by individuals, reflected not only in 'rights' but also 'responsibilities', and any social practices which influence degrees of social inclusion (Marshall, 1950: 28; Turner, 1993: 2). Though there is wide acceptance that T. H. Marshall's classic essay 'Citizenship and Social Class', which differentiates between civil, political and social forms of citizenship, suffers from an excessively teleological, Anglocentric, liberal progressivist orientation, this need not invalidate use of the idea of citizenship as such, nor Marshall's achievement in beginning to understand citizenship as the sum of individuals' entire social existence (Marshall, 1950; Bulmer and Rees, 1996). Citizenship helps to articulate how people conceive who should acquire status as full and equal members of their society.

There is currently extensive debate over whether and how theories of citizenship can be adapted to account for late twentieth-century dilemmas (Turner, 1993, 1997), to address feminism and gender (Walby, 1994; Lister, 1997; Werbner *et al.,* 1997), sexuality and same-sex sexualities (Richardson, 1998). Theorists of sexuality have recently coined the concepts of 'sexual citizenship' (Evans, 1993) and 'intimate citizenship' (Plummer, 1995). Each of these concepts has problematic implications due to its formulation within a particular framework (Waites, 1996). This chapter uses 'sexual citizenship', without adherence to the particular understandings of Evans, to describe the ways in which individuals are included and excluded from communities on grounds of their assumed or real 'sexual' identities, thoughts, feelings and/or behaviours. Contrary to Bryan Turner's insistence, citizenship must be understood as international, not solely defined in relation to the nation state (Turner, 1993: 1–2, 162–87, cf: Meehan, 1995).

THE AGE OF CONSENT

The forms and purposes of laws regulating sexual acts for different age groups have changed so dramatically in the course of the past century that finding a language to theorize them is difficult. The term 'age of consent', used in public debates, does not exist in law, but is a convenient expression which can be used with caution to describe *minimum ages* below which certain sexual acts are *prohibited* (Policy Advisory Committee on Sexual Offences, 1981: 3–4, 11–12). But each articulation of a legal boundary between groups of people above and below a particular age involves mutually-constituting, relational cultural definitions of those age groups. These definitions, linked to a range of assumptions about the gender and sexuality of these groups, amount to articulations of the degrees and forms of sexual citizenship granted by the state. Hence debates over the age of consent can provide a lens through which to analyse the forms and degrees of sexual citizenship granted to persons both above and below the age of consent over time. Combining sociological understandings of shifting gender identities (Connell, 1995) sexual identities (Weeks, 1985; Seidman, 1996) constructions of childhood (James *et al.,* 1998) and ageing processes (Finch, 1986) with a historical study of changing age of consent legislation in the UK offers the possibility of new understandings of the relationship between the age of consent and citizenship.

The age of consent is usually discussed in terms of its meaning and effects in relation to people aged below it. Hence the question arises: how, historically, have articulations of the 'age of consent' represented the sexual citizenship of those below the legal boundary? A history of the age of consent could help us to rethink how our society has historically understood youth and sexuality. This is a vital task at a time when child abuse scandals, fear of paedophiles, and panics over young people's sexuality have become endemic foci of cultural anxiety. Recent examples include: campaigns to use the 'paedophile register' created in 1997 to 'out' former sex offenders to local communities;[1] the paedophile scandal which rocked Belgium in August 1996 (Ryback, 1997); controversy over the recent groundbreaking ITV drama 'No Child of Mine', portraying the sexual abuse of a young girl;[2] and strong criticism from the NSPCC, Esther Rantzen, and the *Sun* newspaper of journalist Dea Birkett's excellent feature article 'Monsters with Human Faces' in the *Guardian*, and Channel Four documentary *The Devil Amongst Us*,[3] using interviews with paedophiles to question their demonization (Birkett, 1997). Meanwhile dissenting voices such as lesbian/gay/bisexual/queer activist group Outrage campaign for a lower, and equal, age of consent at 14.[4]

The age of criminal responsibility in the UK is 10, the lowest in Europe. Since the abolition of the presumption that boys under the age of 14 are incapable of sexual intercourse by the Sexual Offences Act 1993, 10-year-olds can be tried for rape.[5] Yet the UK's laws prohibit consensual 'heterosexual' intercourse for young people aged less than 16, and consensual 'homosexual' sexual acts for young men aged below 18. In both cases the law not only makes consent irrelevant, but assumes it does not exist: intercourse is defined by sections 14 and 15 of the Sexual Offences Act 1956 as an 'indecent assault' against people of both sexes aged under 16. There is confusion at the heart of conceptions of the shift from childhood innocence to adult citizenship. Are we imposing responsibilities upon children without rights?

Academic research on the age of consent, and debates over the 'consenting' sexual behaviour of children and young people below the age of consent is rare, though long-standing vitriolic debates over children's sexuality and paedophilia between conservative moralists, feminists and sexual liberationists have slowly achieved wider prominence (NAMBLA, 1980; Jackson, 1982; Sandfort *et al.*, 1990; Evans, 1993: 209–39). More discussion and research is required on these issues. Where discussion of the age of consent exists, it tends to focus solely upon what the law implies for children and young people below the age of consent, and upon the dilemma of how high or low the age of consent should be. What has generally been omitted is a more detailed consideration of the changing rationales for age of consent laws, and in particular of what it means to be *above* the age of consent. Hence one question this chapter seeks to raise is how, historically, has the sexual citizenship of those above the age of consent been articulated?

This chapter outlines the exclusionary nature of age of consent legislation in relation to women and people with same-sex sexualities, and shows that understandings of the age of consent have begun to shift in response to their resistances and claims for full sexual citizenship. It suggests that while age of consent legislation created for 'heterosexuals' in 1885 and male 'homosexuals' in 1967 was oriented to *protecting* young people, it has begun to be reinterpreted in popular understandings as implying the gaining of a *right to consent*, an element of adult citizenship. The chapter traces the emergence of 'the consenting sexual citizen', and hence evaluates recent claims that, in late modernity, intimacy is being more democratically negotiated (Giddens, 1992; Plummer, 1995).

LAW AND CONSENT

When the age of consent is discussed in the media and political debates today, it is commonly assumed that the meaning of the law and its rationale remain the same as when the present 'age of consent' of 16 for sexual intercourse between a man and woman came into being in 1885. But the contexts in which the 'age of consent' operates, and understandings of the meanings it holds, have changed significantly over the past century.

'Consent' means 'voluntary agreement'. But the conditions necessary in law for an individual to be recognized to have given such agreement are widely seen to be inconsistent, and 'consent' has come under increasing scrutiny (Law Commission, 1995). In recent years theorists have demonstrated with increasing sophistication how categories in law form part of the social process through which new gendered and sexualized subjectivities are invented and situated (Moran, 1995, 1996). Using such approaches it is possible to interpret the legal debates surrounding the age of consent at different historical moments which defined and hence regulated consensual and non-consensual acts (Moran, 1997).

Various literatures exist on the interpretation of 'consent' in the criminal law in relation to a wide range of activities, including rape (Smart, 1995: 110–14; Jamieson, 1996; Edwards, 1996), sado-masochism (Thompson, 1994; Smart, 1995: 114 20; Stychin, 1995: 117 26) and HIV transmission (Bronitt, 1994). The meaning of consent in relation to sexual behaviour is hotly contested (Archard, 1998). There is increasingly careful engagement between sociologists, social theorists and legal scholars, attempting to link the ways in which 'consent' is framed in legal texts and interpreted by the courts through traditions of legal positivism, to historical understandings of changing social contexts. Lynn Jamieson, for example, discusses the way in which Scottish law has delimited the right of women to refuse consent to sexual intercourse (Jamieson, 1996: 55–73). On 19 January 1994 the rape conviction of Brian Jamieson was quashed by the Scottish Court of Criminal Appeal, on the grounds that a man who 'honestly believes' a woman has consented cannot be guilty of rape, even if he has no reasonable grounds for his belief. Hence the parameters of consent for women in Scottish rape law are determined by the intentions of men, and women have no absolute right to consent. Such examples show how law embodies assumptions about who can consent, which reflect form of social power.

To understand the contemporary meaning of the age of consent in relation to its history means reflecting upon the changing subjectivities to which that term has applied, the changing contexts of its application, and the social forces which have brought change about. As will become clear, a key issue is to decide whether the changing knowledges through which people both above and below the age of consent have been imagined reflect genuine changes in how society views the experiences of these people, or whether the emergence of a language of citizenship and consent merely obfuscates the absence of change.

THE AGE OF CONSENT FOR 'HETEROSEXUAL' WOMEN

On 14 August 1885 the Criminal Law Amendment Act created the 'age of consent' in UK law for young women engaging in 'heterosexual' sex which still stands on the statute book (Bland, 1995; Walkowitz, 1980, 1992; Weeks, 1989). The act was passed in the context of a public outcry over prostitution among young girls, magnified by a series of articles entitled *The Maiden Tribute of Modern Babylon* by W. T. Stead, editor of the *Pall Mall Gazette* (Walkowitz, 1992). The change in the law occurred as the movement for social purity began to overcome previous *laissez-faire* Victorian attitudes to the role of the state in governing intimate relationships. Sexual behaviour had previously been seen largely as 'a private matter'. As feminists have long argued, this definition preserved men's sexual access to women, denying women the rights to personal and domestic privacy granted to men by the liberal ideology of the time.

The Act prohibited sexual intercourse with a woman aged less than 16, where previously, since 1875, intercourse had been prohibited below the age of 13. It created the offence of 'defilement' of a girl aged under 16:

Any person who –
(1) Unlawfully and carnally knows or attempts to have unlawful carnal knowledge of any girl being of or above the age of thirteen years and under the age of sixteen years; ... shall be guilty of a misdemeanor, and being convicted thereof shall be liable at the discretion of the court to be imprisoned for any term not exceeding two years, with or without hard labour.[6]

A further offence of 'defilement of a girl under thirteen years of age' was made punishable by life imprisonment. While women below the age of consent were not punishable, males of all ages were punishable, creating a stark contrast between the 'innocence' of girls under 16 and the culpability of boys the same age.

Though the new law was discussed as an 'age of consent', feminist commentaries have demonstrated that this was a misnomer, since the rationale behind the law was prohibitive rather than empowering in its attitude to women. As the language of 'defilement' and 'carnal knowledge' reveals, it was conceived in paternalistic terms as an 'age of protection', below which the state was responsible for protecting young women – a negative prohibition, placing limits upon the rights of men to sexual access. It did not create any *right to consent* to sexual intercourse above that age, as the existence of legal rape within marriage prior to the Criminal Justice and Public Order Act (1994) demonstrated. The law represented a limit upon male agency, rather than a recognition of women's equal agency.

What we now think of as the 'heterosexual' 'age of consent' was formulated in 1885 prior to the invention of the concept of hetero-sexuality (Katz, 1995). The law was intended to protect only women, not men, a fact which belies the assumption of mutuality when a 'heterosexual age of consent' is discussed in contemporary public debates. Furthermore the existence of same-sex sexual behaviour was not contemplated. Although the Labouchère amendment, which created the crime of 'gross indecency' between males, was passed as a last-minute adjunct to the Criminal Law Amendment Act, this did not influence debates over the age of consent. The Labouchère amend-ment in any case did not encode 'homosexuality' as such into law, and ignored female homosexuality (Weeks, 1977; Moran, 1996).

The age of consent legislation in the Criminal Law Amendment Act was founded on a polarized view of male and female sexuality whereby 'the beast' of male lust required legal containment to preserve the virtue of a passive, innocent female sexuality. Prevailing views of gender saw men as both more rational, yet also more potentially lustful. Women were divided neatly between the virtuous virgins and mothers and the whores who became the most demonized figures in popular iconography. The morality of women was reconciled with their less rational status through the common understanding that women were governed by emotions linked to their essential womanly nature (Bland, 1995: esp. pp. 48–91). The question of an age of consent for men did not arise, due to the overwhelming assumption that women did not initiate sexual activity. The law which remains on the statute books today was thus profoundly gendered in its conception, and has remained so in its enforcement.

Given that 'consent' is usually considered to be meaningful when it is informed, one must also question the meaning of an age of consent at a time when there was much confusion in popular beliefs about sexuality, no sex education in schools, and when girls were given minimal information about sex to protect their 'innocence'. Even when the *British Medical Journal* responded to the *Maiden Tribute of Modern Babylon exposé* by calling for commencement of sex education in schools, it remained ambivalent about such education being extended to girls, for fear of undermining their purity (Bland, 1995: 59). Many girls above the so-called age of consent engaging in sexual acts would therefore not have known what they were consenting *to*, including the risks of pregnancy and sexually transmitted diseases.

Yet to understand the age of consent's formation and effects in 1885 involves examining the reality behind representations of young women as passive victims. Judith Walkowitz and Jeffrey Weeks are agreed that the portrayal of young girl prostitutes as sexually innocent passive victims of individual evil men ignored the opportunities offered to young women by prostitution to combat poverty and dismal employment prospects, with the consequence that social purity's moral campaigns ignored the need for structural social reforms (Weeks, 1989: 88; Walkowitz, 1992). Weeks argues that campaigns which continued until the 1930s to raise the age of consent, even to 21, assumed that young girls needed protection from being dragged into prostitution.

The dominant axis of debate over the 1885 Criminal Law Amendment Act was the opposition between male libertarians who sought to protect their sexual prerogatives, and the forces of social purity who favoured regulation. However, both sides contained those who linked their proposals to greater autonomy for adult sexual subjects, and both contained more reactionary forces who opposed sexual freedom.

In general the ideology of social purity did not support the legitimacy of consenting adult subjects, but involved a generalized scepticism towards sexual progressivism (Weeks, 1989: 81–3). However, some feminists allied to social purity were already beginning to place greater emphasis on women's sexual agency, despite seeking to protect young girls. Such differing emphases within social purity were mirrored in debates over prostitution, where a minority of feminists led by Josephine Butler argued for women's right to choose for themselves, despite believing prostitution to be evil. Bland (1995) notes the positive effect which social purity campaigns had in enabling women to speak of sex for the first time, foreshadowing more 'sex-positive' forms of feminism in the early twentieth century. A reduction in ignorance about sexuality, and the beginnings of a more public negotiation of appropriate sexual behaviour between men and women, initiated a process of constituting women as having rights, needs and desires. However, the thrust of much of social purity was to repress debate, and many of the new voices which did emerge were inadvertent effects, paradoxically generated by the movement. Social purity was on the whole disempowering with regard to both young people's sexuality and to women's sexuality (Bland, 1995: xvii).

Many of those who opposed social purity's demand to raise the age of consent, including MPs, did so in a manner which did not support the rights of all adults to actively consent to sexual relations. Their motive was to protect the power of men. But there were a few, such as Charles Hopwood, MP for Stockport, who did so on the basis that legislation violated the right of free choice, despite supporting the social purity view of prostitution (Weeks, 1989: 89).

Thus, on both sides of the debate in 1885 can be found arguments influenced by liberal democratic emphases upon the rights of the individual citizen. These represented early attempts to apply the emerging ideals of liberal democratic citizenship to the realm of intimacy and sexual relations. In the arguments of Hopwood and others it is possible to find emergent elements akin to contemporary feminist perspectives which focus upon protecting the sexual autonomy of young women, rather than diminishing their agency. They sought to uphold the right of young women to say yes or no. However, as the work of Frank Mort and Lucy Bland has shown, the unique political configurations of the time make it extremely difficult to read back a liberal progressivist narrative, without a careful analysis of gendered power. Mort and Bland place more emphasis upon women's experiences and feminist narratives which they see as disrupting liberal assumptions of 'progress' (Mort, 1987; Bland, 1995).

Sexuality was conceived by the Victorians as essentially a private matter, within a 'private sphere' of the patriarchal family central to the bourgeois imaginary. Prior to social purity, the conservative state's ethos was essentially '*laissez-faire*'. But social purity subsequently sought to prohibit certain activities, particularly in the public realm, while preserving the sanctity of the family. However, while this process of moral regulation, evident in the raising of the age of consent, demonstrated a recognition of collective social responsibility, it involved no concurrent protection of sexual rights.

Walkowitz rightly links her critical analysis of the 1885 debates to contemporary debates over 'victim feminism' and the desire for a feminism which favours sexual empowerment rather than constraint (Walkowitz, 1992). Yet perhaps to assess the 1885 Criminal Law Amendment Act in these terms is to underemphasize the significance of the state recognizing its responsibility to protect young women, and the importance of contraception and medical knowledge developed during the twentieth-century which have made possible a more empowered female sexuality.

THE MALE HOMOSEXUAL AGE OF CONSENT

In 1957 *The Report of the Committee on Homosexual Offences and Prostitution*, subsequently known as the *Wolfenden Report*, was published (RCHOP, 1957). The report, from a Home Office departmental committee which had spent three years investigating homosexuality and prostitution, advocated the partial decriminalization of homosexual acts between consenting males in private (RCHOP, 1957: 115). It provided the dominant rationale and framework employed when this measure eventually came about after sustained lobbying in England and Wales in 1967, though not in Scotland until 1980, or in Northern Ireland until 1982.[7] The Sexual Offences Act 1967 stated:

> ... a homosexual act in private shall not be an offence provided that the parties consent thereto and have attained the age of twenty-one years.[8]

Decriminalization thus created a minimum age for male homosexual activity at 21, the age of majority (voting age) when the report was written, but did not encode the concept of an 'age of consent' as such into law. When the age of majority was subsequently reduced to 18, in 1969, the homosexual age of consent at 21 remained as a clear anomaly (Jeffery-Poulter, 1991: 8–89; Weeks, 1977: 156–82; Weeks, 1989: 239–48; Hall, 1980; Greenwood and Young, 1980; Grey, 1992; Moran, 1995; Moran, 1996; Higgins, 1996).

Decriminalization did not represent homosexuals being granted equal citizenship with regard to the age of consent. As the *Wolfenden Report* said:

> It is important that the limited modification of the law which we propose should not be interpreted as an indication that the law can be indifferent to other forms of homosexual behaviour, or as a general licence to adult homosexuals to behave as they please.
>
> (RCHOP, 1957: 44)

The *Wolfenden Report's* formula was conceived to further a strategy of control rather than of pure liberalization. Though differing in their emphases, Stuart Hall, Jeffrey Weeks and more recently Les Moran have argued that the objective of the Wolfenden committee was to eradicate the problem of homosexuality from public view, rather than to instigate further steps towards equality (Weeks, 1977, 1989; Hall, 1980; Moran, 1996; Waites, 1997).

Decriminalization encoded 'homosexuality' as such into law for the first time. The posing of the problem of homosexuality generated a quest by the Wolfenden committee for new definitions and sources of expertise (Moran, 1995). Decriminalization and the invention of a homosexual age of consent were therefore intertwined with new conceptions of scientifically defined homosexual subjects. As a result, a homosexual age of consent implied a sphere of consent for a very particular kind of medically defined legal subject.

Much regulation of consensual activities between adults remained after 1967, making the idea of an 'age of consent' misleading. Partial decriminalization did not remove the Labouchère amendment which installed 'gross indecency' in law. Rather, it exempted a tightly defined category of acts from prosecution. Buggery and 'indecency' (sexual acts between men other than buggery, such as fellatio and mutual masturbation) remained illegal except in strict 'privacy', which, contrary to the Wolfenden committee's intentions, was defined more strictly than for heterosexuals by a late House of Lords amendment, to mean no more than two men present (RCHOP, 1957: 25). Sodomy laws remained on the statute book, and new stricter sentences for buggery were introduced where decriminalization did not apply. Soliciting (cruising or propositioning men) and procuring (inviting, encouraging and facilitating homosexual acts) were unaffected by the 1967 Act, and remained completely illegal. A legal judgement in 1972 by the House of Lords decided that the 1967 Act exempted homosexuals over 21 from criminal penalties without making their actions 'lawful in the full sense' (Weeks, 1989: 275). The merchant navy and armed forces remained exempted from decriminalization. The law also imposed new regulations upon consensual public behaviour such as importuning, and with regard to 'minors' below the new age of consent.

It is also significant that consensual sexual acts committed in public were not governed by the fair rule of law which might be expected to apply as one of the most basic of civil rights constituting citizenship. Recently released transcripts of police evidence presented to the Wolfenden committee, together with letters and other documentation held at the Public Record Office, illustrate that the police – 'very decent chaps' – were permitted to proceed with their use of *agents provocateurs* unchallenged, despite the chairman having 'not the least doubt that it occurs' (Higgins, 1996: 45–8).

Decriminalization represented a pragmatic decision to recognize that the law was not a deterrent, largely on the basis of the *Wolfenden Report*'s conclusion that homosexual identity in adults was a *fait accompli.* It did not represent the granting of a general right to consent above the age of 21. It signalled, as Jeffrey Weeks has argued, an ethic of limited tolerance, and efficient regulation of public behaviour, rather than equal rights and equal respect (Weeks, 1989).

Despite the scope of the *Wolfenden Report* potentially including female 'homosexual offences', lesbianism was largely ignored. Sexual offences by women against women continued to largely escape criminalization by British law due to assumptions of women's lack of sexual agency. There was no attempt to create a female homosexual 'age of consent', despite a lack of clarity as to whether an age of consent existed for lesbian acts. The Wolfenden committee did consider whether the offence of 'indecent assault' encoded in the Sexual Offences Act (1956) – 'an assault accompanied by circumstances of indecency on the part of the person alleged to have been assaulted' (RCHOP, 1957: 36–8) – could apply to lesbians.[9] It carried a maximum sentence of two years imprisonment, compared with 10 years for men. But the committee were unable to find a single instance of such an act having been directly committed against another female, and continued to assume 'homosexual offences' were male (RCHOP, 1957: 38; Moran, 1996: 97–101). Their decision not to propose new legislation represented ignorance rather than an endorsement of women's right to consent. The idea of older women as potential abusers of young girls was anathema.

The *Wolfenden Report* stated, in accordance with the near-unanimous view of its medical witnesses, that a young man's sexual orientation is fixed 'in the main outline' by the age of 16, although its call for more research and advocacy of hormone treatments suggests residual doubts about the fixity of sexual orientation. However, it argued that he could only take decisions which might set him apart from society after the age of 21 (RCHOP, 1957: 25–8).

> a boy is incapable at the age of sixteen of forming a mature judgement about actions of a kind which might have the effect of setting him apart from the rest of society.   (RCHOP, 1957: 25)

This suggests an interesting disjunction between physical maturity, the fixity of desires, and rational/ethical maturity, the attainment of moral responsibility. According to the argument used by the committee, this mind/body split implied that only the attainment of certain mental capacities could legitimize the acquisition of the legal 'right' to choose as a full citizen. However, recently released committee records suggest a more messy compromise. Chairman John Wolfenden insisted on 21 against a majority of his committee in favour of 18 and, despite being demonized by Patrick Higgins, may well have been right to choose this pragmatic course to achieve even partial decriminalization (Higgins, 1996: 65, 73).

The disjuncture between the fixity of desires and the attainment of citizenship articulated in the report must be understood in the context of pragmatic politics. It was the product of a compromise between universalist humanistic intentions, evident in the committee's positive response to meeting homosexuals face to face and their language of a universal citizens' right to privacy, and the desire to contain the 'problem' of homosexuality, to 'make it go away'. The committee's recommendation for an age of consent at 21 was not rationalized on principle, but determined by what committee members – particularly the chairman – believed to be attainable. The committee recognized that the symbolic importance of the age of majority as an age for ethical decision-making by adults would be powerful in convincing MPs of the case for decriminalization. They drew upon liberal impulses to extend autonomy to individuals in a modern society of value-conflicts, in sexual matters as elsewhere. But it is clear that for most of the committee the abstract principle of linking the age of consent to the age of majority was less of a priority than practical issues, particularly how to avoid criminalizing young people, while simultaneously minimizing the dangers of seduction into homosexuality. The committee's beliefs on desirable age of consent legislation were pragmatically oriented by a view of law as a crude tool necessary for the management of social policy, rather than a vehicle for ethical transformation. Their actual recommendation, as distinct from their majority view, was similarly a product of political pragmatism. Despite the age of majority being appropriated, there was little support for the idealistic view that age of consent law should be linked to an age of maturity, at which young people are deemed capable of decisions as citizens. The committee saw the law on sex in a much more utilitarian light, as a tool to manage rather than transform society.

Comparisons with the rationale for legislation in 1885 are problematic. Superficially, it would appear that, whereas the age of consent for young women in 1885 was defined largely by their biological maturity, a need for protection, male homosexuals in 1967 were accorded consent on the grounds of ability to exercise ethical choice as adult citizens. But it is evident that the 1967 formulation did not represent consent in relation to sexuality being increasingly linked to other adult rational and ethical capacities. Rather, the high age of consent reflected the strong fear of seduction of young men among heterosexual male MPs and opinion-formers. If the Wolfenden rationale is understood as an effort to contain homosexuality and preserve heterosexuality, the high age of consent linked to the age of majority must be understood less as a recognition of adult homosexual citizenship, and more as a measure of fear against a stigmatized homosexuality. There was no question that adult homosexuals could join the dominant adult moral community on equal terms, or that their freedoms had equal value. Homosexuals over 21 were not imagined as fully rational beings, or deserving of equal citizenship status.

The sphere of consent was the sphere of privacy, a carefully delimited realm, tightly patrolled at the boundaries where public order and decency were threatened (RCHOP, 1957: 9–10, 12, 20). Though the formal definitions of both consent and privacy were intended to be the same as for heterosexuals by the Wolfenden committee, this disguised a contrary intent. While consent in private for heterosexuals was seen to contribute to the flourishing of the family, society, and good citizenship, consent in private for homosexuals was intended to manage and contain irrevocably deviant individuals. A universalistic, humanist language of an equal right to consenting acts in privacy for all citizens was employed (RCHOP, 1957: 20). But this disguised contrary intentions with regard to real, meaningful citizenship: of enhancement and promotion on the one hand, of containment and dissappearance on the other (Hall, 1980; Greenwood and Young, 1980; Weeks, 1989; Moran, 1996). The *Wolfenden Report* stated that lesbian and male homosexual acts are:

> … reprehensible from the point of view of the family … We deplore this damage to what we regard as the basic unit of society … This argument [for decriminalization] is not to be taken as saying that society should condone or approve male homosexual behaviour.
>
> (RCHOP, 1957: 22)

The male homosexual age of consent was conceptualized in negative terms of protection similar to those which had structured the age of consent for young women in 1885. But while the former was explicitly rationalized through being linked to the age of majority, the latter had never been formulated in such terms. The contrast was rooted in scientific and popular understandings of male and female bodies, desires and aetiologies. While in 1885 the imagined sexual innocence of women aged under 16 was an assumption paralleled by wider assumptions about the lack of female desire, the rationale for the decriminalization of male homosexual sex involved a complex relation between the presumed latent heterosexual desires of young boys and the surplus of adult homosexual desires requiring a legal outlet. The discrepancy between the ages of 21 and 16 reflected the contrasting implications of hegemonic heterosexual male perspectives with regard to the two groups: strong homophobia and fears of seduction in relation to male homosexuality, compared with reluctant denial of male access to young women. Both laws, however, represented prohibitions upon activity below the age of consent, without endorsement of equal sexual citizenship for those above. The cultural taboo against paedophilia, historically stronger in relation to male 'homosexual' acts than in relation to 'heterosexual' acts, played an important part in ensuring a higher male homosexual age of consent.

Nevertheless, liberal ideology and humanist assertions of the universal rights of citizens did play their part. In 1967, far more than in 1885, ideas of individual rights and privacy were used in relation to sexuality, as in other areas of social life. In 1885 such ideas had been largely irrelevant, in an era when women were not even regarded as responsible or rational enough to be granted basic citizenship rights such as the vote. But in 1967 ideals of individual autonomy for adult citizens played a part alongside a prohibitive logic of protection of the young. Adult male homosexuals remained excluded from such citizenship due to a range of cultural understandings of homosexuals as driven by deep bodily desires and compromised by weak-willed, effeminate minds.[10] Male homosexuals were thought to lack the capacities for rational, responsible, strong-willed ethical decision-making required by full citizens. The adult homosexual subject could never be a full sexual citizen, but would remain necessarily compromised by deviant sexual desires requiring judicious constraint.

THE GAY AGE OF CONSENT

By 1994 sexual acts between male homosexuals were the only activities in the UK prohibited for young people until the age of 21. Ages for purchasing cigarettes and alcohol, marriage or gaining a driving licence were all no higher than 18. The age of 21 was also the highest age of consent in Europe, and there was an equal age of consent in 21 out of 28 Council of Europe states (Stonewall, 1993b). Following campaigns for lesbian and gay equality, the male homosexual age of consent was reduced from 21 to 18 (427 votes to 162 in favour), but not to the 'heterosexual' age of 16 (307 to 280 votes against). Equality was denied, but for the first time people with same-sex sexualities – lesbians, gay men, bisexuals, queers and otherwise-identified – had led their own fight for a just age of consent, and demanded equality rather than tolerance. The vote in parliament on 21 February 1994 followed the first full parliamentary debate on the subject since 1967 (Waites, 1995).[11]

During the 1994 debate, following transformations initiated by the sexual liberation movements of the 1970s, the idea of a 'gay age of consent' was being 'invented'. Those engaged in the debate sometimes seemed unconscious of the historical shifts which had taken place. Media reports sometimes neglected to clarify how the Sexual Offences Act 1967 continued to make a wide range of consensual sexual acts between men illegal, and the language of an 'age of consent' was used uncritically to describe existing laws regulating both heterosexual and male homosexual acts.

More positively there had been a shift from 'homosexual' to 'gay'. Previously the 'homosexual age of consent' had been conceived as permitting a very limited set of actions for a medicalized sexually deviant group. Now claims were being articulated in 'gay' terms, with all the positive connotations of equality which that implied through the legacy of gay liberation, though in the same essentialist language, emphasizing the fixity of homosexual desires. Where a 'homosexual age of consent' had applied to a medicalized category of deviants, as a pragmatic legal response to their affliction, the 'gay age of consent' implied some recognition of the agency of gay men and lesbians, and their capacity to make claims to citizenship and define themselves. Yet 'gay' and 'age of consent' remained in tension, since the aspiration to equal citizenship embodied in 'gay' was contradicted by the continuing prohibition of various consensual sexual acts between men.

The language of the 'age of consent' had been appropriated from 1885 and 1967, but given new meaning. Both the male homosexual subject and his consenting sexual acts had been reinterpreted. Where previously the consenting homosexual subject of the *Wolfenden Report* had been granted partial citizenship only as a means to govern deviant desires, now the gay sexual subject was articulated by supporters of equality as deserving equal rights precisely due to his fixed desires. Equality supporters still insisted upon the fixity of desires, indeed Stonewall and others cited the evidence for this produced by the *Wolfenden Report* in 1957, a strategy which damagingly marginalized many bisexual, queer, and lesbian and gay voices (Stonewall, 1993b;

Waites, 1995). But the language of perversion and deviancy was replaced by a language of equality, thus reframing the meaning of medical claims for the fixity of fixed sexual orientation.

For equality supporters the right to perform consensual sexual acts became an indicator of equal citizenship, a measure against hetero-sexuality. But this did not imply for them that the age of consent should be linked to the attainment of 'adulthood', the 'age of majority' or a newly accepted 'age of maturity', hypothesized by some as an age of competence for a variety of ethical decisions. In fact there was little debate and little consensus on what the age of consent, once equal, should be. Most equality campaigners argued their case in terms of pragmatic social policy: the health needs of young gay men, and the desire to avoid criminalizing them.

The emphasis of pro-equality campaigns was often on the problems of criminalization rather than a right to have sex, and there was ambivalence as to whether sex for adolescents was necessarily 'a good thing'. However, a movement from pragmatic decriminalization in 1967 to claims for a 'right to consent' was occurring. People with same-sex sexualities argued that they should be entitled to legal sex if they chose it. Though these claims to sexual citizenship were not claims to full adult ethical responsibility, they were claims to a degree of sexual autonomy at an early phase in the life-course. Unlike in 1885, and to a greater extent than in 1967, the age of consent was discussed as a matter of sexual citizenship for those above the legal age, rather than a matter of protecting those below.

Elements of the Conservative right and Labour traditionalists con-tinued to successfully articulate the homosexual age of consent as an age of protection from seducing older men. Hence the male homosexual age of consent remained unequal to that for heterosexual intercourse, at 18. Yet such views were clearly on the wane, and must be seen in the context of a declining Conservative Party fighting a rearguard action to preserve the distinctiveness of its fractured ideology.

Despite some confusion over the law on the age of consent for heterosexual boys, disinterest in amending the gendered legislation of 1885, and some conservative arguments about the late maturation of boys requiring special protection, it was widely assumed that the law should recognize that men and women are equally capable of giving active consent. Following feminist transformations, women were no longer conceived as passive. Questions were raised as to why men below the age of consent for same-sex behaviour are criminalized (by 'gross indecency'), when men indecently assaulted by older women are treated as innocent victims. Lesbianism, however, remained largely off the agenda, due to the continuing mainstream invisibility of both lesbian desire and lesbian sexual abuse.

A significant disjunction between concepts of paedophilia and homosexuality had occurred, with homosexuality becoming included in what is normal and acceptable, while paedophilia remained illicit. But the image of the seducing older male homosexual continued to be critical. Some commented that the gay age of consent should remain higher and unequal to the heterosexual age, because young men needed extra protection since they matured later than young women. This led to the interesting response that perhaps the age of consent for men to engage in heterosexual sex should also be raised, a suggestion which was widely debated. In this context it seemed that men were seen as in need of greater protection than women, in contrast to a century before. However, lack of concern for the seduction of young women, evident in the rareness of prosecutions against older heterosexual men, did not go unnoticed by equality campaigners such as Conservative MP Edwina Currie, who demanded women's equality in the terms of a popular feminism.

TOWARDS EQUALITY?

A reduction of the 'male homosexual age of consent' to 16 is now imminent. When the Labour government pledged on 14 July 1997 to allow a free vote in Parliament, on the same day as speculating about raising the minimum age for purchasing tobacco to 18, debates ensued on the inconsistency of the law and attitudes to young people's rights and responsibilities. Increasing sympathy was evident for more consistent attitudes and even possibly a single 'age of maturity'.[12] On Tuesday 7 October 1997 the European Commission on Human Rights ruled, in favour of Euan Sutherland (supported by Stonewall), that an unequal age of consent for male homosexuals is discriminatory and contravenes the right to privacy enshrined in Article 8 of the European Convention on Human Rights. Following the case, the government promised a vote 'at the earliest opportunity'.[13] An amendment to the Crime and Disorder Act (1998) was accepted by the House of Commons in June 1998, but subsequently rejected by the House of Lords (Hansard: HC 22.6.98 cols 754–811; HL 22.7.98 cols 936–76; HC 28.7.98 cols 176–211). In the Queen's Speech of 24 November 1998, the Government signalled its intention to introduce legislation 'equalizing' the age of consent during the 1998/99 parliamentary session. Reporting these developments, the *Independent* illustrated the common misconceptions which this chapter has sought to problematize, claiming that a reduction to 16 would mean '*giving gays the same right heterosexuals have had since 1885*'.[14]

The legacy of the Labouchère amendment in 1885, the partial decriminalization of male homosexual sexual acts in 1967 and the lowering of the male homosexual age of consent in 1994 is a framework of legislation on male same-sex sexual activity built upon prohibitive exclusions from citizenship, mitigated by liberal tolerance, utilitarian pragmatism and piecemeal reform. Meanwhile the law on the age of consent for sexual acts between women remains ambiguous. There is no 'right to consent' to same-sex acts.

CONCLUSION

Each of the historical moments outlined bears witness to complex forms of power and resistance. Power is evident in the very definitions of gender and sexual identities, and in the definition of the age of consent. Resistance has taken the form of claims to sexual citizenship by women and people with same-sex sexualities who have argued that their biology and desires do not compromise their ethical and rational capacities for autonomous decision-making.

In the light of the argument above, one is drawn to look afresh at familiar international comparisons of the age of consent, such as those employed by equality campaigners in 1994 (Stonewall, 1993a; Tatchell, 1992). How must the individual national trajectories of law, and the different cultural formations informing them, compromise such easy comparisons between states? Does the age of consent have the same meaning, or does it operate in the same way, if the histories of the age of consent in each country reveal similarly distinctive formations?

What does the history of age of consent legislation in the UK tell us about transformations in understandings of sexual citizenship? In relation to 'consensual' sexual relations for people below the current age of consent there is little evidence of any desire to 'expand' sexual citizenship in accordance with the arguments of sexual liberationists. What Giddens describes in *The Transformation of Intimacy* as the emergence of 'the pure relationship' between adults and children in late modernity, characterized by negotiation and equality of participation, shows little sign of changing the law on the age of consent, despite finding echoes in new thinking on children's rights and participation in decision making (Giddens, 1992; Lansdown, 1995; Schofield and

Thoburn, 1996). There may be greater recognition that the desires and experiences of young people should be a part of the process of decision-making, but this is not interpreted widely to mean a lowering of the age of consent.

Male children's right to protection from abuse has been increasingly recognized. The crime of 'indecent assault', though articulated in the Offences Against the Person Act (1861) with the intention of applying only to same-sex acts between men, has been appropriated for use as an age of consent for boys aged less than 16.[15] Public attitudes continue to be deeply gendered however. When a 33-year-old woman, ran away to Florida with a 14 year-old virgin boy in July 1997 she was found guilty of abduction, gross indecency and indecent assault, but escaped a prison sentence with two years' probation. The *Sun*'s report (Friday 5 December 1997: 1–3), headlined: 'Boy, 14: My Sex, Sex, Sex with a Mum, 33', illustrated the difference in cultural understandings of sex for underage boys, who are always expected to want sex, in contrast to girls, whose innocence requires protection from it.

There have recently been at least two cases of lesbians being prosecuted for 'consensual' sex with females aged under 16, charged as 'indecent assault', indicating attempts to reinterpret nineteenth-century laws to create a 'lesbian age of consent' for the first time (Stonewall, 1997: 6).

With regard to people *above* the age of consent, there is some evidence that the principle of informed consent remains fragile. The law continues to delimit the scope of consent for adults. Particular offences applying to consensual same-sex acts between males remain where not conducted in strict privacy. The realities of trials for violent sexual offences including rape undermine the rights of male and female victims to consent or say 'no', for example by making reference to irrelevant sexual histories. In the R. v Brown 'Spanner' case, 15 men were arrested and five jailed in 1990 for consensual acts of sado-masochism. However, following the case, the Law Commission has recommended that such acts become legal (Thompson, 1994: 1–13; Law Commission, 1995). Renewed attempts are afoot to criminalize HIV transmission through consensual sexual activity. Both sado-masochistic acts and HIV trans-mission are understood through definitions of 'harm' which are believed to invalidate the principle of informed consent, and government responses in both cases illustrate the fragility of that ideal.

Nevertheless, developments point to a strengthening of the idea that individuals should have the 'right to consent', as sexual rights become seen as a matter of citizenship. There is legitimate debate over whether formally entrenched rights, such as the European Convention on

Human Rights, or a future Bill of Rights revising and updating this convention, are necessary devices to achieve effective individual rights in practice. But what is evident is a widespread shift in public beliefs in favour of the various juridical, political and social institutions of the state upholding individual adult sexual autonomy as a practical outcome. The 1994 debate provided evidence that the idea of an 'age of consent' has been reinterpreted in the aftermath of feminism and gay liberation. Women and homosexuals have claimed equal respect and thus become increasingly regarded as capable of decision-making. The consenting sexual acts of male homosexuals are seen more positively, rather than as pragmatically managed in a private space. Sexual relations in general, and rights to consent in particular, have increasingly become issues of citizenship.

The right to privacy in the language of nineteenth-century liberal political theorists, which once upheld the rights of men over women within the home and family, denying married women the right to consent, has been reinterpreted to uphold the right of all individuals to consent to sexual acts (Kymlicka, 1990: 247–62). The European Convention on Human Rights is being incorporated in UK law,[16] while the right to privacy enshrined in Article 8 is simultaneously being invoked to outlaw discrimination against people with same-sex sexualities in relation to the age of consent, and possibly other iniquitous laws such as gross indecency and buggery. To a significant extent, existing gendered laws on the age of consent stand as legal anachronisms, preserved by political inertia rather than public demand.

The 'negative freedom' from rape and abuse has been expanded in scope, to include married women and male rape victims, via the Criminal Justice and Public Order Act (1994).[17] These measures changed the context of 'age of consent' legislation, which increasingly represents a meaningful 'right to consent', in a legal framework which gives due recognition to the seriousness of assaults where consent does not exist.

Taken together, such measures represent steps towards recognizing the sexual autonomy of every citizen alongside other rights and responsibilities. The capacity to consent to sexual acts is becoming seen as a positive and integral element of citizenship. The concept of an age of consent has been appropriated and transformed in accordance with changing ideals about adult sexual autonomy.

The ages of consent for both women and homosexual men have been reinterpreted, to a degree, in the popular imagination to imply a right to consent for those above the age rather than a prohibition against acts with the under-aged. This optimistic, progressive outlook mirrors the conclusions of both Anthony Giddens' *The Transformation of Intimacy*, and Ken Plummer's account of 'intimate citizenship' in *Telling Sexual Stories* (Giddens, 1992; Plummer, 1995). These argue that sexuality is increasingly being negotiated by democratic principles of liberty and equality. However, Giddens, and to a lesser extent Plummer, present seductive narratives which should be approached with caution (Jamieson, 1996). The inclusion of non-heterosexuals and heterosexual women as full sexual citizens deemed capable of consent on the same terms as heterosexual men remains an incomplete process. It should not disguise the continuing failures of society to address sexual violence, gendered power and sexual hierarchies, and to uphold consent in practice rather than as an ideal. The diverse sexual identities, traditions and lifestyles of individuals in contemporary society do not necessarily imply more reflexive democratic choices by individuals, or more consensual behaviour.

Understanding recent developments necessitates a more complex narrative than the expansion of sexual citizenship throughout society. Since the 1960s there has been a movement towards gender equality and homosexual equality; a limited and uneven withdrawal of the state from regulation of adult sexual relations, and a strengthening of the public ideology that individuals should have the right to consent and to have their decisions enforced by the law through the punishment of non-consensual acts. There has been minimal movement towards increasing the scope of consent for younger age groups.

Contemporary moves towards the withdrawal of state regulation of adult behaviour in favour of a neutral state framework which preserves individual autonomy may simply reflect a pragmatic retreat by the state in the face of intractable value-conflicts. It represents a limited advance, from traditional sexual ideologies to a neutral state, rather than the positive construction of any new form of shared citizenship. The legality of choice is not articulated as approval of promiscuity, for example; indeed many traditional cultural attitudes persist. Citizens are free of legal regulation, but there is only a limited collective sense of respect for the rights of other citizens to consent to whatever actions they choose. The emergence of a consenting adult sexual subject in the public imaginary in part signals the weakening of a shared sense of citizenship and community in a society of radical difference, although removal of paternalistic traditional legal frameworks also opens a space for constructive democratic dialogue. The language of citizenship employed by Stonewall and equality supporters in 1994 may be destroying the state's role in articulating shared citizenship ideals in the face of radical difference, rather than generating new forms of shared sexual citizenship.

The history of the age of consent demonstrates that a narrative of progressively expanding consent cannot capture the profoundly different frameworks of meaning within which consent has been conceptualized in the past. Yet examination of past debates in 1885 and 1967 does reveal the beginnings of sexual citizenship in the making; voices of women and homosexuals claiming the right to make decisions, beginning to apply principles of active autonomy to sexual life. Despite the historical exclusion of women and homosexuals from sexual citizenship, it is possible to trace back the historical emergence of ideals of sexual autonomy to which they have increasingly gained access as adult sexual citizens.

ACKNOWLEDGEMENTS

This chapter is derived from PhD research funded by an Economic and Social Research Council Research Studentship Award. I am grateful for this financial support.

When I presented the original version of this chapter as my first conference paper to the BSA, in April 1997, I had to evade tabloid journalists and photographers to reach my panel. The *Daily Mail* had published an article that morning under the inflammatory headline 'Children's Right to Sex, by Sociologist'. I thank Brian Heaphy, formidable bodyguard Nicola Boyne, and everyone who supported me at the conference and afterwards. The lessons? Postgraduates should be aware how easily their work can be misrepresented. The BSA must learn to advise its members and deal with the press. And our society must learn to talk about young people's sexuality.

[*Editors' note*: The experience undergone by Matthew has led directly to an immediate review of the BSA's press and media liaison policy. The BSA is also planning to host training events on dealing with the media.]

NOTES

1. *The Sun*, Monday 9 June 1997, demanded in its editorial that 'The police should be free to warn parents about paedophiles' (p. 2).
2. 'No Child of Mine', produced and directed by Peter Kosminsky, was eventually screened, after postponement, at 10.40 p.m.–12.15 a.m. on Tuesday, 25 February 1997, on ITV. See: 'Last Taboo TV Drama Shocks with Actress, 12', *The Observer*, Sunday 9 February 1997.

3. 'Witness: The Devil Amongst Us' was screened on Channel Four on Thursday, 8 January 1998, 10–11 p.m.
4. Peter Tatchell, 'Is Fourteen Too Young for Sex?', *Gay Times*, June 1996, pp. 36–8.
5. 'Boy, 11, on Rape Charge', *Guardian*, Tuesday 21 October 1997.
6. See: *The Public General Statutes*, vol. XX1, Chapter 69, pp. 358–65. The Criminal Law Amendment Act was later recodified in the Sexual Offences Act, 1956.
7. A first-hand account of the battle for decriminalization by the former secretary of the Homosexual Law Reform Society can be found in Grey (1992). Some of the key parliamentary debates over the 1967 Sexual Offences Act can be found in *Hansard* as follows: (1) Parliamentary Debates: Commons Standing Committees, House of Commons Official Report, Session 1966–7, vol. X, Standing Committee F. Sexual Offences (no. 2) Bill. Wednesday 19 April 1967, cols 1–42. (2) Parliamentary Debates: Commons, Official Report, Fifth Series, 1966–7. (i) vol. 748. 23 June 1967, cols 2115–200. (ii) vol. 749. 3 July 1967, cols 1403–526.
8. See: *Public General Acts and Measures*, 1967, Part II (London: HMSO), chapter 60, p. 1269.
9. The offence of 'indecent assault' against a female, recodified in the Sexual Offences Act 1956, derived from the Offences Against the Person Act 1861, itself a consolidation of previously existing legislation. See: *Public General Acts*, 1861, chapter 100, p. 829, 'Rape, Abduction and Defilement of Women', sections 50–2.
10. For an indication of the cultural stereotypes at work, see Hauser (1962).
11. This discussion of the 1994 Age of Consent Debate incorporates research for a Masters thesis in 1995, which included a survey of national newspaper reports for a month prior to the vote in parliament on 21 February 1994, and for a week afterwards (Waites, 1995). The full House of Commons debate and votes recorded by MPs can be found in Hansard (Hansard, HC, 21 February 1994, cols 74–123), together with the subsequent House of Lords debate (Hansard, HL, 20 June 1994, cols 10–67; 74–108).
12. 'Gay Sex at 16 May be Made Legal', *Daily Telegraph*, Monday 14 July 1997, p. 1; 'Gays Win Key Battles' (p. 1) and editorial (p. 15) *Independent*, Tuesday 15 July 1997; 'Gays Win Sex at 16 Battle' (p. 3), Editorial (p. 14), and Jonathan Freedland, 'Age of Consent Goes Up in Smoke' (p. 14), *Guardian*, Tuesday 15 July 1997; 'Letters: Young Ones' Right to a Fag and a Shag', *Guardian*, Wednesday 16 July 1997, p. 16; 'So When Does a Child Turn into an Adult?', *The Observer*, Sunday 20 July 1997, p. 12, editorial (p. 5); and Simon Edge, 'Proudly, Openly, Equally Gay' (pp. 22–3), *New Statesman*, Friday 18 July 1997.
13. *Guardian*, 8 October 1997, p. 7.
14. *Independent*, 8 October 1997, pp. 7, 23.
15. See: *Public General Acts*, 1861, chapter 100, p. 833, 'Unnatural Offences', section 62.
16. A White Paper, 'Rights Brought Home', and a Human Rights Bill were published by the government on 24 October 1997.

17. Criminal Justice and Public Order Act (1994), Part XI, Sexual Offences; in *Current Law Statutes* (1994), volume 3, chapter 33, pp. 142–148 (London: Sweet & Maxwell).

REFERENCES

Archard, D. (1998) *Sexual Consent* (Oxford: Westview Press).
Birkett, D. (1997) 'Monsters with Human Faces', *Guardian Weekend*, Saturday 27 September 1997, pp. 22–30.
Bland, L. (1995) *Banishing the Beast: English Feminism and Sexual Morality, 1885–1914* (London: Penguin).
Bronitt, S. (1994) 'Spreading Disease and the Criminal Law', *Criminal Law Review*, no. 21.
Bulmer, M. and Rees, A. M. (eds) (1996) *Citizenship Today: The Contemporary Relevance of T. H. Marshall* (London: UCL Press).
Connell, R. W. (1995) *Masculinities* (Cambridge: Polity).
Edwards, A. (1996) 'Gender and Sexuality in the Social Construction of Rape and Consensual Sex: a Study of Process and Outcome in Six Recent Rape Trials', in J. Holland and L. Adkins (eds), *Sex, Sensibility and the Gendered Body* (London: Macmillan), pp. 178–201.
Evans, D. (1993) *Sexual Citizenship: The Material Construction of Sexualities* (London: Routledge).
Finch, J. (1986) 'Age', in R. G. Burgess (ed.), *Key Variables in Social Investigation* (London: Routledge), pp. 12–30.
Giddens, A. (1992) *The Transformation of Intimacy* (Cambridge: Polity).
Greenwood, V. and Young, J. (1980) 'Ghettoes of Freedom: an Examination of Permissiveness', in National Deviancy Conference (ed.), *Permissiveness and Control: The Fate of the Sixties Legislation* (London: Macmillan), pp. 149–74.
Grey, A. (1992) *Quest for Justice: Towards Homosexual Emancipation* (London: Sinclair-Stevenson).
Hall, S. (1980) 'Reformism and the Legislation of Consent', in National Deviancy Conference (ed.), *Permissiveness and Control: The Fate of the Sixties Legislation* (London: Macmillan), pp. 1–43.
Hauser, R. (1962) *The Homosexual Society* (London: Bodley Head).
Higgins, P. (1996) *Heterosexual Dictatorship: Male Homosexuality in Post-War Britain* (London: Fourth Estate).
Jackson, S. (1982) *Childhood and Sexuality* (Oxford: Basil Blackwell).
James, A., Jenks, C. and Prout, A. (1998) *Theorizing Childhood* (Cambridge: Polity).
Jamieson, L. (1996) 'The Social Construction of Consent Revisited', in L. Adkins and V. Merchant (eds), *Sexualizing the Social: Power and the Organisation of Sexuality* (London: Macmillan), pp. 55–73.
Jeffery-Poulter, S. (1991) *Peers, Queers and Commons: The Struggle for Gay Law Reform from 1950 to the Present* (London: Routledge).
Katz, J. N. (1995) *The Invention of Heterosexuality* (London: Penguin).

Kymlicka, W. (1990) *Contemporary Political Philosophy: An Introduction* (Oxford: Oxford University Press).

Lansdown, G. (1995) *Taking Part: Children's Participation in Decision Making* (London: Institute for Public Policy Research).

Law Commission (1995) *Consent in the Criminal Law*, consultation paper no. 139 (London: HMSO).

Lister, R. (1997) *Citizenship: Feminist Perspectives* (London: Macmillan).

Marshall, T. H. (1950) *'Citizenship and Social Class' and other Essays* (Cambridge: Cambridge University Press).

Meehan, E. (1995) 'Citizenship and the European Union', *Contemporary Politics*, 1(2), p. 139.

Moran, L. J. (1995) 'The Homosexualization of English Law', in D. Herman and C. Stychin (eds), *Legal Inversions: Lesbians, Gay Men and the Politics of Law* (Philadelphia, PA: Temple University Press), pp. 3–28.

Moran, L. J. (1996) *The Homosexual(ity) of Law* (London: Routledge).

Moran, L. J. (1997) 'Enacting Intimacy', *Studies in Law, Politics and Society*, 16, pp. 255–74.

Mort, F. (1987) *Dangerous Sexualities: Medico-Moral Politics in England since 1830* (London: Routledge & Kegan Paul).

NAMBLA: North American Man-Boy Love Association (1980) 'The Case for Abolishing the Age of Consent Laws', in M. Blasius and S. Phelan (eds), *We Are Everywhere: Historical Sourcebook of Gay and Lesbian Politics* (London: Routledge), pp. 459–68.

Plummer, K. (1995) *Telling Sexual Stories: Power, Change and Social Worlds* (London: Routledge).

Policy Advisory Committee on Sexual Offences (1981) *Report on the Age of Consent in Relation to Sexual Offences*, Cmnd 8216 (London: HMSO).

Report of the Committee on Homosexual Offences and Prostitution, Cmnd 247 (1957) (London: HMSO)

Richardson, D. (1998) 'Sexuality and Citizenship', *Sociology*, 32(1), pp. 83–100.

Ryback, T. W. (1997) 'Crying out Loud', *Independent Magazine*, reprinted from the *New York Times Magazine*, Saturday 15 March 1997, pp. 26–30.

Sandfort, T., Brongersma, E., and Naerssen, A. van (eds) (1990), Special Issue of *Journal of Homosexuality: Male Intergenerational Intimacy: Historical, Social-Psychological, and Legal Perspectives*, 20(1/2) (New York: Haworth Press).

Schofield, G. and Thoburn, J. (1996) *Child Protection: The Voice of the Child in Decision Making* (London: Institute for Public Policy Research).

Seidman, S. (1996) *Queer Theory/Sociology* (Oxford: Blackwell).

Smart, C. (1995) *Law, Crime and Sexuality: Essays in Feminism* (London: Sage).

Stonewall (1993a) *Age of Consent Briefing*, unpublished paper (London: Stonewall).

Stonewall (1993b) *The Case for Change: Arguments for an Equal Age of Consent* (London: Stonewall).

Stonewall (1997) 'Legislation Round-up', *Stonewall Newsletter*, 5(2), April 1997: p. 6.

Stychin, C. F. (1995) *Law's Desire: Sexuality and the Limits of Justice* (London: Routledge).

Tatchell, P. (1992) *Europe in the Pink: Lesbian and Gay Equality in the New Europe* (London: Gay Men's Press).

Thompson, B. (1994) *Sadomasochism* (London: Cassell).

Turner, B. (ed.) (1993) *Citizenship and Social Theory* (London: Sage).

Turner, B. (1997) 'Citizenship Studies: a General Theory', *Citizenship Studies*, 1(1), February 1997, pp. 5–18.

Waites, M. (1995) 'The Age of Consent Debate: a Critical Analysis', unpublished dissertation submitted for MA Sociology of Culture to Department of Sociology, University of Essex.

Waites, M. (1996) 'Lesbian and Gay Theory, Sexuality and Citizenship', *Contemporary Politics*, 2(3), Autumn, pp. 139–149.

Waites, M. (1997) 'Rethinking (Homo)Sexual Citizenship in the UK: the 1957 Wolfenden Report – Decriminalization and the "Permissive Moment"', unpublished paper delivered at the European Sociology Association Conference, University of Essex, 27–30 August 1997.

Walby, S. (1994) 'Is Citizenship Gendered?', *Sociology*, 24(2), pp. 379–95.

Walkowitz, J. (1980) *Prostitution and Victorian Society* (Cambridge. Cambridge University Press).

Walkowitz, J. (1992) *City of Dreadful Delight: Narratives of Sexual Danger in Late Victorian London* (London: Virago).

Weeks, J. (1977) *Coming Out: Homosexual Politics in Britain from the Nineteenth Century to the Present* (London: Quartet).

Weeks, J. (1985) *Sexuality and its Discontents: Meanings, Myths and Modern Sexualities* (London: Routledge & Kegan Paul).

Weeks, J. (1989) *Sex, Politics and Society: The Regulation of Sexuality since 1800*, 2nd edn (London: Longman).

Werbner, P., Yuval-Davis, N., Crowley, H. and Lewis, G. (1997) *Feminist Review, Citizenship: Pushing the Boundaries*, no. 57, Autumn.

6 'I Hadn't Really Thought About it': New Identities/New Fatherhoods

Carol Smart and Bren Neale

INTRODUCTION

It has become almost clichéd to remark upon the so-called crisis in fatherhood in western societies in the 1990s. There are a burgeoning number of studies on both masculinities and fatherhood(s).[1] Social policy and family law have turned their attention to fathers and fathering, and pressure groups continue to press for a greater recognition of fathers' rights. Fatherhood has been problematized and virtually redefined as having minority group status (Dennis and Erdos, 1993). The reasons for this shift are complex and interrelated and we shall explore some of them in this chapter. What is clear, however, for most commentators, is that it is divorce or separation that seem to trigger the crisis, and that the apparent decline in the status of fatherhood is inexorably linked with recent advances in women's status (Morgan, 1995; Phillips, 1997). Divorce exposes the taken-for-granted nature of gender relationships in heterosexual partnerships. Just as divorce exposes women's vulnerability to poverty and their lack of standing in the labour market (Eekelaar and Maclean, 1986; Maclean, 1991), so too does divorce render visible the pretence of fatherhood as an active relationship rather than a passive status. By this we mean that, for the majority of heterosexual couples who follow traditional child-care arrangements, fatherhood still does not routinely provide an identity for a man nor necessarily an active, involved relationship with children. Although we acknowledge that men's behaviour may well be changing, we would still suggest that, for the majority of fathers, fathering is something that they have to fit into a schedule dominated by paid employment, which tends to mean that their core identity is generated elsewhere.[2] Consider the following quotation, which comes from one of the fathers in our study of parenting after divorce (we discuss this more fully below):

118

LEON: I hadn't really thought about it. We were still living in the house together for about a year when we were going through really difficult times, moved into separate rooms. It was a case of I'd always worked really hard, I'd come home, gone up to the study and the children were there. My role as a father was to go out to work, to bring the money in, to try and look careerwise and the children were young and it was a case of just saying 'Hello, sit on my knee, then off to bed'.[2] And I was just there and I probably didn't pay them much attention at all. *It was only when I realised that they might not be part of my life that gave me a real shock and it made me more aware and during that year I made more effort to spend time with the children.*

This father acknowledges the taken-for-grantedness of fatherhood during marriage and was well aware that had his marriage continued he would have gone on being estranged from his children while nonetheless living with them. He had been a 'traditional' distant father during the marriage but became quickly aware that this style of fathering was going to be fruitless after divorce, at least if he wanted to have any kind of meaningful relationship with his children. Leon had 'bought into' the old gender contract only to find that he was ill-served by it in the face of divorce.

For many fathers, of course, the recognition that old-style fathering has many drawbacks struck them as being exceptionally unfair (and we shall discuss this sense of unfairness more below). But mothers also felt a sense of unfairness when they too had 'bought into' the old gender contract only to find that its terms were changed on divorce. This comment comes from one of the mothers in our study:

FELICITY: Well, that was last summer and we'd had a really big row. It was when he started fighting for having an equal share of the children and I was saying '*Look, I gave up my job in order to be their mother and I do my little bit of freelance to keep ticking over but basically my role is to be their mother. And you've got not only a full time job but various other things as well*, you've got a highly successful career and yet you're expecting to have them half the time'. We really couldn't agree about this and thumped the table and shouted and screamed for the very first time.

These two quotations perhaps sum up the crisis of fatherhood. In the first the father recognizes that being a traditional distant father during marriage has not prepared him for post-divorce fatherhood and he is probably going to have to adjust. However, as the second quotation reveals, if he does change he comes into conflict with the equally legitimate demands of the mother who wishes to keep her side of the established gender contract, especially when it has cost her so dear and when she has invested so much in being a traditional nurturing mother. Unfortunately for mothers, while fathers' claims are now seen as laudable, there is little sympathy for women who have difficulty with the unanticipated reversal of the gender contract.

How should we interpret this clash? The dominant paradigm for interpreting this scenario is a psychologistic one. The father is seen as a kind of prodigal who suddenly recognizes that there are better ways of being a father (Burgess, 1998). He is valorized because he is engaged in a kind of personal growth which will benefit his children. His anger against a system or person who makes it difficult for him easily to effect his transition is seen as legitimate. The mother, on the other hand, is often portrayed as a kind of dog in the manger. She, it is said, fails to appreciate the father's transformation because she is too involved in her own emotional world to realize how important the father's transformation is for the children (Willbourne and Geddes, 1995; Rosenblatt and Scragg, 1995). She is depicted as wanting to live in the past and as unable to recognize that it is in the interests of her children that she jettisons the promises entailed in the old gender contract and gets on with the new. The mother's declarations about injustice are seen as merely self-serving and misguided. This psychologistic framework constructs this clash between parents in entirely personal and individual terms. The solution is therefore identified as residing with mediation or some kind of therapy which will help the mother come to terms with the new reality. Such an approach is typified in Simpson *et al.*'s (1995) study of fathers after divorce. They state:

> Once again it would appear that an inability to move beyond the emotional fog of failed spousal relationships appears to stifle the possibility of continuing to share a relationship as parents.
>
> (1995: 32)

In this system of interpretation, new styles of fatherhood can only be promoted by diminishing motherhood and mothers. Again, quoting from Simpson *et al.*:

Although such sentiments (of not wanting the children to see the absent parent) may be deeply felt by mothers ... they would appear to be rarely shared by fathers and children in the aftermath of divorce. (1995: 39)[3]

Thus mothers are depicted as the obstacles to proper post-divorce fatherhood. Moreover it is assumed that there are achievable 'solutions' to this dilemma because the problem is defined as an individual's failure to adjust. Once the adjustment is made, the problem, it is assumed, promptly disappears.

From a more sociological perspective, however, the situation looks rather different. We wish therefore to 're-interpret' the above scenario and offer other ways of understanding the crisis of fatherhood which is, in any case, just as much a crisis in motherhood. This approach will not offer simple solutions because we do not understand these shifts in the meaning of motherhood and fatherhood as isolated events, but as processes which cannot be 'fixed' by psychological interventions while everything else around the family is undergoing massive structural transformations. We shall be drawing on insights and interview material from a study of divorced and separated parents who experienced negotiating over their children in the context of the Children Act 1989. In this study[4] we interviewed 31 mothers and 29 fathers on two occasions separated by 12–15 months. Our focus in the research was to try to ascertain whether the new structure for post-divorce parenting introduced by the legislation was influencing how parents approached the question of where children should live and how much contact they should have with the non-resident parent. We were interested to find out whether assumptions that mothers should have 'custody' were changing, and whether the new legislation altered fathers' expectations about, and their chances of, gaining the residence of children.[5]

POWER, GENDER AND PARENTHOOD

Feminist analyses of the history of fatherhood have pointed to the way in which the historically privileged legal status of the married father – which gave him absolute rights over *his* children – also gave him almost absolute power over his wife (Mason, 1994; Reiss, 1934; Harrison and Mort, 1980). The fact that until the middle of the nineteenth century a woman who had to leave her husband because of his violence could not take her children with her clearly gave the father immense control over her behaviour. Thus Caroline Norton, who began the first feminist campaigns to change the laws on guardianship in the 1830s, stated:

> Mr Norton held my children as hostages; he felt that while he had them, he still had a power over me that nothing could control. ... [H]e had still the power to do more than punish – to torture – the wife who had been so anxious to part from him. I never saw them; I seldom knew where they were.
>
> (Norton 1982; originally published 1854)

This power relationship has been depicted as classic patriarchal power under which the wife has no legal redress and under which she is at the mercy of her husband's benevolence.

This classic patriarchal power was gradually diminished as a consequence of two developments. The first was the growing status of motherhood which began to be identified with special qualities and responsibilities. The second was the changing understanding of childhood and the emphasis on the special needs of children, especially in relation to nurturance. In Britain these developments reached their height in the post-war Bowlby era in the 1950s when it became a conventional wisdom that young children should not be separated from their mothers (Brophy, 1982, 1989). These wisdoms, which were oppressive of women in a number of ways, nonetheless shifted the balance of power in married households such that, on divorce, most mothers could readily assume that they would win the custody of the children. As Delphy (1984) and others have argued, this arrangement often left the mothers impoverished and unable to enter into full-time work, but it was a counterbalance to the absolute patriarchal power of husbands in the nineteenth century.

By the end of the 1980s this situation was changing again. As if to counterbalance the power of the ideology of motherhood, there grew a new ideology of (new) fatherhood. This was composed of a number of competing and contradictory strands. For example one element was the orthodox psychoanalytical approach which argued that the absence of a father in a family would make it impossible for boys to become properly masculine. It was assumed that a feminine household would emasculate the boy.[6] The New Right, on the other hand, argued that a feminine household lacked discipline so that the boy would become exaggeratedly masculine – a barbarian with no sense of responsibility. The Fathers' Rights Movement, on the other hand, might tacitly support either of these positions, but their main argument was that men could be just as good at caring for children as women, and that the principles of sex equality demanded that they should have just as much right to the residence of children on divorce as mothers. Thus they insist that they should have at least 50 per cent of the children's time and attention. These positions on fatherhood are quite distinct and even contradictory. Yet together they seem to constitute an ideological whole which valorizes fatherhood no matter which form it actually takes. These three competing styles should also be differentiated from a fourth kind of fatherhood which really does entail the shared care of children as well as a shared responsibility for their well-being. There is no political movement composed of these fathers, namely men who are mobilizing to reduce their hours of work, to demand longer paternity leave and leave for family reasons, nor who demand to share their pensions and other masculine privileges with their partners. Yet this desirable figure (to which no doubt a minority of men may conform) is also mixed into the brew which is now seen as an ideal and undifferentiated social phenomenon, namely the new fatherhood. These four ingredients can thus be summed up as follows:

Elements of the New Fatherhood
1. Providers of masculine identity (potentially regressive stance).
2. Enforcers of patriarchal power (highly reactionary, backward-looking).
3. Carriers of rights (self-interested, individualized power).
4. Sharers of responsibilities (collective, potentially progressive stance).

It often seems to be the case that different writers on the new fatherhood invoke only one of these ideal types when they frame their understanding of developments. Thus feminists have perhaps only seen the resurrection of the *enforcers of patriarchal power* and have sought to challenge any acceptance of the new fatherhood. On the other hand, the Institute for Public Policy Research seems only to see the new father as the *sharer of responsibilities* and thus welcomes him (Burgess and Ruxton, 1996). Although the IPPR acknowledges the existence of the *new carriers of rights*, it sees the hostility and conflict that this variety of new fatherhood induces merely as epiphenomenal and caused by some mothers being intransigent.

It should not be surprising that feminists are alarmed by the new fatherhood. On a simple calculus it is possible to see that, at one stage in the history of marriage and divorce, men had *both* the money and the children. Then in the post-Second World War era women gained access to the children, but not to the money. But men are now demanding the children back, and women still have no economic security. However, while there is a basic truth in this calculus, it is too simple a model to provide an understanding of the developments we are witnessing. We cannot, for example, explain these developments as if there is simply an ongoing and unchanging power play between men and women, removed from other kinds of social and economic developments. Nor should we assume that women and men at the end of the twentieth century want the same things and experience parenthood in the same way as their forebears did at the end of the last century. It might therefore be useful to consider some of the broader sociological explanations that have been provided for the recent changes in fatherhood.

EXPLAINING THE RISE OF THE NEW FATHER

Hochschild (1995) has argued that in the American context the traditional (breadwinner/authority) father has been marginalized by two new developments. The first is the new father and the second is the deadbeat dad. The first has emerged as a consequence of broad economic changes arising from the globalization of capitalism. These have reduced men's wages and have also drawn women into the labour market more extensively. At the same time the lowered birth rates and other improvements in the status of women have allowed women to participate more fully in paid work. This change gives rise to new fathers who become more involved with their children and who are likely to share more extensively in their care. (This is our category of *sharers of responsibilities.*) The second development, however, relates to rising rates of divorce, which Hochschild suggests have weakened men's links with their children because on divorce so many fathers withdraw completely. This in turn, she argues, is related to the rise of children born outside wedlock where, because of the fragility of these relationships, the fathers divest themselves even more of emotional ties with their children.[7]

For Hochschild there is now an immense diversity of fathering styles, and she stresses that this range is a new development. Even though individual fathers may have been 'involved' or 'disengaged' in the past, she suggests that fatherhood itself had a limited set of meanings and possibilities. Now, she argues, it has become a matter of active choice with a range of different models available to men. Within this context she points to an irony in which middle-class men may now subscribe most vociferously to the ideal of the new father, while in practice being unable to act as a new father because of their career structures.[8] On the other hand, working class fathers may subscribe more to the ideal of the traditional, distant father while in practice becoming much more involved with their children because of the working patterns of their wives and the impact of unemployment.

Given Hochschild's emphasis on the economic engine that has produced these changes, it is perhaps surprising that she ultimately focuses on the idea of 'social programmes' which support active fathering as a way of responding to the crisis in fatherhood. She wants to see more mediation and counselling to keep fathers in touch with their children after divorce, and she also wants children who have lost contact with their fathers to be in touch with 'fatherly men' in various volunteer projects. These interventions may or may not be a 'good thing', but having identified global social change as the source of the crisis in fatherhood, it seems incongruous to suggest highly psychologistic interventions at the individual level. This contrasts quite considerably with the approach taken by Beck and Beck-Gernsheim (1995), who constantly warn against framing social change as if individualized solutions can resolve the problems it generates.

> Look at some common suggestions on how to stick the disintegrating marriages together again: take part in 'family training' or get professional help in choosing your spouse; all we lack is enough marriage counsellors and the difficulties would banish; the real threat to married life lies in pornography, or legal abortion or feminism, we must do something to stop them. And so on. Social contexts and historical developments are simply passed over. (1995: 143)

Beck and Beck-Gernsheim offer a different understanding of contemporary fatherhood. While Hochschild suggests that high rates of divorce leads to disinvestment by men in their children, Beck and Beck-Gernsheim suggest that the impermanence of the marital (sexual) bond gives rise to a greater investment in the parent–child bond since this is seen to be the only remaining permanent relationship. Their argument is complex because at every point they recognize that there are competing pressures on both men and women. Some social trends push women into marriage and motherhood, while others push them into the labour market. For both men and women there are pressures towards complete individualization and autonomy from ties of kinship and location. But at the same time there develops a greater need to bond with a significant other to defeat the isolation that this generates. Thus, for example, they argue:

> The logic behind modern life presupposes a single person, for market economies ignore the needs of family, parenthood and partnership. Anyone expecting employees to be flexible and mobile without paying any regard to their lives as private individuals is aiding the break-up of family life by putting the market first. The fact that work and family are incompatible remained concealed as long as marriage was synonymous with woman at home and man at work; it has surfaced with great turbulence now that each couple has to work out its own division of labour.   (1995: 144)

They further add:

> Life as a single person generates a deep longing to love and be loved by somebody but at the same time makes it difficult or impossible to integrate this somebody into a life which is really 'one's own'.   (1995: 145)

The significance of Beck and Beck-Gernsheim's analysis is that they do not separate out what is happening to men/fathers from what is happening to women/mothers, and both are understood to be occupying subject positions which are influenced by social forces but are also seen as agents of their own lives. What is equally important is that, while they recognize the extent to which women's lives have changed, they do not fall into simplistic assumptions about equality. This means that they never see gender conflict as a form of atavistic behaviour, nor as women's 'fault', nor as arising from individual problems or pathologies. While they seek to place issues of identity, feelings and emotion on the agenda, these are not seen primarily as individual qualities nor as being generated in any context save a social context.

In this sociological account the growing conflict between men and women over children on divorce does not come about because men are good people who have the welfare of their children at heart while women are bad people who behave selfishly and irrationally because they are emotionally immature. Rather a new site of conflict has materialized because, amongst other things, there are new identities available to men which are to do with active fathering, and these may be replacing older identities as breadwinners as employment becomes more unstable. In addition, men – like women – may be identifying the most permanent and satisfying relationship they may have as the one with their children rather than with their spouses or workmates. This re-evaluation of the father–child bond, coupled with the recognition that the world of paid labour is a place of diminishing satisfaction, often strikes men at the point of divorce.

> Becoming a father is not difficult, but being a divorced father certainly is. At the moment when it is too late, the family personified by the child becomes the centre of all hope and concrete effort; the child is offered time and attention in a manner which during the marriage was allegedly out of the question, 'although I really would like to spend more time with him/her'. Divorce confronts the man with his own feelings as a father; he is the one to mourn for, having realized too late what liberation means, just as its objective slips away.
>
> (Beck and Beck-Gernsheim, 1995: 154)

Beck and Beck-Gernsheim recognize that it is at the point of divorce that for most men fatherhood becomes an issue, as shown by the quotation from Leon in the introduction to this chapter. However, they also realize that it is at this moment that men realize that the mother of the child is in a more powerful position than they are. It is this reversal of power relations that they see as giving rise to much rage and frustration on the part of men. Thus Beck and Beck-Gernsheim understand this moment as arising from a process of historical change so that it carries with it all the significance of past gender relations as well as new social forces. The relationship between men and women is thus now seen as suddenly new and equal, with women on exactly the same footing as men. In addition, the authors understand the conflict that arises at this moment in both structural and emotional terms, but they do not give precedence to the emotional hurt that men may feel as if its intensity is a sign of some kind of purity of motive. While men's anger becomes explicable sociologically, it is at the same time not divorced from questions of power. This is why we regard Beck and Beck-Gernsheim's work as so significant.

In almost all the legal, professional and popular literature on the question of fatherhood after divorce that is being published in the UK, the issue of power has vanished. If it is raised at all, it is because women are thought to have too much power and fathers too little.

We therefore want to outline some of the developments that are occurring as a consequence of this profoundly un-sociological understanding of fatherhood, and to draw on our own research to see to what extent it supports or undermines some of the ideas of Beck and Beck-Gernsheim.

THE NEW CONTEXT OF FATHERHOOD IN THE UK

In 1992 the Children Act 1989 introduced new principles into the management of post-divorce parenthood. The old system of awarding custody to one parent and access to the other was abolished. It was decreed that divorce would no longer alter a parent's legal relationship with a child and that, just as parents were jointly responsible for children during marriage, they should remain so after divorce. The new legislation stressed that parents should not need court orders but should be encouraged to negotiate privately over the way they would raise their children. Certain guidelines were introduced to protect the welfare of the child which balanced competing concerns and interests. Yet, out of a list of seven elements, one in particular has become the determining feature of modern divorce law; this is the assumption that the welfare of the child can be secured only if the child retains a relationship with both parents.

This presumption has taken concrete shape as case law has developed. Although the Act was meant to reduce conflict between parents on divorce, and to discourage them from going to court, what appears to have happened may be an increase in litigation over children. One issue has become particularly significant. This is the problem of the so-called implacably hostile parent. The implacably hostile *mother* (because it is now always assumed that it is the mother who assumes this stance) is the woman who refuses to facilitate contact between the father and the children. This mother is seen as emotionally immature and as unable to recognize the best interests of her child. She is seen as giving priority to her negative feelings towards her former partner over the benefits which would accrue to her child of retaining contact with the father. She has thus been depicted as needing psychiatric help and counselling, and more recently she has been depicted as simply delinquent and in need of punishment (Rosenblatt and Scragg, 1995; Willbourne and Geddes, 1995).

In this context there are two recent cases that merit attention. The first is Re O (*Contact: Imposition of Conditions*) [1995] 2 FLR

124. In this case an unmarried mother was ordered to facilitate indirect contact between her child and the child's father. This consisted of writing regular reports, informing the father of important changes to the life of the child and any illnesses it might have. She was also to give the child any presents the father sent and was ordered to read to the child all the letters he sent without being selective in what she read. The judge had formed a favourable impression of the father, but felt that the mother had formed an 'irrational repugnance' towards him. (In fact the father had harassed her to the point where she had had to take out a restraining order against him. He had broken the conditions of this order and had actually been imprisoned.) This case was important because it established that no interests of the parents should be considered by the court in these cases. The only thing that the courts should consider was defined as the welfare of the child. Thus it would not matter how difficult it might be for the mother to sustain contact with the father, nor would it matter that she was compelled to read his letters and accept his gifts. As far as the court was concerned the mother's future quality of life was immaterial and also, seemingly, unrelated to the quality of her child's life.

Following this case the courts became more and more stern with so-called implacably hostile mothers until, in October 1996, a mother (Dawn Austin) was imprisoned for contempt of court for refusing to take her daughter to a contact centre to meet her father. The courts increasingly took the view that these mothers are indifferent to the welfare of their children because they do not appreciate how necessary it is for the children to see their fathers. These mothers are seen as attempting to wield unjustly the power they have as residential parents, against the good father who merely wishes to meet the needs of his children. However, what was often overlooked in these cases was the fact that the mother's repugnance towards the father might actually be reasonable. In Dawn Austin's case her partner was violent and had hospitalized her. He had also served a prison sentence for violence to a previous partner. But, as far as the courts were concerned, this could not override the need for father/child contact, nor did it disqualify the man from being a good father.[9] Thus, from the perspective of the courts and the father, the implacably hostile mother is trying to use her power illegitimately. But from a sociological perspective the decision to imprison the victim of an excessively violent man because she feels the father is a damaging influence, and not truly interested in her welfare, looks more like the state supporting the illegitimate and violent power of men. This is especially a matter of concern when the assumption that domestic violence is harmless to children is being promoted by fathers' rights activists.[10] We shall return to this point below.

FINDINGS FROM THE STUDY

In his book *Risk Society*, Beck (1992) makes the following observation:

> In the marital support model, to put it schematically, the woman is left after divorce *with* children and *without* an income, the man by contrast *with* an income and *without* children. In the two-earner model, little seems to have changed at first glance, other than that the woman has an income *and* she has the children (following prevalent law practice). But to the degree that the economic inequality between men and women is decreased – whether through professional activity of the woman, the support regulations of divorce law, or old-age assistance – *fathers become aware of their disadvantage*, partially naturally and partially legally. ... The men who free themselves from the 'fate' of a career and turn to their children come home to an empty nest. This is clearly illustrated by the increasing number of cases ... in which fathers kidnap children not awarded to them in divorce proceedings.   (1992: 113)

This passage suggests that, while divorce reveals the different position of men and women in relation to children, the experience of injustice comes as men 'realize' (or imagine) that women have got both careers *and* children. Hence men's sense of disadvantage is based on a recognition that women now 'have it all'. We want to suggest, however, that while this may be how many fathers, including the fathers in our study, 'see' the situation, it was frequently a misrepresentation of the actuality of their personal circumstances. Thus it appeared that men might well have the image of the liberated, salaried woman in mind against whom they were struggling to preserve their identity; however this woman was symbolic rather than real. Their actual wives did not have careers and well-paid jobs but stayed at home to raise the children. So in this situation the men's demands for equality are in relation to a *mythic* woman rather than the *actual* woman they are divorcing.

Looking at this engagement from the woman's point of view we can see that she signs the gender contract and leaves work to care for the children and then, at the point of divorce, she is treated as if she has had all the opportunities and advantages that full-time work would have given her. In this situation it seems undeniable that men are very angry because they feel a deep sense of injustice against the *mythic* woman. But what is surprising is that so few of the mothers are angry at all that they are perceived as being so privileged when they are manifestly not. Rather, mothers seemed to concede that fathers are disadvantaged and want to facilitate their contact with their children. Thus, although the legal, professional and popular literature persists in presenting the mothers as obstacles to good post-divorce fathering, these armies of implacable hostile mothers seem to be figments of an imagination fuelled by media myths of equality that has gone too far and ideas about how men are disadvantaged.

Invoking the Mythic Woman and the Ideal Father

I think in the old days, traditional [ideas] were that they stay with the mother but now it's not like that. More and more women are breadwinners, having to go out to work. (Anthony)

I think there's a big difference between a lot of fathers than there was twenty years ago. There's a lot more fathers now who are willing and able to look after their children and bring them up whereas twenty years ago it was just assumed that men worked and women looked after children. Now I think it's changed. (Tim)

I knew in my own mind that I could give the children the same or better care than Paula and I thought that we're in a modern world now and everyone's talking about 'new age men'. I'm a totally modern kind of parent. (James)

In these extracts it is clear that these fathers believe that the gendered relations of parenthood have changed. Although a small number of fathers in our study claimed to have shared equally the care of their children during their marriages, none had given up work or reduced their working hours to do so. Thus their actual experience of taking responsibility for their children had not changed dramatically from that of their fathers. Yet, they were convinced that *things* were different now.

The women in our sample seemed quite willing to accommodate sudden changes in their husband's involvement with the children.

Graham was a workaholic and still is in some ways, but he now wants to spend more time with the children. I feel that if that's the case then that's got to be looked at.   (Sally)

If he says, 'Well, the children need their father', then I quite agree. Why should the children see less of their father because I feel it's not fair on me? I take the point really.   (Felicity)

It was quite rare, except in cases of violence, for mothers to reject a change of heart where fathers were concerned. This was one of the exceptions:

He kept saying, 'Well, I think I should have some responsibility for their education again.' I said, 'Why? You never cared about it when you were with them. You always said it was up to me. Well, it's up to me now, I don't see why you should have anything to do with it.'   (Tina)

From these accounts we can see that there is some substance to Beck and Beck-Gernsheim's argument that divorce produces a reappraisal of fatherhood and of the value of children. We found that, out of our sample of 60 marriages, 21 fathers were trying to gain the residence of their children, in other words in a third of cases fathers wanted the children living with them. Of these 21 fathers, one-third (seven) were in full-time work. The remaining two-thirds were either unemployed or had flexible work patterns (i.e. were self-employed or working shifts). Thus their lives were either not dominated by the labour market with their identity constituted as breadwinner, or they had considerable control over their working lives. At least one father chose to give up his job when his wife left him, and others had become unemployed or had been made redundant shortly before the relationship breakdown. These men were very enthusiastic about men's ability to care for children and about how men were changing in relation to caring. However, if we look at the wives of these 21 men we find that only one of them had worked full-time during the marriage. Of the others, 14 were full-time mothers, five worked part-time and one was a student. The men's sense of the over-privileging of mothers who had 'too much' equality was therefore not based on the actuality of the division of labour in their own households. Their sense of unfairness about women 'having it all' had nothing to do with the situation of their own wives. Take, for example, the two quotations from the following fathers, both of whom had succeeded in getting the residence of their children:

You couldn't really class her as an unfit mother [but] I thought, 'We're in a modern world now and everyone's talking about new age man – I'm just going to see how true it is.' She wanted the children [aged 2 years and 10 months] but I beat her out of the door with them. She'd asked for Jimmy back but I'd refused totally, I said 'If you want him you can take me to court to get him'. (James)

We just did the norm. I went out to work and she just stayed at home and looked after the kids. ... She were a good wife and mother, ... she kept the house spotless, she were everything really. When I was working away for 4 months she got to know this other fella ... so *that's* what sort of mother she was. The rule of thumb is, they stay with their mother, but you get bad mothers as well as bad fathers. ... They were *my* kids, ... why should she dictate to me and say 'Look they're out of your life or the majority of it'? She keeps saying 'I love them, I miss them'. If she did love them, I don't think she'd have done what she's done, especially a woman to do that. I don't think she should ever see them again. Those kids are going to grow up without one of their parents. (Keith)

These fathers sound as if they have found a justification for doing what they wanted to do rather than in being concerned to become caring, sharing new men. The fact that they had done none of the caring prior to their separations was not seen as relevant to their cases. The courts treated them and their wives as equal and had no interest at all in the power relations that might be being played out between the parents.

It might be argued that it is inappropriate to make decisions about children in response to issues of power between adults. However, it is our concern that the various strands of thinking over fatherhood have come together to produce a completely unrealistic valorization of fatherhood in which it now seems that men can do no wrong and women are almost always found wanting. Thus we return to the issue of domestic violence which, as we pointed out above, tends now to be disregarded in considerations of children's welfare.

ARE VIOLENT MEN STILL GOOD FATHERS?

Well, you get serial killers and rapists still having contact with the kiddies, doesn't mean to say they're a bad parent. (Anthony)

When I told [my solicitor] of the allegations he said, 'Men who sexually abuse their children and IRA terrorists are allowed contact with their children, so if you don't [allow contact] you'll no doubt go to prison for contempt'. I was terrified so I agreed. (Kathy)

It would seem from these quotations that *any* father is seen as better than no father and that *any* masculine role model is regarded as better than none. Family law in the UK seems to have moved into a position where it is almost impossible to conceive of a father who is harmful to children unless he inflicts direct violence on them. This is at variance with public law, in which social workers are concerned for the welfare of children in homes where there is domestic violence.

We seem therefore almost to have returned to the 1830s. Caroline Norton campaigned for rights for mothers precisely in order to allow them to leave violent husbands. She recognized that women would not leave without their children, and if they were forced to stay with their children they would go on being abused. In the 1990s we face a situation in which women may divorce their violent husbands, but they are required to go on co-parenting with them, having regular direct or indirect contact with them. Moreover they are often required to facilitate his fathering of the children, even if they think the father may be a dangerous influence over the children.

But the idea that a violent husband can be a good father is, apparently, widely held. In our sample of 60 parents the majority made precisely this distinction.[11]

Well I do believe if there's been violence towards the wife that doesn't necessarily say that's gonna be subjected towards the kids as well. Men can be violent towards their wives in ways – sexual, physical – but still be the most fantastic fathers. (Jessica)

Only a minority felt that a violent husband was a dangerous or damaged person who would be an unfit parent.

[I]f it's persistent violence there's usually a reason for it and the man's got a problem and if that problem hasn't been dealt with then it's obviously gonna pose problems for the children. (Justine)

But even though most parents agreed with the current ethos, there was a contradiction in their approach to male violence. While they felt that contact should be maintained, none could imagine a situation in which a mother would leave the children with a man who had been violent towards her. They could not comprehend a situation in which she could let him be responsible for them in order that she could escape the violence. Thus it is clear that in cases of domestic violence it is assumed that mothers must take the responsibility for the children, and moreover they must take the responsibility of facilitating fathering after divorce. The father may be an unreliable or irresponsible person, but it seems that he must not be denied contact with his children; rather the mother must take on this additional burden.

This permissive attitude towards wayward fathers manifested itself in another aspect of our research. When we interviewed solicitors[12] about parenting after divorce, the majority were in favour of tough measures against mothers who attempted to deny contact, even where there had been violence. Contact should be enforced, it was argued, because it was in the interests of the child. However, the majority felt that if a father did not want to see his children, nothing could or should be done about it. None felt it would be appropriate to force fathers to see their children; force was reserved for mothers. As two of our solicitors remarked:

> I think it's part of our brief to say to father, 'Well, is there any good reason why you don't want contact?' I won't moralise or take it any further, just gently cajole them. If it's mother who says she wants father to have contact .. I have to say to her, 'You can't even bring the horse to water, let alone make it drink. You can't force the issue'. (BO, male solicitor)

> [You] talk to the father and at the end of the day respect their decision. ... My personal view is that it could cause as much damage by imposing that in a family unit as anything else.
> (OH, male solicitor)

It would therefore seem that society's expectations of men as fathers are still incredibly low. It would also seem that, with the partial exception of financial support for children, fatherhood is a matter of personal choice, not an obligation. If fathers choose to be involved then the legal system will coerce mothers into agreement, but if they do not wish to take on this responsibility they might be 'gently cajoled' but no pressure would be exerted as this would restrict their freedom of choice.

CONCLUSIONS

It is not clear to us that fatherhood *in general* yet constitutes an identity if, by identity we mean a form of conscious self-recognition combined with active commitment towards the behaviour culturally associated with the subject position of father. There may be, however, an identity emerging of *post-divorce fatherhood*. This identity is formed as a reaction against motherhood in a context in which it is understood that motherhood is powerful. Thus, this *post-divorce fatherhood* constitutes itself as a disadvantaged, minority status. It is forged in the furnace of perceived injustice and thus it is its own justification. But even without this tautological moral justification, it has the full support of the legal and 'psy' professions and, it would seem, of many mothers too:

> [Because] of Brian's behaviour, Jack began to associate Daddy with shouting and Mummy with crying. And people I trust, like my sister who's a psychiatrist, would tell me 'Kate, you've got to stop the contact now. Don't keep putting him back.' But I felt – fathers' rights blah, blah, blah and that it was somehow wrong to do that, and that I must keep sending him back.   (Kate)

If there is such a consensus over fathers' rights on divorce, and if the majority of professionals and mothers agree that, virtually regardless of the circumstances, men must have contact with their children after divorce if they themselves wish it, what might feminist responses be to this situation? Some, like Ros Coward, have started to stress the importance of fathers in terms of the psychic and emotional needs and development of sons and daughters (Coward, 1996). Others, like Bea Campbell (1996), are more sceptical that any father figure is a good father, and suggests that what is required is that men start to co-operate in the caring for children. Yet others, like Hester and Radford (1996) argue that, by ignoring the significance of domestic violence and giving priority to fathers' desire for contact after divorce, the needs of women for protection are ignored (see also Kaganas and Piper, 1994). In these circumstances they argue that women are condemned to live in a perpetual state of fear. Moreover, feminists like Mullender and Morley (1994) are concerned that violent husbands do not make good fathers at all because they reproduce violent behaviour through the legitimation of the use of force.

Arguing against this newly valorized fatherhood is, however, now synonymous with arguing against virtue. Even if one is arguing against the resurrection of the old-style *enforcers of patriarchal power* or the self-interested *carriers of rights*, it is assumed that one is against those few men who really do share the responsibility for their children. Or worse, it is assumed that one is indifferent to the suffering of children. Yet the conditions under which mothering takes place (at least in Britain) are almost certainly worsening as fatherhood is increasingly valorized. The risks of motherhood are becoming high again. These risks are already well documented in economic terms (Joshi, 1991) and they are set to become higher as women realize that the cost of having children may involve an indelible contract (and extensive contact) with men whose behaviour is violent or oppressive.

As feminists have pointed out, motherhood is not an ideal condition but an experience of ambivalence (Rich, 1985; Ribbens, 1994). But motherhood has always been constituted in altruistic terms, and women expect to give up a great deal for their children. However, the new *post-divorce fatherhood* is not constituted in this way at all. Rather it is constituted in terms of a refusal to give up anything at all – including the children. Anecdotal evidence from Court Welfare Officers begins to support the suggestion that the *post-divorce fatherhood* is about 'having' rather than 'caring':

> We deal relatively more now with young men – who, themselves, often have a great deal of growing up to do – seeking contact with young children in situations that call for much subtlety, patience, and restraint if there is to be any chance of such contact working. It is often very difficult to judge whether contact can work and whether it should be set up in the first place. An allied problem is that relatively more applications seem half-hearted. (Pugsley 1995: 381)

Moreover, some fathers too seem uncomfortable with the idea that men can do it all, and that mothers should be dismissed or diminished:

> I feel quite comfortable having my son here and I would give up work or do what is needed. That would be very good for me, whether or not it would be ideal I don't know. I was born in 1959 and if someone should say to me 'Who should the child go to live with?' then I would say the mother. Looking at myself intellectually I don't know if that is a social condition or an intellectual statement. I sit here and think that when I went for residence I thought 'Am I being a bastard here? I shouldn't be doing it because it's not right'. Me mother says that a child should be with its mother. (Kevin)

But not all court welfare officers are worried by the sudden growth in fathers' interest in their children, and not all fathers are as reflexive as Kevin. The current system of family law in England, and the sudden public adulation of fatherhood, legitimates demands, rather than requests, from fathers that they should be able to alter the gender contract that served them well until the point of divorce. It seems important, therefore, for feminists to keep differentiating between the types of fatherhood that are currently being promoted. In as much as many mothers want co-operation from fathers during and after divorce, it seems important to support this demand, but during marriage as much as after it. However, it is equally important to find ways to identify harmful fathering and to challenge the dominant assumption that women-beaters are good fathers. At the very least, men's violence should not be disregarded as if it were inconsequential behaviour. If new identities for fatherhood are being forged at the point of divorce, rather than at the point of childbirth, then it is important for feminists to challenge this combative, self-justifying identity which seems, quite simply, to be an old way of oppressing women in a new guise.

ACKNOWLEDGEMENTS

We acknowledge the support of the ESRC, who funded the research project on which this chapter is based. We also thank all the parents and solicitors who took part in the study. All the names used here have been changed to preserve anonymity.

NOTES

1. See for example Burgess (1998), Burgess and Ruxton (1996), Burghes *et al*. (1997), French (1993), Moss (1995) and Simpson *et al*. (1995).
2. This presumption has recently been supported by work by Ferri and Smith (1996).
3. There is in fact no evidence that we can find that residential fathers are more willing than residential mothers to allow the children to see the absent parent, or that they feel entirely happy about contact. In our research, from which we cannot generalize, we found that residential fathers were often highly obstructive of contact and voiced exactly the same sort of sentiments as some of the residential mothers we interviewed. We therefore feel that this 'emotion' is not linked to

gender (i.e. an attribute of womanhood) but is linked to the situation in which certain parents find themselves. We regret that Simpson *et al.* are unintentionally fostering such negative views of mothers without the necessary research on residential fathers to support such a statement.

4. 'An Investigation into the Moral and Legal Ordering of Households in Transition', funded by the ESRC (R000234582).

5. A full discussion of this study can be found in Smart and Neale (1999).

6. In its most extreme form this stance argues that lesbian households produce homosexual boys.

7. These deadbeat dads are, in the New Right account, the sons of fathers who were forced out of the family by over-dominant mothers, and who were not provided with a proper authoritarian breadwinning father figure who would have inculcated more responsibility into their sons had they remained in the family.

8. See the recent report from the Family Policy Studies Centre, *Parenting in the 1990s*, by Ferri and Smith (1996), which shows that men's working hours mitigate against their involvement with their children. Middle-class men in particular are 'distant', and this is not fully explained by their commitment to work.

9. There is evidence that some judges are rejecting this harsh doctrine. See Hall (1997); also Re D (*Contact: Reasons for Refusal*) [1997] 2 FLR 48.

10. See Mullender and Morley (1994), for arguments against this assertion.

11. In the second round of interviews with the parents we showed them a sequence of vignettes about a divorcing couple and asked them what they thought should be done at various stages of the divorce process. At the end of the vignettes we asked whether they would have offered different advice if they knew that the husband had been violent to the wife. The majority thought that this should not alter the father's right to contact, even though it might be difficult for the mother. However, none of the parents could imagine that a mother might leave her children with her husband if he was violent. In other words they did not think that he should have their full-time care but he should be able to have an ongoing relationship with them.

12. We interviewed 37 family lawyers (20 women and 17 men) from different kinds of practices in the Yorkshire region in 1995.

REFERENCES

Barker, R. (1994) *Lone Fathers and Masculinity* (Aldershot: Avebury Press).
Beck, U. (1992) *Risk Society* (London: Sage).
Beck, U. and Beck-Gernsheim, E. (1995) *The Normal Chaos of Love* (Cambridge: Polity).
Brophy, J. (1982) 'Parental Rights and Children's Welfare: Some Problems of Feminists' Strategy in the 1920s', *International Journal of the Sociology of Law*, 7(2), pp. 149–68.

Brophy, J. (1989) 'Custody Law, Child Care and Inequality in Britain', in C. Smart and S. Sevenhuijsen (eds), *Child Custody and the Politics of Gender* (London: Routledge).

Burgess, A. (1998) *Fatherhood Reclaimed* (London: Vermillion).

Burgess, A. and Ruxton, S. (1996) *Men and their Children: Proposals for Public Policy* (London: Institute for Public Policy Research).

Burghes, L., Clarke., L. and Cronin, N. (1997) *Fathers and Fatherhood in Britain* (London: Family Policy Studies Centre).

Campbell, B. (1996) 'Good Riddance to the Patriarch', *Guardian*, 15 April.

Coward, R. (1996) 'Make the Father Figure', *Guardian*, 12 April.

Delphy, C. (1984) *Close to Home* (London: Hutchinson).

Dennis, N. and Erdos, G. (1993) *Families without Fatherhood*, 2nd edn (London: Institute of Economic Affairs).

Eekelaar, J. and Maclean, M. (1986) *Maintenance after Divorce* (Oxford: Oxford University Press).

Ferri, E. and Smith, K. (1996) *Parenting in the 1990s* (London: Family Policy Studies Centre).

French, S. (1993) *Fatherhood* (London: Virago).

Hall, Mr Justice (1997) 'Domestic Violence and Contact', *Family Law*, 27, pp. 813–18.

Harrison, R. and Mort, F. (1980) 'Patriarchal Aspects of Nineteenth-Century State Formation: Property Relations, Marriage and Divorce, and Sexuality', in P. Corrigan (ed.), *Capitalism, State Formation and Marxist Theory* (London: Quartet Books).

Hester, M. and Radford, L. (1996) *Domestic Violence and Child Contact Arrangements in England and Denmark* (University of Bristol: Policy Press).

Hochschild, A. (1995) 'Understanding the Future of Fatherhood', in M. van Dongen, G. Frinking and M. Jacobs (eds), *Changing Fatherhood* (Amsterdam: Thesis Publishers) pp. 219–30.

Joshi, H. (1991) 'Sex and Motherhood as Handicaps in the Labour Market', in M. Maclean and D. Groves (eds), *Women's Issues in Social Policy* (London: Routledge).

Kaganas, F. and Piper, C. (1994) 'Domestic Violence and Divorce Mediation', *Journal of Social Welfare and Family Law*, 3, pp. 265–78.

Maclean, M. (1991) *Surviving Divorce* (Basingstoke: Macmillan).

Mason, M. A. (1994) *From Father's Property to Children's Rights* (New York: Columbia University Press).

Morgan, P. (1995) *Farewell to the Family?* (London: Institute of Economic Affairs).

Moss, P. (ed.) (1995) *Father Figures: Fathers in the Families of the 1990s* (Edinburgh: HMSO).

Mullender, A. and Morley, R. (eds) (1994) *Children Living with Domestic Violence* (London: Whiting and Birch).

Norton, C. (1982) *Caroline Norton's Defence* (Chicago, IL: Academy; originally published 1854).

Phillips, M. (1997) *The Sex Change State* (London: Social Market Foundation, Memorandum no. 30, October).

Pugsley, J. (1995) 'Legal Aid – the Continuing Deluge', *Family Law*, 25 (July), pp. 380–2.

Reiss, E. (1934) *The Rights and Duties of English Women* (Manchester: Sherratt and Hughes).

Ribbens, J. (1994) *Mothers and their Children: A Feminist Sociology of Childrearing* (London: Sage).

Rich, A. (1985) 'Anger and Tenderness: the Experience of Motherhood', in E. Whitelegg *et al.* (eds), *The Changing Experience of Women* (Oxford: Blackwell).

Rosenblatt, J. and Scragg, P. (1995) 'The Hostile Parent: a Clinical Analysis', *Family Law*, 25, pp. 152–3.

Simpson, B., McCarthy, P. and Walker, J. (1995) *Being There: Fathers after Divorce* (Relate Centre for Family Studies, University of Newcastle upon Tyne).

Smart, C. (1984) *The Ties that Bind* (London: Routledge & Kegan Paul).

Smart, C. and Neale, B. (1999) *Family Fragments?* (Cambridge: Polity Press).

Willbourne, C. and Geddes, J. (1995) 'Presumption of Contact – What Presumption?' *Family Law*, 25, pp. 87–89.

7 State Power, Children's Autonomy and Resistance: the Juridical Context

Carole Smith

INTRODUCTION: HOW THE LAW THINKS ABOUT CHILDREN

In this chapter I am concerned to explore the way in which the law 'thinks' about children (King and Piper, 1995), particularly with regard to how the expression of children's autonomy rights is managed within the juridical field. However, it must be recognized that the law does its thinking in a social and political context; the juridical field is, in its operations, centrally influenced by a responsiveness to those characteristics which are thought to constitute childhood and to the weighty significance of its role in social regulation. I must acknowledge here the sustained debate about whether the law 'thinks' in any consistent way at all. It has been suggested that those essential and mutually reinforcing elements which define the law as a discrete discourse have been eroded and diffused by changing patterns of social regulation and an extension of juridical practice into administrative and discretionary areas where it is ill-equipped to intervene (see Cotterell, 1992: Chapter 9). Thus, it is argued that the law no longer operates as a singular channel through which the State exercises power as a legitimate form of social control. Instead, its regulatory function has been largely displaced and dispersed by a variety of disciplinary mechanisms which grow into the very fabric of the State. These mechanisms, or technologies of government, critically hinge upon expert definitions of normal and deviant conduct. The application of expert knowledge encourages and supports the development of conditions which allow continuous surveillance of the population, monitoring at a distance and over time, and self-regulation rather than punishment and overt control (Foucault, 1977). Referring to Foucault's (1979) conceptualization of 'governmentality' as an attitude or mental orientation, Miller and Rose describe the subtle process of social regulation in the following way:

> The classical terminology of political philosophy and political sociology – state vs. civil Society, public vs. private, community vs. market and so forth – is of little use here ... at the technical level, operationalising government has entailed the putting into place, both intentionally and unintentionally, of a diversity of indirect relations of regulation and persuasion that do not differentiate according to such boundaries. In particular the capacities that have been granted to expertise – that complex amalgam of professionals, truth claims and technical procedures – provide versatile mechanisms for shaping and normalising the private enterprise ... in ways which are simply not comprehended in these philosophies of politics.
>
> (Miller and Rose, 1990: 8)

Additionally, as the law has extended into areas of social welfare, it has increasingly relied upon government by administrative regulation and decision-making by expert advice. As seepage occurs, in both directions, between the juridical field and areas of administrative and expert discretion, the boundaries between legislative and executive power tend to lose their practical effect (Poulantzas, 1978). The juridical field, historically characterized by formal rules which are impartially applied to the resolution of disputes and for the protection of citizens who are held to be equal under the law, finds itself drawn into the arena of 'social' law where instrumental rationality is tarnished by discretionary judgements about needs, welfare, deserts, preferences and positive discrimination (Ewald, 1986). This critique, however, has attracted a counter-argument which suggests that the law protects its autonomy by acting as a self-referential system. Juridical practices reflect a focus on making judgements about particularly legal issues, that is, the rightness or wrongness and legality or illegality of the matter at hand. This process is facilitated by an interlocking series of legal rules, procedures, concepts and modes of reasoning which cannot accommodate other forms of knowledge, other than by colonization and interpretation within a legal framework (see for example, Luhmann, 1985; Teubner, 1986, 1988). An expert witness providing the court with advice drawn from, for example, a psycho-logical discourse, will find his/her evidence translated into a form which the juridical field can assimilate and apply to its particular mode of thinking and practice. As Teubner suggests:

They are not imported into the law bearing the label 'made in science', but are reconstructed within the closed operational network of legal communications that gives them a meaning quite different from that of the social sciences.   (Teubner, 1989: 749)

It is my contention, however, that it is possible to trace how the law 'thinks' about children, not only from a position of applying universal rules, but within a legislative and policy framework which requires the exercise of discretion, judgements about best interests, and engagement with expert discourses lying outside the juridical field. Leaving aside juridical ambivalence about those children who exhibit challenging and disruptive behaviour (Harris and Timms, 1993; Smith and Gardner, 1996) or who fall under the criminal law, juridical intervention is arguably characterized by the twin imperatives of paternalistic protection and benign control. As I will demonstrate, the regulatory mantle of protection and control, mediated by the language of welfare and best interests, must necessarily collide with a recognition not only that children have rights under the law, but that the juridical field should recognize and implement a wide range of rights for children to which citizens generally are entitled. Hence the stage is set for a struggle between the operational influence of rights and interests, autonomy and control, and the power to demand or to resist discursive dissolution and change. The juridical field, as I will show, plays a central role in both managing this struggle and in determining its outcomes. In order to elucidate juridical thinking in this context, the following discussion will concentrate on three related areas. First, the way in which childhood is discursively constituted; second, the nature of juridical intervention as this both reflects and serves to confirm a particular discourse of childhood; and third, the operation of power and resistance in relation to escalating pressure for a recognition of children's autonomy rights.

THE SOCIAL CONSTRUCTION OF CHILDHOOD

The Child as an Object of Concern

A growing sociological interest in the study of childhood has emphasized the extent to which philosophy and psychology have assumed a pre-eminent role in determining both the status of childhood and, in relation to this, its epistemological parameters as an area of philosophical and empirical enquiry. Archard (1993) notes John Locke's conception of childhood as a time during which the cumulative effects of maturation, experience and education develop and refine the child's latent capacity to reason. Similarly, Hendrick (1990) and Jenks (1996) point to Rousseau's portrayal of childhood as incorporating the flowering potential of reason, spirituality and morality from natural virtues and predispositions. A broadly psychological approach has been concerned to investigate and describe childhood as a significant period of cognitive and emotional development. Thus, Piaget (1924) sought to demonstrate experimentally how children grow towards cognitive competence by progressing through a necessary and sequential series of mental and physical adjustments to their experienced world. While Piaget's work has been critically examined in relation to its questionable epistemological foundations (Venn and Walkerdine, 1978; Rose, 1990; Jenks, 1996) and its empirical reliability (Donaldson, 1978; Lyon, 1993), it continues to exercise a powerful influence over how we conceptualize childhood and how we respond to children's formal educational 'needs' (Walkerdine, 1984; Urwin, 1985; Alderson and Montgomery, 1996). Additionally, psychoanalytic and psychodynamic schools of thought have designated childhood as a battleground on which libidinal impulses vie with the need for social integration and emotional acceptance, while the fear of abandonment is quieted by ambivalent attachment. Children are likely to emerge from this maelstrom as reasonably competent human beings only if they have enjoyed an appropriate balance of affection and discipline, consistent attachment and secure separation, immediate and deferred gratification, disappointment and satisfaction, and all the emotional, social and educational experiences which facilitate effective socialization and the internalization of moral and behavioural norms (see, for example, Erikson, 1950; Bowlby, 1969, 1973, 1980; Wollheim, 1971; Freud, 1973 and 1977; Klein, 1987; Gay, 1988).

Philosophical and psychological conceptions of childhood tend to neglect children as having ontological status and concentrate, instead, on investigating and charting their developmental progress towards adulthood. Childhood performance is understood not in terms of children's activities in constructing a social world with others, but only in relation to their achievement of incremental steps on the long road towards adult competence. Jenks describes the perspective thus:

> As a consequence of the adult member being regarded within theory
> as mature, rational and competent (all as natural dispositions), the
> child is viewed, in juxtaposition, as less than fully human, unfinished
> or incomplete.   (Jenks, 1996: 21)

Even where sociologists have applied themselves to the study of childhood, their attention has been caught by those particularly social
processes through which children mature to assume the mantle of
citizenship. They are primarily concerned, therefore, with the effective-
ness of socialization as this is managed within the family, the education
system and other social networks, where the child is nurtured and
honed as human capital for the future. Sociologists too have failed to
identify children's ideas, constructions and activities as warranting
attention, and have contributed to a discourse of childhood in which
children are merely of teleological interest as 'becoming' adults
(Prout and James, 1990; Jenks, 1996).

Prout and James (1990) suggest that a number of trends in social
scientific understanding and epistemology have directed attention
away from those grand meta-narratives (Lyotard, 1992) which seek to
theorize childhood with reference to universally valid explanations or
developmental themes. They identify broadly interpretive methodologies as having particular significance in this respect and point to
Aries' (1962: 17) historical analysis as 'blasting a large hole in
traditional assumptions about the universality of childhood'. These
developments open the way to exploring a new paradigm which
concentrates enquiry on the social construction of childhood, both
in relation to the role which children themselves play in socially
constructing their world, and in understanding how and why
childhood is discursively constituted in particular ways. This approach
relies heavily on Foucault's (Foucault, 1972; Rouse, 1994) notion of
discourse as situating and expressing power relations through
language, social practices, symbolic communication and the discursive
generation and transmutation of knowledge forms. Operationally, a
discourse identifies, therefore, what we 'know' about children's needs
and the ways in which these should be met through a variety of
institutional arrangements in the private and public spheres.

Put simply, Layder describes the idea of a discourse as:

> all that can be thought, written or said about a particular thing such
> as a product (like a car, or a washing detergent), or a topic or
> specialist area of knowledge (such as sport or medicine). In this

sense, the ability to employ a discourse reflects a command of knowledge of a particular area. (Layder, 1994: 97)

What must also be understood, however, is that Foucault does not refer to a discourse as being simply a reflection or coherent version of everything that is known or expressed, in various forms, about something. Rather, a discourse is active in constituting and generating the very nature of a topic area through language and symbols which are used to describe, analyse and refer to it. A discourse thus constitutes its own meaning and, in so doing, becomes suffused with power relations, both internally and in relation to other discursive constructions, which may have a challenging and reformative influence. Thus, the discursive construction of childhood determines the ways in which we understand, think about, describe and investigate childhood and the ways in which we interact with, respond to, and form relationships with children, in a range of emotional, social, educational and disciplinary encounters. In short, a discourse constitutes how we 'know' childhood and the power relations which inherently characterize a particular way of 'knowing'.

The Child as a Person

Despite epistemological and empirical critiques of the way in which the study of childhood has marginalized children as objects of investigation and adults 'in the making', it is arguable that this discourse remains influential in constituting the knowledge claims of those 'experts' who routinely monitor, assess and intervene in the lives of children. However, this discourse has been increasingly challenged over the past 20 years by the emerging language of rights. Children are to be understood as persons and not acted upon as objects of concern (see the Cleveland Report, 1988). In this sense it has been argued that children, no less than adults, have a legitimate interest in, and claim upon, autonomy rights which guarantee a minimum degree of interference consistent with living in a society of others. Of course, there is a practical question here, in that it is difficult to determine at what point children come to share an equivalence of interests with adults and cease to need the physical protection and emotional nurture provided by significant carers. However, this problem, far from diminishing the power of 'rights talk', simply enters into the discursive realm where it becomes another element in the shifting, complex and emergent constitution of childhood.

THE JURIDICAL CONTEXT

The definition of children, as persons with a legitimate claim to
autonomy rights, is most transparently mediated in the juridical field. I
want to illustrate how the law thinks about children in this context by
reference to convention, statute law and case law, and then to consider in some detail a child's right to consent (or to refuse consent) to
medical treatment and a child's right to initiate or to participate in
certain legal proceedings under the Children Act 1989.

The United Nations Convention on the Rights of the Child was
adopted in November 1989, and ratified by the United Kingdom
government in December 1991. It requires ratification by 20 countries,
following which it assumes the status of international law and is
binding on those countries which have signed. The Convention has
43 Articles in all. Article 12 is of particular relevance for a juridical
recognition of children's rights:

1. States Parties shall assure to the child who is capable of
   forming his or her own views the right to express those views
   freely in all matters affecting the child, the view of the child
   being given due weight in accordance with the age and maturity
   of the child.
2. For this purpose, the child shall in particular be provided the
   opportunity to be heard in any judicial and administrative
   proceedings affecting the child, either directly or through a
   representative or an appropriate body, in a manner consistent
   with the procedural rules of natural law.

Although the Convention is framed in terms of children's *rights*, it is
hedged about with references to their welfare and interests. Article 3,
for example, requires that:

In all actions concerning children, whether undertaken by public or
private social welfare institutions, courts of law, administrative
authorities or legislative bodies, the best interests of the child shall
be a primary consideration.

The Convention's preamble emphasizes a child's need for 'special
safeguards and care', including appropriate legal protection, by virtue
of the child's physical and mental immaturity. The 1996 European
Convention on the Exercise of Children's Rights attempts to avoid the

potential conflict between interests and rights by asserting that fulfilment of the former is dependent upon realization of the latter:

> The object of the present convention is, in the best interests of children, to promote their rights, to grant them procedural rights and to facilitate the exercise of these rights by ensuring that children are, themselves or through other persons or bodies, informed and allowed to participate in proceedings affecting them before a judicial authority.   (Representing Children, 1995: 10)

Against this backcloth the Children Act 1989 was implemented in 1991, having learned some tough lessons from the Cleveland Report (1988) about over-zealous State intervention in the lives of children and their families. The Act did pay attention to children's rights, in allowing that they could initiate and participate in certain legal proceedings; that they had to be consulted by any local authority which was 'looking after' them and their wishes and feelings taken into account; that they should have access to a formal complaints procedure and that, in public law proceedings, they could refuse to undergo a 'psychiatric or medical examination or other assessment' even if a court had made directions to this effect. However, a child's ability to exercise certain of these rights is dependent upon a discretionary judgement about whether the child has 'sufficient understanding' to do so, and Section 1 of the Children Act requires that, in making any decision about a child's upbringing, the court must give paramount consideration to the child's welfare. Thus, the formality of rights and associated obligations is tempered by conditional and discretionary interventions arising from an assessment of developmental factors ('sufficient understanding'), needs and interests (Mnookin and Szwed, 1983; Timms, 1997). Sir Thomas Bingham summarized the intentions of the Children Act as follows:

> The purposes of the Act were not, however, solely legislative. They were in part declaratory of the attitudes and purposes that were to inform and direct the courts and other agencies in dealing with children. The child's welfare was to be treated uniformly as the paramount consideration. Delay was to be avoided. Basic freedoms were to be emphasised and officiousness discouraged, through application of the rubric that no order should be made in respect of a child unless the court considered that to do so would be better for the child than making no order at all. Every opportunity was to be afforded for the

child's own views to be communicated and, where appropriate, explained through independent representation.

(Re S (A Minor) (Independent Representation) [1993] 2 FLR 440)

In the context of common law, arguments about children's rights largely turn upon the legal presumption that children lack capacity (or competence) while adults are presumed to have capacity, until and unless, evidence is brought to rebut this presumption. Thus in Re X [1975][1] Latey J quoted *Halsbury's Laws of England* as follows:

An infant does not possess full legal competence. Since he is regarded as of immature intellect and imperfect discretion, English Law, while treating all acts of an infant which are for his benefit on the same footing as those of an adult, will carefully protect his interests and not permit him to be prejudiced by anything to his disadvantage.

Compare the above with Lord Donaldson's conclusion in Re T [1993]:[2]

Prima Facie every adult has the right and capacity to decide whether or not he will accept medical treatment, even if a refusal may risk permanent injury to his health or even lead to premature death. Furthermore, it matters not whether the reasons for his refusal were rational or irrational, unknown or even non-existent. This is notwithstanding the very strong public interest in preserving the life and health of all citizens. However, the presumption of capacity to decide, which stems from the fact that the patient is an adult, is rebuttable. (115)

– and the comments of Thorpe J. in Home Secretary vs. Robb [1995]:[3]

The right of an adult of sound mind to self-determination prevailed over any countervailing interest of the State. (678)

The Law Commission (1995a) has no plans to change the fundamental legal distinction between children and adults. In considering the matter of consent in the criminal law, the Commission notes that it will begin, in true juridical fashion, by identifying the rules which are required to ensure that non-voluntary consents are treated as ineffective. It states:

> This exercise will involve making special rules for the young and the disabled: in certain circumstances the state will be entitled to dictate that there is an age below which no consent shall be valid, but this must be determined on a case by case basis.   (20)

Furthermore:

> The law combines a respect for the autonomy of those who are growing up with the need to protect them from the consequences of certain decisions until they have reached an age at which Parliament decides they really are old enough to take decisions for themselves without Parliamentary protection   (50)

Where adults are deemed to lack capacity, courts will make decisions based upon their best interests. Thus children, and adults without capacity, are treated in the same way; as subject to a discretionary judicial assessment of what will be in their best interests and therefore lawful (see Re F(HL) Sterilisation: Mental Patient [1989] 2 FLR 412).

It is important to note here a final source of juridical power, which derives from directly delegated responsibility from the Sovereign to the courts. While one may appreciate Foucault's unwillingness to locate power alongside the meta-narratives of class, State, sovereignty and so on, and his insistence that power and associated resistance is everywhere found in discursive relations (Sarup, 1988; Clegg, 1989; Cooper, 1994), the *parens patriae* jurisdiction of the High Court provides a distinctive challenge to his approach. In reaching judgements, courts are bound by the procedural, evidential and substantive requirements of statute law, that is by legislation which has been approved by Parliament. However, in areas where Parliament has not legislated, or where the intentions of Parliament are less than clear, the High Court and the Courts of Appeal will apply their inherent powers to resolving matters before them. This exercise involves reference to historical legal precedent, to matters of policy and public interest, to what Parliament may have intended had it considered the issue and, in the case of the *parens patriae* jurisdiction, to the courts' particular protective responsibilities in relation to children. Essentially then, the *parens patriae* jurisdiction represents a special aspect of the judiciary's ability to make its own law. Insofar as it relies on a court's inherent powers it constitutes judicial, rather than Parliamentary, consideration and resolution of important issues. In England the *parens patriae* jurisdiction relates only to children and is, as Lord Donaldson commented in Re R [1992],[4] theoretically without limit. He explains it thus:

> It is also clear that this jurisdiction is not derivative from the parents' rights and responsibilities, but derives from, or is, the delegated performance of the duties of the Crown to protect its subjects and particularly children who are the generations of the future.   (25)

In Lord Donaldson's view the *parens patriae* jurisdiction allows a court to override the views of parents or child, if it considers that this would be in a child's best interests. In Re X [1975][5] Latey J. explains the jurisdiction in this way:

> All subjects owe allegiance to the Crown. The Crown has a duty to protect its subjects. This is and always has been especially so towards minors. ... And it is so because children are especially vulnerable. They have not formed the defences inside themselves which older people have, and therefore need special protection. They are also a country's most valuable asset for the future. So the Crown as *parens patriae* delegated its powers and duty of protection to the courts. Those powers and that duty so derived are not the creation of any statute and are not limited by any statute.   (52)

This jurisdiction has been applied particularly in cases involving children's rights to consent, or to withhold their consent, to medical treatment, where statute law is sparse and disputed and the child's protection becomes a central issue for the court. It has similarly been significant in determining other questions where a child's attempts to prove 'sufficient understanding' are contested and the conflict between autonomy and protection must fundamentally inform juridical intervention.

CONSENT TO MEDICAL TREATMENT

Section 8 of the Family Law Reform Act 1969 deals with consent to medical treatment. It states:

S.8(1)   The consent of a minor who has attained the age of sixteen years to any surgical, medical or dental treatment which, in the absence of consent, would constitute a trespass to his person, shall be as effective as it would be if he were of full age; and where a minor has by virtue of this section given an effective consent to any treatment it shall not be necessary to obtain any consent for it from his parent or guardian.

There is no statutory provision relating to medical intervention for children under 16 years old (hence the significance of the Gillick judgement at common law) except partial provision in the Children Act 1989, which need not concern us here. The Gillick judgement,[6] in the House of Lords, determined that a child under 16 years old has a right to seek and consent to medical treatment provided that he/she is of sufficient understanding and intelligence to comprehend the nature and implications of such a decision. That is, if a child can persuade the court that he/she should be treated as having capacity. Lord Scarman referred to Blackstone (1830) as support for the proposition that increasing maturity should reasonably be matched by increasing autonomy:

The underlying principle of the law was exposed by Blackstone. ... It is that parental right yields to the child's right to make his own decisions when he reaches a sufficient understanding and intelligence to be capable of making up his own mind on the matter requiring decision.   (186)

Concluding, more directly, Lord Scarman said:

I would hold that as a matter of law the parental right to determine whether or not their minor child below the age of 16 will have medical treatment terminates, if and when, the child achieves a sufficient understanding and intelligence to enable him or her to understand fully what is proposed.   (188)

The child as a person with, albeit conditional, autonomy rights appeared to have shifted the balance of power relations which characterize the discourse of childhood. However, noteworthy though the Gillick judgement may be, it did not attend to the much more problematic issue of a *refusal* to consent to medical treatment. In Re E [1993][7] a hospital authority sought leave to administer blood

transfusions to a young man of nearly 16 years old. He and his parents
were Jehovah's Witnesses and were adamantly opposed to the treatment, despite the likelihood of death within a few days if medical
intervention was withheld. Ward J. gave leave to the hospital authority
to proceed. He found that, although A was 'a boy of sufficient
intelligence to be able to take decisions about his own well-being', he
did not have a full understanding 'of the whole implications of what
the refusal of treatment involves'. In Ward J's view, A lacked capacity
and he therefore based his judgement on an assessment of A's best
interests. Ward J. commented:

> He is of an age and understanding at least to appreciate the con-
> sequences, if not the process, of his decision, and by reason of the
> conviction of his religion, which I find to be deeply held and
> genuine, he says no to medical intervention which may save his life.
> What weight do I place upon this refusal? I approach this case
> telling myself that the freedom of choice in adults is a fundamental
> human right. He is close to the time when he may be able to take
> those decisions. I should therefore be very slow to interfere. Putting
> the case at its highest as a considered wish to choose for oneself to
> die, is this choice of death one which a judge in wardship can find to
> be consistent with the welfare of a child? ... When, therefore, I have
> to balance the wishes of the father and the son against the need for
> the chance to live a precious life, then I have to conclude that their
> decision is inimical to his well-being.   (393)

A judicial keeness to facilitate life-saving treatment is understandable,
but Ward J. extended the test of capacity way beyond Lord Scarman's
expectations in 'Gillick'. Similarly, the central question which concerned Ward J. was whether he personally, and the juridical system
more generally, could accept the consequences of a minor's autonomous decision whilst being charged with protecting his/her welfare.
He thus chose to allow the anticipated outcome of A's wishes to
determine his assessment of A's capacity. Two years later, when A was
18, he exercised his right to refuse medical treatment, a decision which
resulted in his death.

Re R [1992][8] concerned a young woman, two months off her
sixteenth birthday, who was placed in an adolescent psychiatric unit.
Doctors in the unit wished to administer antipsychotic drugs at their
discretion whether or not R consented to this. R was assessed by an
'approved social worker' as rational and lucid. Lord Donaldson

considered the position of a 'Gillick competent' child who refused consent and unequivocally concluded that Lord Scarman (in the Gillick judgement) had not intended parents to lose an independent right to consent if their child refused to do so. While he found R to lack capacity, his comments are illuminating in this context:

> I do not understand Lord Scarman to be saying that, if a child was 'Gillick competent', to adopt the convenient phrase used in argument, the parents ceased to have an independent right of consent as contrasted with ceasing to have right of determination, that is, a veto. In a case in which the 'Gillick competent' child refuses treatment, but the parent consents, that consent *enables* treatment to be undertaken lawfully, but in no way determines that the child shall be so treated.
> (23, original emphasis)

Re W [1993][9] gave Lord Donaldson a further opportunity to rehearse, and largely confirm, the views which he had earlier expressed in the previous case, Re R. Leave was sought to move J, a young woman of 16 years old suffering from anorexia nervosa, to a specialist medical unit and to give her treatment without her consent. True to form, Lord Donaldson found that J lacked capacity because of the nature of her illness. However, along the way he made it clear that the court's inherent jurisdiction gave it the power to override the refusal of a 'Gillick competent' minor, of whatever age, if it considered that it was in the child's best interests to do so. The court cannot exercise its inherent jurisdiction in opposition to statute law, but Lord Donaldson concluded that S. 8 of the Family Law Reform Act 1969 allowed a child of 16 to consent, but not to *refuse* consent, to medical treatment. So, Lord Donaldson introduced an impenetrable barrier to hopes for children's emancipation. Such is the discursive power of childhood as characterized by children's vulnerability and need for protection, that even a 'Gillick competent' child may find his/her autonomy constrained in the face of alternative definitions of their welfare.

Re K, W and H [1993][10] concerned three children, two of whom were 15 and the other 14, in which case a psychiatric hospital sought authorization to administer medication without their consent. Once again they were found to lack capacity but Thorpe J. made it clear, following Re R (above), that even if the children had been assessed as 'Gillick competent' their refusal could be overridden by an adult with parental responsibility or by the court. Finally, in South Glamorgan County Council v. W and B [1992],[11] Douglas Brown J. gave authorization for a

15-year-old girl, *whom he considered to be 'Gillick competent'*, to be forcibly removed from her home to an adolescent unit against her will. What is particularly remarkable about this judgement is that A, the child in this case, was the subject of an interim care order to the local authority. Under these circumstances, S. 36(8) of the Children Act 1989 makes it abundantly clear that a child may *refuse* any medical or psychiatric examination or other assessment if he/she is of sufficient understanding to make an informed decision, even if the court makes directions. Guidance from the Department of Health (1991) makes a point of emphasizing the child's right to refuse in this situation. The decision that A had capacity, but that her right to decide should be overridden in the face of a clear statutory proscription, led Lyon (1994) to refer to the potentially abusive effects of systems which are designed to protect children's interests.

It is evident from the juridical response to these cases that the courts will not allow *even 'Gillick competent'* children to make autonomous decisions about refusing medical treatment. If the court considers that a child has misjudged what is in his/her own best interests, it will not hesitate to override the decision. Consider this position in relation to an adult, whose presumed capacity renders the basis of any decision which he/she may make his/her own business and of no interest to the court. Although a child who has demonstrated 'Gillick competence' must be equivalent to an adult in terms of capacity, the legal status as a minor allows the court to ignore his/her autonomy rights in a way which would be unthinkable for similarly situated adults.

CHILDREN'S RIGHTS TO INITIATE OR PARTICIPATE IN LEGAL PROCEEDINGS

Although cases involving consent to medical treatment provide quite dramatic illustrations of juridical intervention, those situations in which children may wish to initiate or to be joined in legal proceedings may well have considerable significance for their social and emotional well-being in the longer term. The law and court rules are substantively and procedurally complex in this area. I do not wish juridical mystification to obscure the major themes which are relevant to this discussion. I will therefore gloss over some of the legal technicalities in order to illuminate the way in which childhood is constructed in this juridical field. In proceedings under Part II of the

Children Act 1989 (private law), children may apply for leave to make an application for a section 8 order. These orders refer crucially to arrangements for contact and residence when a child's parents divorce or separate and, less importantly in this context, to a prohibited steps or specific issues order. The court will grant leave to a child only 'if it is satisfied that he has sufficient understanding to make the proposed application'. Such is the significance accorded to a decision about allowing the child to take this step, that any application must be heard in the High Court (President's Direction, 22 February 1993).

Judicial reflection on the extent to which a child may be construed as having sufficient understanding suggests a particular orientation to childhood and to the tender sensibilities of children who may thus become caught up in adult conflicts. In Re S [1993][12] a boy of 11 years old applied for leave to continue proceedings, which concerned issues of residence and contact disputed by his divorced parents, without the Official Solicitor. He wished to instruct a solicitor to represent him and to have all the rights of an adult involved in litigation of this sort. In refusing the child's application, Sir Thomas Bingham provides a compassionate, and at the same time controlling, perspective on childhood having all the hallmarks of a construction which defines the child as an inchoate adult:

> First is the principle, to be honoured and respected, that children are human beings in their own right with individual minds and wills, views and emotions, which should command serious attention. A child's wishes are not to be discounted or dismissed simply because he is a child. He should be free to express them and decision makers should listen. Second is the fact that a child is, after all, a child. The reason why the law is particularly ... solicitous in protecting the interests of children is because they are liable to be vulnerable and impressionable, lacking the maturity to weigh the longer term against the shorter, lacking the insight to know how they will react and the imagination to know how others will react in certain situations, lacking the experience to measure the probable against the possible. (348)

Sir Thomas Bingham clearly recognizes that the concept of childhood must necessarily incorporate 'a babe in arms and a sturdy teenager on the verge of adulthood', and that judicial assessment of 'sufficient understanding' must therefore reflect an individual child in the context of particular proceedings. Nevertheless the 'picture' which he conjures

up is clearly indicative of a discourse in which childhood is characterized by experiential, emotional and rational underdevelopment relative
to adulthood.

A similar situation arose in Re C [1995][13] in which case a girl of
14 sought leave to make an application under S. 8 of the Children Act
1989 so that she could live with her mother. Stuart White J. referred
approvingly to Sir Thomas Bingham's comments above, but then went
on to add another (and some might say irrelevant) consideration to
the condition of 'sufficient understanding'. He said:

> Secondly, it is pointed out, again not without considerable force,
> that one of the reasons why courts ought to be cautious about
> allowing applications of this kind is that, once a child is party to the
> proceedings between warring parents, that leads the child to be in a
> position in which that child is likely to be present hearing the
> evidence of those parents, hearing the parent cross-examined,
> hearing perhaps of many matters which, at the tender age of the
> child, it would be better for her not to hear.   (930)

He did, however, grant the child leave to make an application as she
wished. Re H [1993][14] concerns a child of 15 who was the subject of
care proceedings by the local authority. This boy wished to instruct his
own solicitor rather than being represented by a solicitor, who was
also acting for the *guardian ad litem*, with whom he disagreed. A
guardian ad litem is appointed by the court in specified proceedings to
safeguard the child's interests. This boy wanted to express his views,
and argue his case directly to the court, rather than having his
interests mediated through the recommendations of the *guardian ad
litem*. In assessing the question of 'sufficient understanding', Thorpe J.
expressed his position thus:

> Obviously a child suffering from a mental disability might not have
> such understanding. Obviously a child suffering from a psychiatric dis-
> order might not have such a level of understanding. But I cannot
> follow her (the child's solicitor) to the conclusion that if a child is only
> suffering from some emotional disturbance then really there is little
> room to question his or her ability to instruct a solicitor. It seems to
> me that a child must have sufficient rationality within the under-
> standing to instruct a solicitor. It may well be that the level of
> emotional disturbance is such as to remove the necessary degree of
> rationality that leads to coherent and consistent instruction.   (449)

He is prepared to admit that a child could be sufficiently rational to have the necessary degree of understanding, but suggests that emotional disturbance might interfere with the exercise of rationality. There would have been no such qualms about a person's emotional state had Thorpe J. been talking about an adult rather than a child. Thorpe J. accepted the 'forensic force' of the submission advanced by the child's solicitor that a decision made in the lower court should not be allowed to stand because S had not been legally represented at that stage. However, applying his discretion, he concluded that the result would not have been any different even if S had been afforded the opportunity to argue his case.

Finally, in Re H [1993][15] Booth J. echoes the sentiments expressed by Stuart White J. when she eschews children's involvement in the adult world of adversarial proceedings. She says:

> The court must be satisfied that H, in this instance, has sufficient understanding to participate as a party in the proceedings without a *guardian ad litem*. Participating as a party, in my judgement, means much more than instructing a solicitor as to his own views. The child enters the arena among other adult parties. He may give evidence and he may be cross-examined. He will hear other parties, including in this case his parents, give evidence and be cross-examined. He must be able to give instructions on many different matters as the case goes through its stages and to make decisions as need arises. Thus a child is exposed and not protected in these procedures. (555)

Booth J. did grant leave for the 15-year-old boy involved in these proceedings to conduct his case via his solicitor, but she clearly did so with some regret about the 'loss of innocence' which this would involve. During her judgement she made the important point that in reaching an assessment of 'sufficient understanding' the court should not confuse the conditions of the test with its own view about what would be in a child's best interests; the formal attribution of rights should be distinguished from the discretionary interpretation of interests. It is unlikely that the judiciary in other cases cited above were ignorant about this distinction. What is much more likely, and is supported by a detailed reading of their judgements, is that they chose to conflate capacity and best interests in a way which is unacceptable in cases involving adults, and which is specifically abrogated in the Law Commission's (1995b) deliberations on assessing adult capacity.

CAPACITY AND RIGHTS

Common law principles and the application of judicial discretion have been hotly criticized by those who wish to see an effective protection of children's rights. It is argued that the legal distinction between children and adults is insupportable, in terms of a philosophical analysis of autonomy (Lindley, 1986; Alderson, 1992; Lansdown, 1994; Dickenson and Jones, 1995) and an empirical demonstration of children's capacity to absorb information, weigh alternatives, and make reasoned decisions in their own best interests (Alderson, 1994; Franklin, 1995; Alderson and Montgomery, 1996). In any event, the probability that some (older) children lack experience, emotional stability and reflective sophistication is hardly a sound basis on which to distinguish children from adults, since many adults would be unlikely to pass the stringent tests of capacity which the courts are prone to set for children. Additionally, the courts have been berated for their willingness to find that children lack 'Gillick competence' (capacity) and for their paternalistic reliance upon the *parens patriae* jurisdiction to override children's wishes on those rare occasions when they are successful in persuading a court of their competence (Douglas, 1992; Bainham, 1992; Eekelaar, 1993; Lyon and Parton, 1995).

However, those who wish to argue that the presumption of childhood incapacity cannot be sustained beyond the formal categorizations of the juridical field, betray a curious ambivalence about allowing that children and adults should enjoy the same autonomy in making crucial decisions about their own well-being. Lansdown (1994) argues that the law should start from the premise that children have a moral right to self-determination and that any interference with this right should require adults to justify their intervention. This principle should be overridden only where there is clear evidence that a failure to intervene would be contrary to the child's best interests or would lead to conflict with another's rights. She says:

> What needs to be recognised, however, is that children have civil rights which must form the framework against which decisions and judgements are made. A presumption of competence should prevail and where it is overridden all actions should be tested against the promotion and respect for those rights. (44)

Crucially, however, Lansdown accepts that a restriction of self-determination may still be imposed where adults assess that this is necessary in the child's best interests. The issue of best interests does not become relevant to a court's determinations in respect of adults until the presumption of capacity has been rebutted: best interests is not a condition for disallowing autonomy. Lansdown thus conflates self-determination and best interests in such a way that children's autonomy remains subject to discretionary control. Similarly, Alderson and Montgomery (1996) assert that adults frequently under-estimate children's ability to make reasoned decisions, and they suggest that the presumption of childhood capacity should be linked to compulsory school age. They set out a detailed administrative procedure for protecting children's autonomy in cases of consent to medical treatment, but cannot quite bring themselves to give children the same rights as adults when a decision is required. So, they argue, the test of competence must depend on a child's ability to understand the consequences of refusing treatment; the more serious the consequences, therefore, the less likely it is that a child would be found competent to decide. Final intervention lies with the court:

> The refusal by children would only be overridden in cases involving serious irreparable harm. It would not be automatic that their refusal would be overridden in such cases, as the alternative to the serious irreparable harm of non-treatment may be an equally unsatisfactory situation if treatment is attempted. However, such harm is the minimum threshold for disregarding the child's views. (92)

Thus, a competent child's wishes may still be overridden in cases involving serious irreparable harm. As I have shown, this is not the case for adults, where capacity is the *only test* which legitimates interference with autonomy rights. Douglas (1992) mounts a trenchant criticism of Lord Donaldson's views in Re R (considered above), suggesting that they 'strike at the very core of the Gillick principle of respect for the decision-making of mature minors', or as it is put in Re R, 'Gillick competent' children (571). Despite her wish to protect the autonomy rights of competent children, however, she still proposes that it is necessary to identify some acceptable means of overriding a child's refusal to accept medical treatment in life-threatening situations. This might be achieved by either finding a child too immature to decide, on the premise that children generally would wish to be so protected, or through legislation to determine the minimum age at which a child's refusal would be binding.

It is understandable that those who argue for children's autonomy rights should baulk at accepting the logical conclusions of their own arguments. They want to dismantle the legal distinction between children and adults, but when it comes to the crunch they find themselves unable to allow children and adults equivalent rights over decisions which will centrally impact upon their lives (or deaths). The discourse of childhood is riddled with ambiguity and ambivalence. Throughout juridical and knowledge fields, language and practices struggle with the imperatives of rights versus interests, experience versus protection, self-knowledge versus expert assessment, certainty versus risk, adult responsibility versus childhood independence, and the child as subject versus the child as object.

CONCLUSION: DISCOURSE AND THE JURIDICAL FIELD

As I have attempted to show, the law does 'think' about children in a particular, albeit ambivalent, way. While statute law at least makes some reference to children's autonomy rights, its overriding concern is with how best to protect their welfare. Common law principles and judicial discretion clearly point to a juridical recognition that children are to be treated as subjects but, at the same time, provide a framework in which children's interests are likely to be preferred over their rights. There are two consistent and mutually reinforcing presumptions which characterize juridical intervention in children's lives. First, that children lack the experience, emotional stability and cognitive sophistication enjoyed by adults and are therefore prone to misjudge what is in their own best interests. Second, that children lack the mental and emotional stamina, fortitude and worldly toughness to compete with adults in adversarial proceedings and that they should be protected from the formal and litigious settings in which disputes are resolved. This perspective clearly reflects and reinforces a discourse of childhood where language and practices constitute the child as developmentally immature and as an adult 'in the making'. In this way the juridical field becomes essentially entangled with, and a contributor to, the discursive construction of childhood. It combines with experts and their knowledge claims to inform the government of childhood and the power relations which this supports. Miller and Rose (1990) describe this discursive activity thus:

The government of a population, a national economy, an enterprise, a family, a child or even oneself becomes possible only through discursive mechanisms that represent the domain to be governed as an intelligible field with its limits, characteristics whose component parts are linked together in some more or less systematic manner.   (6)

However, as we have seen, the 'domain to be governed' is becoming increasingly ambiguous. The juridical field itself is beset with conflicts about rights and interests (although tending towards the latter), and expert knowledge has been challenged over the way in which it constitutes childhood as a cognitively and emotionally immature version of adulthood. Childhood as a discursive construction becomes less 'intelligible' insofar as language and practices represent the child as having legitimate claims to autonomy rights whilst, at the same time, needing protection in his/her best interests from the consequences of his/her decisions.

Foucault's idea of discourse is helpful here since it captures the way in which language and practices from a number of sites (social, juridical, expert) interact to constitute childhood in a particular way. The whole thus becomes more than the sum of its parts until, as we have seen, competing denotations and practices threaten to fragment the discourse and leave the way open for a variant discourse to emerge. In this context the juridical field is both a contributor to, and a product of, discursive formation. It is helpful, too, to conceptualize power not as a fixed commodity which is 'owned' by an institution or group, but as essentially emergent in discursive constructions. Thus, rather than understanding children and the juridical field as being locked in a battle for power, with one or the other holding power or engaged in resistance, we can see that a particular discourse of childhood gives rise to power relations which must inform any judgement or debate about children's rights. Those battles which are fought in court are but a reflection of a much bigger war in the discursive construction of childhood. This accords with Foucault's (1980) description of the operations of power in terms of 'strategies, tactics, struggle and conflict' (Layder, 1994). However, although a Foucauldian perspective identifies discursive construction as a way of clarifying and understanding the current debate (and ambivalence) about childhood, children's autonomy rights, protection and welfare, it falls short of capturing the whole picture. For we have to concede that power relations are not only constructed through discourse and that children's rights are defined through the practical operations of the State via legislation and juridical intervention. The *parens patriae* jurisdiction of the High Court legitimates discretionary power which can strike at the very heart of parents' and children's rights.

Power and resistance, as these characterize the conceptual and practical struggle over children's rights, must therefore be understood as arising from the process of discursive construction and as existing in the institutional machinery of the State. Both perspectives can be accommodated, and are indeed necessary, in order to grasp our ambivalence about childhood and children's rights and to take account of the location of power as this is displayed in the juridical field. This avoids the criticism that, if left to Foucault, power would be mere ephemera (Hall, 1986; Best and Kellner, 1991) and acknowledges that even Foucault cannot avoid reference to the legitimating functions of the Sovereign State (Barron, 1990; Larrain, 1994).

NOTES

1. Re X (A Minor) (Wardship Jurisdiction) [1975] AC Fam. 47.
2. Re T (An Adult) (Consent to Medical Treatment) [1993] AC Fam. 95.
3. Home Secretary v Robb [1995] 1 FLR 412.
4. Re R (A Minor) (Wardship: Consent to Treatment) [1992] CA Fam. 11.
5. See note 1 above.
6. Gillick v West Norfolk and Wisbech Area Health Authority [1986] AC 112.
7. Re E (A Minor) (Wardship: Medical Treatment) [1993] 1 FLR 386.
8. See note 4 above.
9. Re W (A Minor) (Consent to Medical Treatment) [1993] 1 FLR 1.
10. Re K, W and H (Minors) (Medical Treatment) [1993] 1 FLR 854.
11. South Glamorgan County Council v W and B [1992] 1 FLR 574.
12. Re S (A Minor) (Independent Representation) [1993] 2 FLR 437.
13. Re C (Residence: Child's Application for Leave) [1995] 1 FLR 927.
14. Re H (A Minor) (Care Proceedings: Child's Wishes) [1993] 1 FLR 440.
15. Re H (A Minor) (Role of Official Solicitor) [1993] 2 FLR 552.

REFERENCES

Alderson, B. (1992) 'Rights of Children and Young People', in A. Coote (ed.), *The Welfare of Citizens* (London: Rivers Oram Press), pp. 153–86.
Alderson, B. (1994) 'Researching Children's Rights to Integrity', in B. Mayall (ed.), *Children's Childhoods Observed and Experienced* (London: Falmer Press), pp. 45–62.

Alderson, P. and Montgomery, J. (1996) *Healthcare Choices: Making Decisions with Children* (London: IPPR).

Archard, D. (1993) *Children: Rights and Childhood* (London: Routledge).

Aries, P. (1962) *Centuries of Childhood* (London: Jonathan Cape).

Bainham, A. (1992) 'The Judge and the Competent Minor', *Law Quarterly Review*, 108, pp. 194–200.

Barron, A. (1990) 'Legal Discourse and the Colonisation of the Self in the Modern State', in A. Carty (ed.), *Postmodern Law, Enlightenment, Revolution and the Death of Man* (Edinburgh: Edinburgh University Press), pp. 107–25.

Best, S. and Kellner, D. (1991) *Postmodern Theory: Critical Interrogations* (London: Macmillan).

Blackstone (1830) *Commentaries* (17th edn), vol. 1, chs 16 and 17.

Bowlby, J. (1969) *Attachment* (London: Hogarth).

Bowlby, J. (1973) *Separation, Anxiety and Anger* (London: Hogarth).

Bowlby, J. (1980) *Loss, Sadness and Depression* (London: Hogarth).

Clegg, S. (1989) *Frameworks of Power* (London: Sage).

Cleveland Report (1988) *Report of the Enquiry into Child Abuse in Cleveland 1987* (London: HMSO).

Cooper, D. (1994) 'Productive, Relational and Everywhere? Conceptualising Power and Resistance within Foucauldian Feminism', *Sociology*, 28(2), pp. 434–54.

Cotterrell, R. (1992) *The Sociology of Law* (London: Butterworths).

Department of Health (1991) *The Children Act 1989, Guidance & Regulations*, vol. 1: *Court Orders* (London: HMSO).

Dickenson, D. and Jones, D. (1995) 'True Wishes: the Philosophy of Developmental Psychology and Children's Informed Consent', *Philosophy, Psychiatry and Psychology*, 2(4), pp. 287–303.

Donaldson, M. (1978) *Children's Minds* (Edinburgh: Fontana).

Douglas, G. (1992) 'The Retreat from Gillick', *Modern Law Review*, 55, pp. 569–76.

Eekelaar, J. (1993) 'White Coats or Flak Jackets: Doctors, Children and the Courts – Again', *Law Quarterly Review*, 109, pp. 182–7.

Erikson, E. (1950) *Childhood and Society* (New York: W. W. Norton).

Ewald, F. (1986) 'A Concept of Social Law', in G. Teubner (ed.), *Dilemmas and Law in the Welfare State* (Berlin: de Gruyter), pp. 41–75.

Foucault, M. (1972) *The Archaeology of Knowledge* (London: Routledge).

Foucault, M. (1977) *Discipline and Punish* (London: Allen Lane).

Foucault, M. (1979) 'On Governmentality', *Ideology and Consciousness*, 6, pp. 5–22.

Foucault, M. (1980) *Power/Knowledge: Selected Interviews and Other Writings 1972–1977*, edited by C. Gordon (Brighton: Harvester).

Franklin, B. (1995) 'The Case for Children's Rights', in B. Franklin (ed.), *The Handbook of Children's Rights* (London: Routledge), pp. 3–24.

Freud, S. (1973) *Introductory Lecture on Psychoanalysis* (Harmondsworth: Penguin).

Freud, S. (1977) *The Dissolution of the Oedipus Complex,* Pelican Freud Library, Vol. 7: *On Sexuality* (Harmondsworth: Penguin).

Gay, P. (1988) *Freud: A Life for Our Times* (London: Dent).

Hall, S. (1986) 'On Postmodernism and Articulation: an Interview with Stuart Hall', edited by L. Grossberg in *Journal of Communication Inquiry*, 10(2), pp. 45–60.

Harris, R. and Timms, N. (1993) *Secure Accommodation in Child Care* (London: Routledge).

Hendrick, H. (1990) 'Constructions and Reconstructions of British Childhood: an Interpretative Survey, 1800 to the Present', in A. James and A. Prout (eds), *Constructing and Reconstructing Childhood* (London: Falmer Press), pp. 35–9.

Jenks, C. (1996) *Childhood* (London: Routledge).

King, M. and Piper, C. (1995) *How the Law Thinks about Children* (Aldershot: Arena).

Klein, M. (1987) *Our Need for Others and its Roots in Infancy* (London: Tavistock).

Lansdown, G. (1994) 'Children's Rights', in B. Mayall (ed.), *Children's Childhoods Observed and Experienced* (London: Falmer Press), pp. 33–44.

Larrain, J. (1994) 'The Postmodern Critique of Ideology', *Sociological Review*, 42, pp. 290–314.

Law Commission (1995a) *Consent in the Criminal Law,* Consultation Paper No. 139 (London: HMSO).

Law Commission (1995b) *Mental Incapacity,* Law Commission Report No. 231 (London: HMSO).

Layder, D. (1994) *Understanding Social Theory* (London: Sage).

Lindley, R. (1986) *Autonomy* (London: Macmillan).

Luhmann, N. (1985) *A Sociological Theory of Law* (London: Routledge & Kegan Paul).

Lyon, C, and Parton, N. (1995) 'Children's Rights and the Children Act', in B. Franklin (ed.), *The Handbook of Children's Rights* (London: Routledge), pp. 40–55.

Lyon, C. (1994) 'What happened to the Child's Right to Refuse' – South Glamorgan County Council v W and B, *Journal of Child Law*, 6(2), pp. 84–7.

Lyon, T. (1993) 'Children's Decision-Making Competency', *Violence Update*, 4, 6 and 9.

Lyotard, J.-F. (1992) *The Postmodern Condition: A Report on Knowledge* (Manchester: University of Manchester Press).

Miller, P. and Rose, N. (1990) 'Governing Economic Life', *Economy and Society*, 19(1), pp. 1–30.

Mnookin, R. and Szwed, E. (1983) 'The Best Interests Syndrome and the Allocation of Power in Child Care', in H. Geach and E. Szwed (eds), *Providing Civil Justice for Children* (London: Edward Arnold), pp. 7–20.

Piaget, J. (1924) *The Language and Thought of the Child* (London: Routledge).

Poulantzas, N. (1978) *State Power and Socialism* (London: New Left Books).

Prout, A. and James, A. (1990) 'A New Paradigm for the Sociology of Childhood? Provenance, Promise and Problems', in A. James and A. Prout (eds), *Constructing and Reconstructing Childhood* (London: Falmer Press), pp. 7–34.

Representing Children (1995) 'European Convention on the Exercise of Children's Rights and Explanatory Report', pp. 9–29.

Rose, N. (1990) *Governing the Soul* (London: Routledge).
Rouse, J. (1994) 'Power/Knowledge', in G. Gutting (ed.), *The Cambridge Companion to Foucault* (Cambridge: Cambridge University Press), pp. 92–114.
Sarup, M. (1988) *An Introductory Guide to Post-Structuralism and Postmodernism* (Hemel Hempstead: Harvester/Wheatsheaf).
Smith, C. and Gardner, P. (1996) 'Secure Accommodation under the Children Act 1989', *Journal of Social Welfare and Family Law*, 18(2), pp. 173–88.
Teubner, G. (1986) 'After Legal Instrumentalism? Strategic Models and Post Regulatory Law', in G. Teubner (ed.), *Dilemmas of Law in the Welfare State* (Berlin: de Gruyter), pp. 299–325.
Teubner, G. (1988) 'Introduction to Autopoietic Law', in G.Teubner (ed.), *Autopoietic Law: A New Approach to Law and Society* (Berlin: de Gruyter), pp. 1–11.
Teubner, G. (1989) 'How the Law Thinks: Towards a Constructivist Epistemology of Law', *Law and Society Review*, 23, pp. 727–57.
Timms, J. (1997) 'The Tension between Welfare and Justice', *Family Law*, 27, January, pp. 38–47.
Urwin, C. (1985) 'Constructing Motherhood: the Persuasion of Normal Development', in C. Steedman, C. Urwin and V. Walkerdine (eds), *Language, Gender and Childhood* (London: Routledge & Kegan Paul), pp. 164–202.
Venn, U. K. and Walkerdine, V. (1978) 'The Acquisition and Production of Knowledge: Piaget's Theory Reconsidered', *Ideology and Consciousness*, 3, p. 79.
Walkerdine, V. (1984) 'Developmental Psychology and the Child-Centred Pedagogy: the Insertion of Piaget into Early Education', in J. Henriques *et al.* (eds), *Changing the Subject: Psychology, Social Regulation and Subjectivity* (London: Methuen), pp. 152–202.
Winnicott, D. W. (1964) *The Child, the Family and the Outside World* (Harmondsworth: Penguin).
Wollheim, R. (1971) *Feud* (London: Fontana).

Part III
Power and Resistance in Intimate Relationships

8 'That's Farming, Rosie...': Power and Familial Relations in an Agricultural Community

Pia Christensen, Jenny Hockey and Allison James

INTRODUCTION

Drawing on an ethnographic study of familial conceptions of dependency in an agricultural community in the north of England this chapter sets out from the proposition that social life necessarily takes place through interdependent social relations, relations which, as Morrow (1996) has argued, remain relatively undertheorized in the sociological literature.[1] What our data indicate is that relations of interdependency are articulated or experienced empirically as either dependent or independent. This, we suggest, is evidence of the ways in which power works to mask their character. In this sense any understanding of interdependence can only be offered at an analytic and theoretical level. This chapter is a contribution to this discussion.

One important factor to be considered is that traditional accounts of dependency have been framed by an inherent and usually unarticulated binarism. The meanings of either 'dependence' or 'independence' are instanced through their implied difference from one another, with the latter seemingly understood to be a more powerful and welcomed state than the former (Hockey and James, 1993). As children we strive to grow up out of 'dependency' and into 'independence'; later life dependency is by contrast resisted for as long as possible. In other words, only through an unspoken comparison with that which they are *not* do these concepts provide interpretive frames for people's everyday experiences. Traditionally,

171

we suggest, this led to particular biases in the literature about dependency which took as its usual focus the 'problems' of illness, disability and ageing because these were seen as threats to personal independence through raising issues of power and control. When tied to concepts of familial care and ageing, for example, dependency was often considered to be that which arises simply through the 'problems' presented by physical/ mental impairment and therefore it was seen as the property of persons – children or older people – as something naturalized at these points in the life-course. In this way the ontological status of dependency was bracketed or rendered temporarily unproblematic and the shifting power relations involved in caring or obligated relationships became the focus for study instead (Walker, 1982; Finch, 1989; Finch and Mason, 1993). The literature on disability, on the other hand, dissociated itself from this 'problem management' perspective. Instead, it profiled dependency as an inherently social construction, seeing it as a stigmatizing concept, the outcome of sets of social relations or particular social, political and economic environments and not as a person-specific issue (Barton, 1989; Oliver, 1990; Swain *et al.*, 1993). Such accounts could, in this way, neglect the empirical details of people's everyday social and physical experiences which may well be constituted through relationships conceived and constructed in terms of ideas of 'dependency' and thus subject to the moral baggage which these entail.

This chapter's examination of relations of interdependency within an agricultural community builds, however, upon more recent work which has attempted to reconcile the formerly divergent orientations of the literature on the care of 'dependent' people and the literature on disability (for example, Butler and Bowlby, 1997). Thus, French (1993), while acknowledging the socially located nature of disability, argues that the reform of a disablist society would not, in itself, overcome the bodily impairments of people who are disabled. Twigg and Atkin (1994) similarly critique the tendency to see 'dependency' as either a property of the person or as a social construction, as reflected in the very different practices which flow from medical as opposed to social models of care.

In providing a comparable bridge across these two literatures, this chapter is concerned to develop a broader theoretical approach to dependency, and offers up for discussion a vignette drawn from our study of farming families. This comprises one farmer's view of his life, social relations and social position and the views offered by family members. In it we trace out the particular relations of power which enable him to see himself and to be seen by others as, at first, a powerfully independent businessman and, later, as more dependent on his family and the local community in which he lives and works. But, as the chapter will show, his very independence, which he values both as a farmer and as a businessman, rests on sets of often unacknowledged and routinized dependencies and relationships of trust. That these are often not recognized by him or his family for what they are is, we suggest, an illustration of the ways in which power works to mask the necessary interdependence of all social life. Thus through a deliberate avoidance of the traditional substantive topics of caring, ageing and disability, yet drawing on their insights (Parker, 1993: 18–20; Morris, 1993: 72–88), in this chapter we will propose a different perspective; one which will enable a wider and more generalized theorizing of dependency (see, for example, Fraser and Gordon, 1994).

Central to this are three issues. First, in agreement with Walker (1982) we argue that dependency should be seen as an essentially relational concept. Put simply, for an individual to be dependent requires another for them to be dependent on. At an analytic level, dependency therefore necessarily entails a social connection which can be constituted both through mutual and reciprocal relations as well as the more hierarchical relations traditionally noted between an independent and a dependent person. Furthermore, dependency may be constructed across a variety of domains – material, social, economic and political dependency – and different connections may be made by different people across and between these different domains. At an empirical level, then, people may experience their lives as ones of dependence or independence, but these are lives which, at an analytical level, should be understood more complexly as necessarily interdependent.

Second, we employ a life-course perspective which will enable dependency to be seen as having temporal dimensions. This allows dependency to be understood as a fluid state of affairs such that people can be seen to move in and out of relations of dependency at different points in their lives. How, why and in what manner they do this may, in part, be a function of particular power relations. This acknowledgement, therefore, allows us to comprehend the processes of becoming 'dependent' or 'independent' by, for example, observing the waning of social relations through people's interactions or the increase in help and assistance being offered to and accepted by a person. These temporally contextualized dependencies may be of an economic, a material or a social kind; they may be characterized by a direct or indirect exchange, taking place at one time or as a kind of delayed reciprocity over time. In sum, a life-course perspective allows us to focus on dependency as an enacted process, and not a state.

Third, dependency can be visualized to have spatial dimensions and to be constituted through situated and local practices. In one setting material dependency may be more heavily marked than social dependencies or knowledge dependencies may outweigh those of a more economic kind. Further, in terms of social space, any one individual may be involved in different kinds of relationships with different people; he or she may be, at any point in time, involved in both dependent and independent relationships. One person's dependency may curtail another's independence, making that person in turn dependent. This is often of a different kind and in a different social space, as the feminist literature on caring has demonstrated in its acknowledgement of the implications for women in relation to their labour-force participation. Caring for a dependent other may mean in time that the carers themselves becomes socially, emotionally and economically dependent on other family members and the state (Dalley, 1988; Hicks, 1988). Thus, though often framed as a binary pair and defined by a necessary oppositional difference, once dependence/independence are not seen as fixed properties of people it becomes possible to see the great variety of ways in which these concepts connect and work to shape people's everyday social relations and social actions.

In sum, a focus on the life-course provides a way of exploring the complex articulation of both dependent and independent social relations through people's everyday social practices. And central to this array are, as we have indicated, questions of power. This does not mean, however, that an easy conceptual mapping can take place; dependency does not foreshadow powerlessness, nor yet are the powerful necessarily independent. Whether particular relations are experienced as dependent or independent relates instead, following Thompson (1984), to the ways in which power is used by individuals to secure 'specific outcomes' in the course of events through specific kinds of interventions and the deployment of specific kinds of resources. These may include the range of structural and cultural resources comprising economic, social and cultural capital, as well as the human 'capital' invested in face-to-face interactions and everyday encounters when the 'affection of the other' may be used to pursue divergent aims (Thompson, 1984). In this sense the model of power which we are employing is of a three-dimensional kind (Lukes, 1974) in which interpersonal relations of dominance, exhibited through behaviour, must be understood within the particularities of the cultural context.

FARMING, DEPENDENCY AND POWER

That farming is a very particular context of power was first remarked by Newby (1975) through his suggestion that the deferential relations characterizing agricultural workers' interactions with farm owners none the less went hand in hand with a fierce sense of self-worth:

> agricultural workers ... who are characterised by a set of beliefs customarily regarded as deferential are vociferous in the defence of their own self-respect. Their relationship to those above them in the social hierarchy, though necessarily inferior, is perceived more as one of partnership than servility. (1975: 145)

In Newby's view this relationship is organic, in the Durkheimian sense of being a 'mutual and harmonious interdependence'; it is 'the way things are'. And, Newby argued, it was precisely this 'organic' aspect which accounts for why deferential relations are sustained. Not only arc they seen as legitimated by traditional authority but any hierarchical differentiation between groups or strata is balanced by a process of identification which is both positive and affective. This process generates a sense of partnership. Managed effectively, the tension between hierarchy and belonging produces a deferential relationship. In the day-to-day encounters of farming, social distance is balanced by social intimacy and it is through the rituals of deference that this tension becomes stabilized.

Newby's account strikes a chord with Thompson's suggestion that power arises through domination which is understood as 'systematic asymmetrical relations', and that is is through the mobilization of particular meanings that these relations are perpetuated. Ideology, says Thompson, is the ways in which meanings (signification) serve to sustain relations of domination, and he notes that this process can take place in three ways: legitimation, dissimulation and reification. It is the latter, the reified or 'natural' domination, which characterizes Newby's account of deference as being that form of social interaction which makes farming what it is: a way of life and not just a job. It is this way of life that we shall now describe through our case-study of Tom Davenport and his relationships with his brother Dick and his son Harry.[2] And it is through this imaging of 'any man' that the chapter thus draws on a particular ethnographic setting to consider those aspects of inter-dependency which are not frequently addressed in the literature: first, the intimate as well as social and economic relations that exist between men, as well as between men and women, and second, the mutually con-stituting and often necessarily interdependent character of hierarchical relationships of power.

MEETING TOM

Tom Davenport is in his early 60s and has lived in the village all his life. He sees himself as a farmer and a successful businessman. Now semi-retired, and experiencing a variety of health problems, he is a man with a large network of social contacts and is a well-known person in the community. Indeed, Tom was the gate-keeper for our project. Early on in the fieldwork he made this offer: 'you tell me who you want to meet, what you want to know' and, though this was not articulated, he implied that he alone would be able to fix it. On a first tour around Tom's farm and his factory units, Tom made his capacity to fulfil this role clear, taking charge of Pia and introducing her: 'This is Pia, she is from the University and she comes from Denmark. She is interested in farming families and has come to work in Needlemore for a year.' Indeed, on that first day, Tom introduced Pia to his wife, some villagers, his factory manager, his brother, his sister-in-law, his son and his daughter-in-law. And, on that same day, he promised to put Pia into contact both with his daughter and her husband's farming family, as well as with older women in the village. He also detailed who were the incomers to the village, the 'townspeople', whom, he suggested, Pia would not need to talk with. He also pointed out who were the 'real' farming families of the village, whom she ought to get to know. And, indeed, Tom fulfilled his promises.

Driving round the area in Tom's car, on that same first day, Tom was able to give visual and material form to his position of power in the community where he owns in excess of 2000 acres of farm land and some pig units:

> That barn over there that belongs to one of my friends. We bought the land together and shared the large fields between us.

This wood, I planted up ... when I came here it was all briars, and we cleared it.

Four hundred and twenty nine acres here and I bought it seven years since. We've just bought as we've been able to buy.

This is the road I put in down here when I bought this farm and built that factory unit.

Beginning with just a smallholding and a produce delivery round, Tom has built up his various businesses over a span of 20 years. Now, carved into the very landscape, is Tom's personal history as a highly prosperous farmer and a businessman.

In his early 20s Tom married Lucy, a farmer's daughter, and they had four children who, themselves now married, have produced five grandchildren. Thus the family name and business are secure; through his eldest son Harry and his eldest son's own newly born son, Tom knows that the 'Davenport' name will remain tied to the land in which he has invested so much. In addition, his brother Dick has returned from a life abroad to settle once more in the village and now manages one of his businesses. All his children and grandchildren live locally, which provides Tom with daily visible evidence of both his past and their future. As an independent member of the local agricultural community, Tom is seen as a central figure. And yet, as we shall show, Tom's 'independence' rests on a whole series of interconnecting dependencies and on his own ability to mobilize particular relations of power through strategic interventions and careful use of the resources available to him.

That Tom's position of power, sketched in briefly here, is clearly not the stuff of the established literature of 'dependency' may raise questions as to whether Tom's experiences actually merit the title of dependencies at all – as we shall see, he himself is only just beginning to be able to be reflexive about his own position in relation to both his family and the wider community. However, focusing on Tom's 'dependencies', which have enabled his 'independence', does, we suggest, allow us to move beyond the narrower focus of the dependency literature. To explore these issues we return to the three aspects of 'dependency' which we signalled for closer attention at the start: its relational, temporal and spatial aspects.

DEPENDENCY AS RELATIONAL: TOM'S FAMILY AND FRIENDS

As a family farmer, Tom's career has been grounded in relationships with the members of the older and younger generations of his family, with his wife and her family and with members of the local farming community. Indeed, it is this very interconnectedness which makes farming a way of life and not just a job. Thus, the business of managing his farms is inseparable from his relationship with his son and daughter-in-law, and indeed with his family identity as a 'Davenport'. Moreover, without his wife's social, familial and domestic support, without his son's financial dependency on him, without the loyalty and admiration of every member of his immediate family and without his farm and factory worker's dependency on him for employment, Tom's representation of himself as 'independent' could not be sustained: it is precisely these dependent relationships – economic, social and material – which provide the context for his own experience of 'independence'. What we need to understand, therefore, is how Tom has been able to limit, control or transform these experiences of 'dependency' so that he is still seen as occupying a dominant, 'independent' position within his family and the local community.

One way has been through a particular kind of engagement with familial and gendered power relations in the family. Over the years Tom's commitment to long working hours, and his refusal to temper his moods, have estranged him from his children. Now he is somewhat distant from them. One daughter explains that she does not feel close to her Dad; her brother says that their dad, Tom, has 'lost touch with us really'. Yet as family members the children acknowledge their own dependency on Tom and the benefits which they have reaped from Tom's commitment to work. And in doing so, they confirm his strengths:

> when we were little, you must understand, it was only a really small farm and it is Dad who has worked in those early years to build it up to what it is now.

At the same time they represent Tom as someone to admire for his drive and independence, and describe how these qualities are inextricably bound up with a moodiness. These qualities are naturalized and hailed as a characteristic of the 'Davenport' family, a set of traits which, like land, have been inherited. They are read as a sign of Tom's power to control and order the lives of his family's members and, at the same time, routinized and accepted. In his children's accounts Tom's parents were seen as the 'scary' grandparents of his children's early lives and, as Tom ages, so his children trace their grandparents' qualities in their father. Thus, though dependent upon fellow family members, Tom maintains a legitimized, independent distance through reference to a family trait which can be traced across the generations.

Crucially, we need to differentiate between these personal and familial experiences of independence and other situations where Tom has made a more deliberate choice to estrange himself from local networks. Thus, for example, though in some ways mirroring the relationships which he sustains within his own family, he has always espoused a strategic business style in his dealings in the community. Rejecting the label of 'nice person', Tom admits that he spares no quarter for adversaries who are often also local people. As a result he has become wealthy, buying up land and building pig units in the locality. Of these relationships Tom now says:

> I have some things in common with them ... but I'd rather meet different people ... I'm not particularly just out to talk farming ... I don't know how to put it really, I don't go out of me way to go to farmers' things, I used to, I used to go to Young Farmers and everything but I've changed a lot. ... Some get a bit jealous of you ... and most of my farming friends are away from here now.

In being separated from former friends and neighbours, Tom can be said to have made himself independent of them. He neither needs anything from them, nor is he tied into any fixed relationship of reciprocal obligation with them.

But in conversations Tom revealed that he himself is wise to the problematic nature of absolute independence of this kind, wrought through the wielding of power. This led him variously to conceal his material wealth and success. For example, initially he refused to own a car and later took to hiding his expensive BMW in the garage, using it only on rare occasions. In such strategies he was supported by his wife Lucy, who still resists any notion that the Davenports are in any way superior to other families within the village. And, although Tom quite explicitly espouses independence in a self-representation as a hard-headed businessman and farmer, he also states his regret that, in some aspects of his life, he has severed his connections to the wider network of interdependencies. Indeed his present independence from family and friends is an aspect of his life which he finds troubling. Thus, in approaching retirement he is making himself more accessible both to his family and others in the community and, indeed, launched our project for us.

Lucy's own view of Tom is as a supportive, hard-working husband who has provided well for his family and given her a secure and now relatively affluent way of life. But this independence, which is his hallmark, can be seen to have been fostered partly through Lucy's commitment to farming and her family and her willingness to make herself therefore dependent upon him, both socially and financially. Lucy describes how their friends are 'more Tom's than mine' and that the people they go on holiday with are Tom's farming associates. In Lucy's opinion if 'the wives get on as well, well that is a bonus'. Lucy herself has lost touch with many of her own friends from her childhood. Recalling one such friend Lucy says:

> She was a farmer's daughter and she married a farmer, very quiet lad, very nice, doesn't drink at all. Tom couldn't cope with that .... and you just seem to drift.

The one close friend she now has is the wife of one of Tom's childhood friends.

The complex web of relations of dependency can be seen clearly here, and they reveal how Tom's own independence in business is built upon particular, more personal dependencies. Thus, though financially he is secure, kinship poses a threat to that feeling of security; though in terms of business he does not need the labour of his son, he is dependent upon his son's goodwill to secure the future success of the business. We can see therefore that not only is he dependent upon his daughter-in-law Rosie to co-operate in fostering good familial relations between father and son, but that this underlines his own dependency upon Lucy, his wife. It was, after all, Lucy who taught Rosie how it is to be a farmer's wife. Whenever Rosie complained about her husband's work absences from the home and his devolving of all the child care onto her Lucy would say: 'That's farming Rosie'.

> If she said 'Oh I never see Harry or something': I would say, 'Well that is farming Rosie.' I used to keep trying to drill it in, that it has to be done and the sooner it is done and finished the sooner you will see him.

Thus Tom's and Lucy's experiences of dependence and independence are shaped by different power relations exercised differentially through the system of kinship and wider community relations. Only through analysis can their interdependent character be made explicit.

DEPENDENCY AS TEMPORAL: TOM, DICK AND HARRY

Though now we encounter Tom with the free time to enjoy, with his wife, his later life and the prosperity he has accumulated across 20 years, this is the result of an ongoing, carefully negotiated involvement in his son Harry's management of their joint land. Thus, his current experience of independence, noted above, needs to be located not just relationally but also temporally in the analysis if his *inter-dependence* is to be fully understood.

From this perspective we find Tom initially at the periphery of the farming community, the son of a smallholder, from a long line of sea-faring people. Though he aspired to farming, there was only the smallholding to pass on to him or his younger brother who was a possible contender for this inheritance. However, time and space articulated in 'age' and 'home' provided a legitimately asymmetrical power-based relationship between Tom and his brother Dick. Tom was eight years older and living at home, and that made him the obvious beneficiary when the meagre legacy of the smallholding was passed on. Across the next 20 years Tom's project was to become a landowner. This made him into the independent farmer he longed to be and placed him eventually at the heart of the local agricultural community. He is not only the owner of farm land and factory farming units, but also the organizer of the local rugby club, and was responsible for providing some of the funding for the building of its new clubhouse.

His current claim to independence is, however, problematic when viewed from a temporal perspective, for Tom's shift from the periphery to the centre of the local agricultural community has been the product of dependent relationships of all kinds. Thus, as already noted, Tom has benefited from the accommodations made by his wife Lucy and his son Harry to the demands of his career. In addition he has been, and remains, dependent upon a wide variety of other people and material things: upon the labour of his brother Dick and his sister-in-law, upon the EEC regulations which determine how and where he can raise pigs, upon the fluctuations of the market, upon his own now ageing body and upon the vagaries of land and weather with which all farmers are confronted. Across his life-course, then, we can see a variety of dependencies coming into play – knowledge, material, physical and social – each of which have helped constitute his social relations. Indeed, it is only where he has been prepared to sacrifice such connections of dependency, in order to promote his business interests, that he can be seen as truly, though somewhat painfully, independent.

For example, Tom is clearly, though not straightforwardly, dependent upon knowledge sources for his success. Although he has managed to accumulate a fortune in land and capital, Tom has had no formal training in the business of farming. Rather, as a boy, he followed quite literally in his father's footsteps as they delivered the smallholding's products in towns and villages throughout the region. Dependent at first upon his father for business know-how, Tom then later drew on the expertise of fellow farmers, information in farming magazines and ideas gleaned from representatives of the seed companies to inform himself of the ways of agriculture.

Taking this knowledge forward into farm ownership, he then encountered a set of material dependencies to do with the land and the weather. As a shrewd businessman, Tom noted the profitability of pigs, while also recognizing that such factory farming is one way of side-stepping the annual cycle of seed-time and harvest which makes farmers so dependent upon the quality of the land they own and the proclivities of the weather. Pigs yield a good crop and, safely housed in their units, can mature independently of weather conditions. Through the profits from pigs Tom was able to finance the purchase of more land. Through his local social connections, fostered through participation in 'leisure' activities such as shooting and visiting the pub, he was able to raise more capital. Thus his skilful use of very modest resources has, over time, transformed his material dependency upon land and weather which he would otherwise share with farmers throughout the region. As Tom observes:

That's what life's about, you've got to take your chances.

Though Tom diminished his dependency upon the environment, as Lucy his wife notes, 'farming is hard physical labour'. Without the ability to draw upon his own bodily resources, Tom's farming businesses would have foundered, regardless of the technology he put to use in farm and factory and notwithstanding the men he was eventually able to employ. Now in his 60s, he suffers from arthritis, as did his father before him – an inheritance which renders him potentially socially dependent. But, though barred from incessant work, he nonetheless continues to draw on the temporal ambiguities of the farming way of life which, with its roots in childhood, extends a working life well beyond customary retirement age. Thus Tom continues his involvement with the running of his farms and factories by drawing on the mediating resources of his land agent and his wife. Tom's vulnerability to ill-health is hence transformed through dependency. Via the land agent, deals are struck which protect him financially whilst still offering a worthwhile package to his son who will do the day-to-day physical work. Metaphorical transformations are achieved by Lucy his wife, who describes him making a fatherly shift 'into the back seat', a strategy which she compares favourably with other farmers who hang on until they die, at which point their son 'is left high and dry because he is thrown in at the deep end'. Tom thus retains his position of independence and power through careful management of economic and symbolic capital.

That Tom is a successful, independent farmer is clear from his own account. But how do others see him? His daughter-in-law Rosie, for example, notes how, early in their marriage, her husband Harry had tried, as she says, 'to get Tom off his back'. To do so he had stopped working for his father and taken a farm independently, some miles away. Rosie's choice of words is illuminating. In Rosie's view Tom was dominating Harry, metaphorically sitting 'on his back', and this was a burden of which Harry wanted to be rid. However, it is also clear that Tom was very dependent upon his son; as noted, he was being metaphorically carried by his son Harry, who had a share in the business and did the everyday farm management. Although the loss of Harry's labour was not an insurmountable problem – Tom could easily have afforded to hire another skilled worker – without his son working the land Tom risked other, less tangible things. For example, he endangered the opportunity for the family name to be continued and he put in jeopardy those generational ties of land and money, which bind the past with the future, the very things for which he himself had worked so long and hard. Tom therefore went out of his way to encourage Harry to return. The farming way of life exerts a powerful familial dependency, and potential vulnerability over time, as Tom himself observes, quoting an old piece of farming lore:

the first generation makes it; the second generation keeps it; the third generation spends it.

DEPENDENCY AS SITUATED PRACTICE

Thus far we have taken an established topic area – dependency – and, via the medium of a vignette, explored the interdependencies which constitute the social life of a prominent and indeed powerful member of an agricultural community. Tom's biography reveals the truth in Gidden's (1991: 54) assertion that a person's identity is to be found in 'the capacity to keep a particular narrative going', but through its details provides a substantive account of how it was that, over time, Tom managed to sustain an 'ongoing story' about the self. However, what we have also shown is that the story of a 'successful business-man' – Tom's current self-identity – must be understood within the context of a whole variety of relationships through which Tom variously represents and experiences his place within the social world – as a dependent, independent and interdependent person. How these representations and experiences of interdependency come into being is, we have argued, a reflection of the ways in which he draws upon his available resources within the context of specific relationships. When we begin to examine these processes across time, we find that this diversity is contingent upon the social, economic and bodily changes which go to make up the life-course.

In this final section of our chapter we bring together the temporal and relational aspects of social life in order to show how the inter-dependency which can be traced at a theoretical level is particular to the local context of practice. First, Tom owns farms and pig units throughout the region he was born in. While the area contains larger farming families, he and his families of birth and marriage nonetheless constitute a core group within the locality. Tom's pig unit is central to the community, both geographically and also as a source of employment. Despite his efforts to erase the visible status symbols of his accumulated wealth, he and his wife feature prominently within local politics, sport and charity work. When we go on to examine the relationships which make up Davenport family life, we therefore need to locate them within this wider set of inter-dependent relationships.

Clearly, for Tom, Dick and Harry, membership of that local community is important not only in terms of active social and economic participation, but also as a marker of personal identity. Tom's business acumen has never taken him outside the region either to acquire land or financial interests; Dick's years abroad have produced only a desire to return to his village of origin to work in Tom's farm business; and

Harry has borne his father's persistent interference in his farm work. His threatened move to Wales has never materialized.

Each of these three men can therefore be seen as tied within a web of interdependencies which connect them not only with each other but also with their wider community. Also, within their own homes, an internal, comparable set of interdependencies is sustained. Tom, Dick and Harry depend heavily upon the services of their wives and the loyalty of other family members, who themselves are reciprocally dependent upon these men for company, transport and financial support. While it is to each other, and to other women within the community, that their wives often take their emotional and child-care needs, their primary commitment is to their farming husbands, to their own roles as farmers' wives, and to farming itself, as a way of life. As we have argued elsewhere, those services which women provide for their husbands and children are sometimes assumed, undervalued and also costly for women themselves, bringing social isolation and lost employment opportunities (Christensen *et al.*, 1997). In this way the dependency of men, such as Tom, Dick and Harry, upon their wives is downplayed, legitimated by a set of traditional assumptions about the nature of men's and women's roles within agriculture. However, in their turn, women discover strategies through which to manage the constraints of a role which only in later life brings them unambiguous benefits.

Thus, as we have shown throughout this chapter, a community constituted through multilayered interdependencies represents a social space within which individuals at various times and in different relationships experience both dependency and independence. A focus on interdependency therefore in no sense obviates the need for an understanding of the relations of power which are played out in every-day community and family-based encounters. By focusing on one of this community's most prominent and indeed powerful members, however, we have been able to indicate the ways in which his local and family connections serve to *constrain* as well as support his achievement of power and status. Tom is a member of an occupational community which lacks an externally imposed hierarchy. Unlike other businesses, rank is not available as a way of legitimately framing difference. Tom is a highly successful farmer. This renders his relationship with less successful farmers potentially problematic as we have shown, particularly since farming is a way of life which permeates every aspect of his family and leisure time. This lack of easy distinctions or clear-cut boundaries renders the exercise of power an ultimately delicate matter. As we saw earlier, if Tom acts in a truly independent fashion, setting his business interests above those of love or friendship, a mode which he has indeed espoused, he risks severing those key interdependencies which sustain a way of life marked by interconnection.

The dependency literature highlights the problems of 'dependency' within an urban cultural milieu where economic and affective life are separated. To care for those we love often brings not only social isolation but, crucially, additional economic dependency. To bring money into the equation, however, casts serious doubt upon our affection. Care is highlighted as an immanent emotion rather than a task, something for which a charge cannot be made. Such mystification cannot, however, be sustained within a community where family bonds and the ties of land are inseparable and where labour and love cannot be differentiated from one another. Without his family Tom would have remained a smallholder with a produce delivery round. Now, as his arthritis worsens, he could be entering a restricted and impoverished social life beyond the realm of the working world. But for Tom this has not happened, precisely because of his interconnectedness with others. Family connections, land, pigs, weather, the rugby club, the shooting fraternity have all sustained his claim to 'independence' and yet, at the same time, in their close and binding proximity they have worked to temper it.

CONCLUSION

We have presented a case-study of a particular member of a farming community in the north of England. However, the patterning of social relations which we have described is not, we argue, specific to this particular setting. Certainly the study of elites such as Tom and his family is somewhat unusual within sociology and anthropology; farming is a very particular cultural setting; and the study of dependency outside the field of medicine and health is an unusual quest. However, the very particularity of this case-study, we suggest, has shown some more general pointers for the ways in which dependency and power might be more effectively theorized. It delineates, for example, the importance of not allowing an empirical binarism to be used as an analytic device. It permits us also to see the ways in which moral/affective positions are sustained through the power relations pertaining to specific interventions in specific events so that dependence and independence can be seen as fluid rather than fixed renderings of particular experiences. Finally, it fosters awareness that interdependence might be the structural connections which sustain a social order, only ever subjectively experienced as a discontinuity between moments of 'dependence' and 'independence' across and within the life-course of an individual.

NOTES

1. This work can be seen as a contribution to the discussions about care and family responsibility initiated by Finch (1989) and Finch and Mason (1993) for the urban context.
2. Tom (as are the other characters) has been glossed with a pseudonym and some of his personal details have been changed to provide anonymity.

REFERENCES

Barton, L. (ed.) (1989) *Disability and Dependency* (London: Falmer Press).
Butler, R. and Bowlby, S. (1997) 'Bodies and Spaces: an Exploration of Disabled People's Experiences of Public Space', *Environment and Planning D: Society and Space*, 15, pp. 411–33.
Christensen, P., Hockey, J. and James, A. (1997) '"You Have Neither Neighbours Nor Privacy": Ambiguities in the Experience of Emotional Well Being of Women in Farming Families', *Sociological Review*, 45(4), pp. 621–45.
Dalley, G. (1988) *Ideologies of Caring* (London: Macmillan).
Finch, J. (1989) *Family Obligations and Social Change* (London: Polity).
Finch, J. and Mason, J. (1993) *Negotiating Family Responsibilities* (London: Routledge).
Fraser, N. and Gordon, L. (1994) 'A Genealogy of Dependency: Tracing a Keyword of the US Welfare State', *Signs*, 19, pp. 309–36.
French, S. (1993) 'Disability, Impairment or Something in Between', in J. Swain, V. Finkelstein, S. French and M. Oliver (eds), *Disabling Barriers – Enabling Environments* (Buckingham: Open University Press).
Giddens, A. (1991) *Modernity and Self Identity* (Cambridge: Polity).
Hicks, C. (1988) *Who Cares: Looking after People at Home* (London: Virago).
Hockey, J. and James, A. (1993) *Growing Up and Growing Old* (London: Sage).
Lukes, S. (1974) *Power: A Radical View* (London: Macmillan).
Morris, J. (1993) *Independent Lives: Community Care and Disabled People* (Basingstoke: Macmillan).

Morrow, V. (1996) 'Rethinking Childhood Dependency: Children's Contributions to the Domestic Economy', *Sociological Review*, 44, pp. 58–77.

Newby, H. (1975) 'The Deferential Dialectic', *Comparative Studies in Society and History*, 17, pp. 139–64.

Oliver, M. (1990) *The Politics of Disablement* (London: Macmillan).

Parker, G. (1993) *With this Body: Caring and Disability in Marriage* (Buckingham: Open University Press).

Swain, J., Finkelstein, V., French, S. and Oliver, M. (eds) (1993) *Disabling Barriers – Enabling Environments* (Buckingham: Open University Press).

Thompson, J. B. (1984) *Studies in the Theory of Ideology* (Cambridge: Polity).

Twigg, J. and Atkin, K. (1994) *Carers Perceived: Policy and Practice in Informal Care* (Buckingham: Open University Press).

Walker, A. (1982) 'Dependency and Old Age', *Social Policy and Administration*, 16(2), pp. 115–35.

9 What Difference Does 'Difference' Make? Lesbian Experience of Work and Family Life

Gillian A. Dunne

INTRODUCTION

This chapter[1] draws on an in-depth study of divisions of labour between lesbian parents to provide alternative insights into the reproduction of gender inequality in work and family life. By focusing on their experiences as women the study seeks to counter a tendency in academic feminism to treat lesbian experience as 'other' or 'different' (see discussion in Dunne, 1997a). A central premise informing the research is that the exploration of the circumstances of non-heterosexual people tell us as much about the workings of gender in the mainstream as it does about the experience of living 'difference'.

Research on work and family life has generally failed to explore and theorize the role of heterosexuality for maintaining the *status quo* between women and men. One reason for this failure is that while theoretically recognizing the overlapping nature of people's 'public' and 'private' lives, empirical studies of the sexual division of labour tend to focus on either the waged (e.g. the labour market) or the un-waged (e.g. the household) dimension. A second reason is that we lack comparative reference points for exploring the significance of heterosexuality itself in reproducing inequality: we know very little about the everyday lives of lesbian and gay people as workers and parents. Thus, the significance of heterosexuality itself for reproducing the differential life-chances of women and men is concealed.

The chapter is organized in the following way. The first section outlines a conceptual framework for theorizing the relevance of lesbian experience for wider feminist concerns about gender and gender relations. The following sections draw on the study. The domestic,

189

caring and employment strategies of lesbian parents are explored and compared with trends for heterosexual parents. In the final section I briefly illustrate some of the social contextual features of same-sex relationship which may act to enhance the construction of more egalitarian relationships.

ADD SEXUALITY AND STIR

In an important study of divisions of household labour, Berk (1985: 199) concludes that gendered patterns of task allocation are so ingrained and taken for granted that they 'hamper our ability to imagine other ways of organizing work'. This leads her to suggest, in a footnote, that science fiction may represent a medium for the exploration of alternative arrangements. This momentary flight from the here and now and into the realms of fantasy reflects an epistemological blind-spot in thinking about gender and the organization of work and family life. Theorizing is informed by empirical research which almost exclusively considers the employment and domestic circumstances of individuals and partnerships who are, or are presumed to be, heterosexual (see Van Every, 1995; Blumstein and Schwartz, 1985 for rare exceptions).

While influential theorists of patriarchy, such as Walby (1990) and Hartmann (1981) include sexuality in the reproduction of gender inequality, how this might actually happen has received scant empirical attention. Methodologies, sample frames and research questions are simply not geared to illuminating the significance of sexuality for shaping life-chances. The invisibility of lesbian and gay experience of work and family life has important implications for feminism more generally. For example, findings from a recent life-history study on lesbian experience of work (Dunne, 1997a) suggest that much of what has been conceptualized as simply gender constraints in the abstract are likely to relate to the heterosexual context which (directly and/or as an anticipated outcome) frames the gendered experience of most women.

The investigation of divisions of labour between partners of the same gender provides an alternative sense of what is achievable in the here and now. Like their heterosexual peers the negotiation of lesbian parenting takes place in an ideological and political context that treats child-care as a private responsibility (Dex and Shaw, 1986; Morris, 1990; Melhuish and Moss, 1991). Paid work opportunities are structured around a 'masculine model of employment' (Bradley, 1989;

Brannen and Moss, 1991) which fails to recognize that parents have responsibilities and time commitments beyond the formal workplace. Thus, my sample of co-habiting lesbian couples with dependent children (the majority of whom were under five) reflect arrangements with the greatest potential for imbalance. Because divisions of labour in lesbian partnerships are negotiated by actors who occupy the same position in the gender hierarchy, and share broadly similar gendered skills and experience, I am in effect holding gender constant. In this we can begin to distinguish between the different sorts of constraints that have been identified as hindering the momentum of change for heterosexual couples. Would the similarities lesbians share as women, and their positioning outside conventionality, enable the construction of more egalitarian approaches to parenting and the allocation of waged and un-waged work? If so, their experience may also provide models for feminists, regardless of how they define their sexuality, without recourse to science fiction.

While it is fair to say that the arrangements of non-heterosexual partners have not been subject to the same level of scrutiny which characterizes some of the best work on heterosexual couples (Oerton, 1998), the invisibility of non-heterosexual experience in the mainstream cannot be explained by an absence of research on the topic. A small but growing body of work highlights the egalitarian nature of lesbian and gay relationships (for example, Blumstein and Schwartz, 1985; Dunne, 1997a; Tasker and Golombok, 1998; Peplau and Cochran, 1990; Peace, 1993). Commonly, when asked what differentiates their relationships from heterosexual ones, lesbian and gay people cite the greater equality that is achievable (Dunne, 1997a; Heaphy *et al.*, this volume). Interestingly, there is some evidence of gender difference in perceptions of equality: for lesbians the source is usually described as rooted in the economic and domestic context of their relationships with women, while for gay men it tends to relate to emotional expression (Heaphy *et al.*, this volume). These differences in standpoint are understandable when we recognize the gender dimension to same-sex relationships. For example, domestic and material balance is much more likely to feature as a gain in women's accounts of the advantages of lesbian relationships. Thus, there are strong grounds for a thorough investigation of divisions of labour in non-heterosexual households. By demonstrating and evaluating claims about equality, rather than taking them for granted, we can move on to more interesting questions about the nature and sources of inequality more generally.

**A Conceptual Framework for the Inclusion of Non-heterosexual
Experience of Work and Family Life**

By drawing together four important feminist insights from across
perspectives we can begin to appreciate why the mapping of lesbian
and gay experience of work and family life can tell us as much about
the workings of gender in the mainstream as it does about the
circumstances of people living 'difference'.

*(i)   Sexuality is a Social Construction (see Extended Discussion in
        Dunne, 1997a)*
The diversity of sexual meanings that exist across time and space fly in
the face of common-sense understandings which link heterosexuality
with the expression of some essential sexual nature. The variety of
different primary relationships formed by people in other times
(Faderman, 1985) and in other places (Ortner and Whitehead, 1981;
Greenberg, 1988) problematizes the naturalness of heterosexuality
and universality of heterosexual partnerships. Instead, we have to
recognize that the ways that we give voice to and act upon our sexual
and emotional feelings are powerfully shaped by our social and economic environments. This insight allows us to critically examine the
processes that construct and police sexual identities just as we have
been doing so successfully for gender (Rubin, 1975; Lees, 1986;
Steinberg *et al.*, 1997; Dunne, 1997a). Key questions include how is
heterosexuality reproduced and whose interests are served by the
dominance of this outcome?

*(ii) The Critique of the Separate Nature of the Public and Private
        Spheres (e.g. Pateman, 1988)*
We cannot understand gender inequalities in the labour market
without reference to the organization of work in the home and vice-
versa. As noted earlier, concepts of work are structured on the basis of
a 'traditional masculine model of employment' (Bradley, 1989;
Brannen and Moss, 1991) thus to be 'successful', or simply committed,
workers must be (or appear to be) free from the time demands of
their domestic lives.

Despite significant changes in women's paid-working lives over the
past 20 years (Walby, 1997), it has been well documented that men have
not made a corresponding shift into women's traditional realm of
domestic and caring work. While there is some evidence that men and

women can form egalitarian domestic relationships (Van Every, 1995), a distinctly asymmetrical division of household labour remains the majority pattern.[2] In the absence of change at home, men and women do not compete in the labour market on the same basis. Thus, a vicious circle is perpetuated. Men can be more single-minded in pursuing employment opportunities while women balance their lives around the competing demands of income generation, the responsibilities of managing a home and, if they have children, for raising them. While it is important to focus on 'Public Patriarchy/Gender Regimes' (Walby, 1997) we must be careful not to lose sight of overlapping and mutually reinforcing nature of constraints on women's lives.

(iii) The Interconnection between Gender and Sexuality
Sexuality and gender connect in a variety of powerful overlapping ways. Together they interact to (a) police the content of masculinity and femininity and (b) shape gender relations by constructing the conditions by which people relate across gender boundaries – I will explore this in the final section (see also extended discussion in Dunne, 1997a, 1998b).

In the first place to have a sexual preference requires the social production of gender as a meaningful category. In contemporary Western societies sexuality is strongly bound to processes of gender differentiation. We do not select partners simply on the basis of their anatomical sex, we are drawn to them as bearers of the social and cultural meanings that are attached to being the possessors of male or female bodies. The likelihood that people will form heterosexual partnerships rests on the social construction of dichotomous and hierarchical gender categories and practices. As Butler (1990: 17) observes, 'The heterosexualization of desire requires and institutes the production of discrete and asymmetrical oppositions between "feminine" and "masculine"'. Likewise Rubin (1975) argues that union between women and men is assured through the suppression of similarities between them, so that a 'reciprocal state of dependency' will exist between the sexes (p. 178). As these reciprocal differences become eroticized, heterosexuality becomes the attraction of opposites (Connell, 1987: 246).

(iv) Heterosexuality is a Social Institution which is Central to the
   Reproduction of Gender Inequality (Rubin, 1975; Rich, 1984)
The role of heterosexuality in reproducing the *status quo* gives it an institutional quality (see longer discussion in Dunne, 1997a). This

insight is fairly under-developed in contemporary academic feminism. By either de-contextualizing sexuality from the material world[3] (Butler, 1990) or becoming embroiled in a critique (Kitzinger *et al.*, 1992) and defence (Segal, 1994) of heterosexual practice, recent thinking tends to remain at the level of the individual at the expense of the more unifying project of developing a sophisticated critique of hetero-sexuality as social institution (Jackson, 1995; Maynard and Purvis, 1995).[4] This alternative conception of heterosexuality is particularly useful for theorizing work and family life. If men's ability to retain their labour market advantage rests on their capacity to appropriate the un-waged labour of women (Pateman, 1988), than we need to recognize the centrality of institutional heterosexuality for providing the logic that translates women's labour into men's material advantage. Linking heterosexuality with the reproduction of inequality somewhat contradicts the accusations of privilege that are often levelled at heterosexual feminists.[5]

By combining these four insights together a new series of questions are opened which are best explored though the lives of lesbian women. With such a sample we can ask: what is the nature of the social processses that enable them to be different and, importantly, what difference does this difference make?

Lesbianism and Empowerment

I began to explore these questions in my book *Lesbian Lifestyles: Women's Work and the Politics of Sexuality*. This was based on a life-history study of continuity and change in the lives of 60 nonheterosexual British women aged 17 to 60. In interviews the women were encouraged to speak of their journey through hetero-sexuality, possibly marriage, and beyond. Woven into this were their remembrances of childhood, of schooling, of adolescent romance, information about their employment and domestic lives. Within all the complexity of respondents' biographies, commonalities could be identified – one of the most striking being the relationship between lesbianism and empowerment. It could be seen, for example, that a lesbian lifestyle both necessitates and facilitates financial self-reliance. In contrast to their heterosexual experience, respondents described their lesbian relationships as based on notions of co-independence. Thus, the capacity to make primary relationships with women, rather than men, necessitates long-term financial self-reliance and the earning of a living wage. This realization informed the decisions of the many respondents who had entered male-dominated craft occupations, or had returned to education or changed their occupations on 'coming out'.

Additionally, women's relationships with women were described as facilitating their engagement with paid employment, through the support and encouragement they experienced from their partners and the more egalitarian domestic arrangements negotiated. I concluded that lesbians may represent a different kind of worker for sociological analysis in so far as their relationship to employment is less distorted by those gender processes which constrain heterosexual women's and inflate heterosexual men's access to opportunities. This was dramatically illustrated by their occupational diversity and the way in which their pay fell roughly half-way between the averages found for women and men more generally.

The implications of these findings for feminist thinking about work, and the relationship between gender and sexuality, are profound. They would suggest, for example, that women who have moved beyond the confines of heterosexuality engage with the 'public' and 'private' under far more favourable conditions than heterosexual women (Dunne, 1997a). Further, the relationship between the lesbian lifestyle and material empowerment seriously undermines notions of sexuality as an individual choice or 'private' issue. I would argue that, as more women become educationally and financially empowered, lesbianism will become an increasingly common choice.

My current research, to which I will now turn, takes up this issue of empowerment in lesbian women's domestic and employment lives by exploring whether such factors hold for lesbian couples with dependent children.[6]

THE LESBIAN HOUSEHOLD PROJECT

The Lesbian Household Project draws on the experience of 37 couples with dependent children. The majority live in urban areas in three northern and three southern cities. The sample is drawn from a wide range of different sources using a snowball technique. The only selection criterion was that partners be living together with at least one dependent child. All who contacted me agreed to participate in the project and were interviewed.

As donor insemination is a relatively recent option for lesbians, couples with children under five years old were well represented, forming 59 per cent of the sample. It is also worth mentioning that, in 14 of these households, co-parents were themselves birth mothers of older children, and in a further four they were planning to become birth mothers. In several instances where one partner experienced difficulties in conceiving, her partner went through the pregnancy instead.[7] To facilitate distinguishing between partners I shall use the term birth mother to identify the mother of the youngest child, and co-parent to describe her partner.

A wide range of qualitative and quantitative methods were employed. A series of two to three hour semi-structured interviews (joint, followed by individual several months later with both partners) were conducted. To explore their perceptions of 'who did what' in the home[8] the first interview centred upon the creation of a 'Household Portrait'.[9] These very detailed perception data were complemented with information from time-task allocation diaries. As household divisions of paid labour have a major bearing on the structuring of work in the home, I was very interested in the organization of employment responsibilities in my partnerships, as well as their strategies towards the allocation of household labour.

To place my findings in context I shall compare them with trends found for couples with children more generally. The relatively small size of my sample means that we must be cautious about the conclusions drawn, particularly as comparisons are difficult because of the many ways that the parents in the study differ from the norm (see Dunne, 1998a for more details). For example, almost all employed respondents work for public sector employers or are self-employed. They are usually professionals, managers, technicians or administrators in occupations such as social work, education, local government, health, and counselling. Consequently, my sample comprises women who have greater control over the circumstances of their lives than women and men more generally. To ensure that the differences identified below do not simply flow from this advantage, I shall, where possible, compare their arrangements with parents in similar occupational groups or levels of education. Nonetheless, respondents face many dilemmas familiar to other parents, for example reconciling the contradictions between the time demands of earning a living and the desire to be available to participate in the work and pleasures of home-life. As we shall see, the similarities they share as women, together with the differences that place them outside conventionality, provide the opportunity to re-think the possibilities of parenting and become, as one couple suggested, 'pioneers behind our own front doors'.

BALANCING EMPLOYMENT AND PARENTING
RESPONSIBILITIES

The Impact of Children on the Working Lives of Mothers and Fathers

There appear to be major contradictions facing contemporary parents. Conceptualizations of fatherhood today are more child-centred than in previous generations (Lewis and O'Brien, 1987), yet British research indicates that the demands of employment continue to make them absent from the home. While couples may hold a commitment to shared parenting and domestic equality, employment constraints limit the extent to which this becomes a reality. Recent research on heterosexual couples indicates that it is still taken for granted that it will be mothers rather than fathers who reduce their employment hours to care for their children.

An analysis of the National Childhood Development Study, by Ferri and Smith (1996), found that in 1991 the great majority (94 per cent) of young married fathers (aged 33) were employed and almost all were in full-time employment. They worked long hours – 66 per cent over 40 hours a week and 27 per cent over 50 hours a week. Likewise, Cappuccini's (1996) longitudinal study of new parents found that all but two of the 104 fathers in her study were employed full-time. Cappuccini's sample was similar to mine insofar as the majority were well educated and two-thirds of both men and women were in professional and managerial/technical occupations (compared with 74 per cent in mine). My analysis of parents with higher qualifications[10] and children under five years old, in the British Household Panel Survey (1993), revealed that 91 per cent of fathers were employed full-time, and only 3 per cent were employed for less than 30 hours a week.[11] The mean paid-working hours for employed fathers with higher qualifications was 47 hours. Thus the possession of higher qualifications does not appear to lead to fathers negotiating a shorter working week. Mothers with higher qualifications are more likely to be employed full-time than other mothers, but the majority re-order their employment lives to care for their children – 33 per cent were at home full-time and 35 per cent were employed less than 30 hours a week. While 83 per cent of the mothers in Cappuccini's study (1996: 95) had returned to paid employment by the end of their maternity leave, 53 per cent went to part-time jobs. Mothers in the National Childhood Development Study tended to be either at home full-time or in part-time employment, with 23 per cent in full-time employment (Joshi *et al.*, 1995). This would

suggest that, despite recent gains in women's employment circumstances (Walby, 1997), the arrival of children continues to introduce
or reinforce polarization between partners in relation to earnings,
employment hours and status, with full-time employment being the
norm for employed fathers.

Level of Employment Participation – Respondents
Given the continuing relevance of gender for predicting who will reduce
their hours of employment to care for children, I was interested in how
employment responsibilities would be allocated between women. To
illustrate the atypicality of their employment strategies, I shall focus on
a sub-sample of the 22 couples with pre-school-aged children, because
this stage in family formation usually represents a time of increased
polarization in the earnings and employment hours of mothers and
fathers (Table 9.1).

The arrival of children clearly had an impact on the employment
patterns of birth mother, 23 per cent were in full-time employment
with 50 per cent favouring part-time employment. However, in contrast to the norm for heterosexual parents, the impact of children was
not confined to birth mothers. Although my co-parents were more
likely to be employed full-time than their partners, 41 per cent were
either employed part-time or not in paid employment. The mean
employment hours for employed co-parents was 34 hours and for birth
mothers it was 28 hours.

As flexibility often characterizes the employment strategies of both
parents in my sub- sample (for example, eight (36 per cent) co-parents
worked shorter hours than their partners) we find a much broader
range of household employment combinations than is usual. Table 9.2
provides a comparative snapshot of my sub-sample with mothers and

Table 9.1   Employment hours: birth mothers and co-parents with children
under five years old ($n = 22$)

Employment hours	Birth mothers (%)	Co-parents (%)
30 plus hours	23	59
10–29 hours	50	27
1–9 hours	0	5
0 hours	27	9

Table 9.2   Household employment combinations: comparing
sub-sample with couples in which both partners have higher
qualifications and children under five

Household employment combination	Lesbian parents (n = 22) (%)	BHPS households, both parents with higher qualifications (n = 70) (%)
Full-time/full-time	14	33
Part-time/part-time	18	0
Full-time/part-time	32	24
Part-time/home	14	4
Full-time/home	23	36
Neither in paid employment	0	3

Source: Lesbian Household Study and the British Household Panel Survey
(1993).

fathers of children under five where both hold higher qualifications
(British Household Panel Survey, 1993). In my sub-sample there are
only three full-time dual-earner households with pre-school children
(14 per cent). As this includes a couple in which the co-parent had
given up a full-time professional job to care for her daughter, but
combined this with a full-time, paid child-minding job, a very high
number – 20 (91 per cent) had at least one partner at home on a part-
or full-time basis.

Attitudes to Home-life Responsibilities

An important reason for these unusual household employment strate
gies is the attitude to home-life of both birth mothers and co-parents.
It was generally felt that child-care is a valuable and enjoyable task
which offers a valid alternative to full-time employment.[12] The
reduction in employment hours was largely through choice, and was
sometimes combined with a return to education (in three cases). A
powerful motivation informing women's employment strategies seems
to be the desire to maximize contact time with their children.

I asked respondents whether the arrival of children had influenced
their views on the centrality of employment. The following answer
illustrates a common attitude. Helen and Maggie[13] made a joint
decision to have children and divide the care of their three-year-old

son between them. Both are employed half-time in professional occupations and Paul is their only child. Maggie explains her changing feeling about the significance of employment:

> It has changed, yes. Yes, and work is not as important to me now. I think the original reason for working part-time was to share Paul. But actually I'm not sure now even if I'd want to go back to full-time – probably not back to being a totally work person, which would be stressful and horrible. … The motivation behind it was to do with Paul, and to make sure that he was equally cared for – because neither Helen nor I wanted to be either the one that was at work or the one that was at home all the time.

What is interesting is that Maggie is not Paul's birth mother. Importantly, this shift in attitude towards paid work was common for birth mothers and co-parents alike. Respondents regularly spoke of seeking balance in their lives. Most employed respondents enjoyed their jobs and, regardless of employment situation, almost all believed that having a working life outside the home was very important – it was a source of stimulation and provided the ability to contribute financially. However, time at home with children and partners was equally, if not more, important. Thus, on the arrival of children, both partners usually lowered their commitment to their careers. Those in full-time employment often spoke of planning or hoping to reduce their hours.

Although Maggie's initial reason for reducing her employment hours was related to child-care, she was in no hurry to return to full-time employment, feeling that as her child grew up she would find other activities to occupy her time. Those parents in the sample with older children, where we find a similarly broad range of household employment strategies, confirmed this view.[14]

Fathers may also feel a strong desire to spend time with their children. However, the existence of powerful ideas that link men's parental responsibilities with breadwinning, together with an employment structure which ignores their parenting needs (Brannen and Moss, 1991) tends to lead men to engage more fully with their paid work. Consequently, processes which construct and maintain gender difference play a crucial role in shaping how men and women come to understand and express their parenting responsibilities.

In contrast, women who bring up children together do not have access to gender-differentiated ideas about how each should enact her parenting. Thus, it is as women that each partner experiences and expresses her parenting and, in common with single mothers more generally, the absence of fathers leads to a redefinition of motherhood to encompass the breadth of parenting styles and practices (bread-winning and caring/mothering) that are more usually contained within the dichotomous categories mother and father.

The interchangeability of roles brings the advantage of facilitating the development of empathic awareness that work in the home and in the labour market has an equivalency in terms of pleasure, drudgery, stress, and relaxation. Routinely respondents challenged the logic behind the following statement: 'surely if one partner has a stressful job and her partner is home-based it is only fair that she should come home to rest?', with comments such as: 'the statement assumes that caring for a small child isn't stressful' or 'getting on with chores at home can be a good way of relaxing'. Lack of specialization, and the capacity for one partner to place herself in the position of the other, is key for understanding their views. Thus, the performance of paid work, the domestic routine and child-care afforded no mystery. This view is well summarized by Winnie. She and her partner May each have half-time employment and share the care of their two pre-school-aged children between them:

> I think that because you have been through the situation yourself you have a real understanding. If you are at home all day with a baby you cannot think of anything that is more demanding than that or more tiring. But if you have been out at work all day you cannot think of anything more tiring than that. But because we have done both, we can really understand. There wouldn't be an argument about who has had the hardest day because we both had a very clear understanding of the experience of being at home all day and the experience of being at work all day. They are both very demanding in different ways.

Respondents' location in predominantly female- rather than male-dominated occupations may also enable the operationalization of greater balance between their domestic and employment lives – although some had struggled to reduce their working hours. For example, one co-parent in teaching negotiated a job share. However, because it took a year for her employers to advertise the other half of her position, she had to squeeze full-time demands into a half-time post. Importantly, for many birth mothers and co-parents, the timing of the arrival of children had been planned to correspond with a point in their working lives at which they could reduce their hours, or take a career break to be at home for children without undue penalty.

Finances

The more extreme divisions of labour found during early family formation in heterosexual partnerships means that this period represents a time when mothers usually experience greatest financial dependence on their partners. If mothers are in paid employment, substantial gender differences in income exist. For example, Brannen and Moss (1991) found that only 5 per cent of mothers in their dual-earner households with very young children earned as much or more than their partners. Joshi *et al.* (1995) found that, in 1991, 24 per cent of employed women aged 33 with dependent children in the National Childhood Development Study had incomes that were similar to or more than their male partners. Regardless of mothers' employment situation most mothers view their male partners as primary or sole providers (Brannen and Moss, 1991; Cappuccini, 1996). This has a major impact on the division of domestic and caring work, and women's judgements about the fairness of their partners' contributions (Doucet, 1991: 24)

My data show a very different situation for lesbian parents with pre-school children. Because earnings differentials between women are usually less than between women and men, and because there are no set rules about who should be the main carer in lesbian relationships, the usual linkage between being a mother and being the lower earner in a partnership is disrupted. Despite birth mothers being more likely to be employed for shorter hours than their partners, 50 per cent earned the same or more than their partners. Even in partnerships in which one woman had a considerably lower income than the other, she was unlikely to think of her partner as the provider.

Men's superior earning capacity is a major problem facing heterosexual couples who wish to share their home-life responsibilities. Often a male wage is essential for family survival, or in the case of better-off households, for the maintenance of a standard of living that they have planned their lifestyles around. For Andrea Doucet's (1995a) largely middle-class sample of married couples committed to sharing, the prioritization of fathers' careers was often viewed by the more ardently egalitarian partners as the result of 'rational' financial considerations rather than conforming to gender norms. Clearly, the entrenchment of gender inequalities in earnings means this outcome is the result of making choices using loaded dice.

Given the existence of financial constraints on decision-making around who should reduce their hours to care for a child, I was interested in exploring this with respondents. I asked Esther, who was planning to return to half-time employment after maternity leave, whether her partner also working half-time made financial sense:

> [M]y job pays more. But I think we actually went not for that [the lowest paid reducing her hours] but for equality – so we both had the same amount of time to spend with Lizzy. It was both of us wanted to have – be able to have a role in bringing her up equally rather than just maximising income in that respect.

Like many of the couples interviewed, rather than earning differentials dictating their caring strategies, a sense of fair play and the desire to share parenting informed their approach to income generation. The common view was that, within limits, time for children was more important than the maximization of earning power. For affluent heterosexual couples seeking more balanced lives, equality may well require the planning for and acceptance of a reduced standard of living.

This awareness is evident in the thinking of some feminist men and women who are actively engaged in creating 'non-sexist' partnerships. For example, Jo Van Every's (1995) study of 'heterosexual women refusing to be wives' found that integral to their journey towards equality was a male critique of the 'traditional masculine model of employment' and the re-evaluation of the role of paid work in the men's lives; she found some male interviewees were working part-time while others were reversing roles with their partners. A North American study of heterosexual feminist partnerships (Blaisure and Allen, 1995) found that the small minority who felt that they had successfully managed to negotiate a satisfactory balance of power were also the ones in which male partners had de-emphasized their involvement in paid work. Fathers may experience a stronger sense of the contradictions between their breadwinner identity and their ability to be involved in active parenting when they have had a fuller role in the early care of their children. Research from Sweden (Haas, 1990), suggests that paid employment takes on a much less central position in the lives of the minority of men who had taken paternal leave compared to fathers who had not. Consequently, the re-evaluation of the significance of employment for most of my co-parents, and mothers more generally, is not a uniquely female characteristic. Through lived experience and/or political reflection, fathers can also develop the will to transform the conditions that shape the degree to which they can share the work and pleasures of the home.

Other households in the study had experienced or expected to experience change in relation to who was the primary carer of their child/ren. For example, Angie, the birth mother of two-year-old Steve, took maternity leave to care for him in his first year. Then Sue, her partner, felt it was her turn to have time at home – despite being the higher earner of the two. Sue gave up a £23,000-a-year job and now works from home as a self-employed childminder. Both agreed that they would be financially better off if they paid for full-time child care, or if Angie – Steve's birth mother – remained at home.

At first sight their arrangements may not make economic sense. However, Angie, whose career was less established, was aware that a lengthy break from the labour market could lead to marginalization in her job. Again the disruption of the givenness of conventional 'gendered' wisdom (which commonly characterized respondents' thinking about work) provides insights for heterosexual couples seeking an egalitarian relationship. Within reason, it may make better long-term sense for both parents, or the parent with the more power-ful labour market position, to shoulder the 'career' penalties that our society associates with caring for children. Failure to do this simply creates or accentuates pre-existing gender inequalities in employment prospects and earnings of women and men.

It is also important to remember that the choices available to parents emerge through a long process of decision-making which often takes for granted a division of labour along lines of gender polarization (see Dunne, 1992, 1997a). For example, Mansfield and Collard's (1988) study of newly-wed couples shows that gender differentiated approaches to employment, earnings and domestic life exist well before parenthood or even marriage. Because lesbian women cannot easily hold these assumptions, they are less likely than heterosexual couples to have fore-closed options through earlier employment decisions. Differences in earnings and employment status between partners in the study were not straightforwardly related to either the choice of who should become, or the position of being, a birth mother. Consequently, lesbian partners usually have greater scope than heterosexual couples for operational-izing their egalitarian ideals in relation to sharing parenting and employment responsibilities.

I now want to integrate child-care and domestic work into the discussion of work, by drawing on my time-use analysis.

TIME-USE DATA

The repetition of time-use studies drawing on large, fairly representative samples allows researchers to chart change over time, and diversity within the population. These indicate that women's employment circumstances have very little influence on men's domestic contributions, which remain consistently low (Berk, 1985; Pleck, 1985; Gershuny and Jones, 1987; Shelton, 1992). Interestingly, if the domestic inputs of single people are compared with those of people in partnerships, cohabiting or married men spend less time on household work than single men, and cohabiting/married women far more than single women (Shelton, 1992). Shelton suggests that there may be a cultural expectation that fathers participate in life at home but, quoting La Rossa (1988), concludes that they are more usually 'technically present, but functionally absent' (Shelton, 1992: 65).

To provide an alternative perspective on their arrangements respondents were asked to complete time-task allocation diaries for one week,[15] and 62 have been returned and analysed. This illuminates how each partner distributes her time across domestic, caring and paid work, and allows us to make comparisons within my own sample, and between this and other time-use studies.[16] To give some sense of the extent to which my sample deviates from patterns found for mothers and fathers more generally I have also analysed trends for married couples with children under 12 from the Social Change and Economic Life Initiative (SCELI). We must bear in mind, however, that comparison is far from perfect; for example, the SCELI data were collected in 1987, and men in professional and managerial occupations comprise 40 per cent of this sub-sample.

The Distribution of Parents' Time Across Paid and Un-paid Work

The diary analysis confirmed the interesting deviations from the norm that I have already noted for my sample. Being the biological mother of the youngest child was a poor predictor of which partner had shorter employment hours. As the availability of time to devote to work in the home can be structured by occupational demands, it makes more sense to discuss my data on the basis of employment

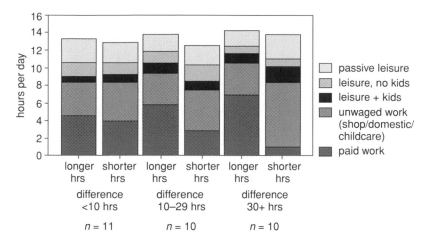

Figure 9.1   Time-use of respondents by differences in hours of employment: households with children under 17

hours rather than birth mother/co-parent distinctions. As the parents in the study have developed more creative approaches to the alloca-tion of employment responsibilities (see Table 9.2 and note 12) I shall present my time-use analysis simply on the basis of differences in employment hours between partners, rather than the full-time/at home, full-time/part-time, full-time/full-time distinctions that are usually used to discuss divisions of labour between women and men. Instead I have divided my parents into three groupings: partnerships with similar paid-working hours (less than 10 hours difference a week); those with greater differences (between 10 and 29 hours); and those with extreme differences (30 hours plus).

As anticipated, specialization is not a strong feature of the time-use patterns for my sample shown in Figure 9.1. First, households are evenly distributed across the three employment groups. There are 11 (35 per cent) households with similar paid-working hours: the average paid-working hours total for both partners is fairly low because this group includes dual-earner part-time as well as full-time partnerships. There are 10 (32 per cent) households in which employment differences are greater (these include my part-time/at home partner-ships as well as my full-time/part-time) and 10 (32 per cent) households in which differences are extreme. Second, the next layer shows that time spent on un-waged work (domestic, shopping and child-care) is fairly evenly balanced between partners except when

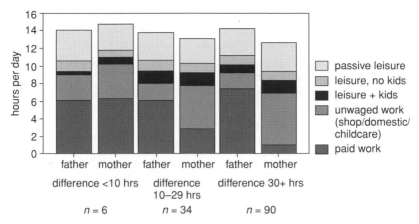

Figure 9.2   Time-use of fathers and mothers by differences in hours of employment: households with children under 12

employment differences are extreme. On average the partner with the longer paid-working hours spends approximately 30 minutes less time on un-waged work than her partner in households with similar employment hours, and 55 minutes when employment hours are greater. In contrast to the patterns revealed in Figure 9.2, each partners' time in the two dual-earner groups is fairly evenly distributed between work that is paid and work that is not.

Examination of time-use patterns for mothers and fathers in Figure 9.2 reveals the extent to which specialization along lines of gender occurs. If we look at the number of cases in each category we can see that very few ($n = 6$) mothers and fathers actually have similar employment hours – reflecting the fact that, even when men and women are both employed full-time (defined as over 30 hours a week), men generally have much longer paid working weeks. The majority, 70 per cent ($n = 90$) have extreme paid work imbalances. If we compare time devoted to paid work with un-waged work we can see that un-waged work usually monopolizes the average working day of mothers, and paid work that of fathers.[17] Regardless of mothers' employment hours, men's average contribution to work in the home is consistently low.

One could argue that these inequalities are explained by men's longer paid-working hours. However, even when partners have similar employment hours, fathers' average contribution of 2.7 hours is 1.25 hours less than mothers' 3.9 hours. Consequently, when time devoted to un-waged work is included, mothers with similar employment hours to fathers have the longest working day in the sample. In a separate analysis (Dunne, 1997b) I found that when respondents' employment hours were similar to the male average they also had considerably longer working days (waged plus un-waged) than men.

My analysis suggests that, unlike men, women's ability to have demanding jobs (those with hours that conform to a masculine model of employment) does not rest on their partners doing the bulk of work in the home. Instead, gendered arrangements in the home help explain why women have been so unsuccessful in gaining well-paid, high-status employment, and why men retain their employment advantage. This also provides insights into respondents' employment strategies, and the desire of many to reduce rather than increase their employment hours – a commitment to sharing home-life responsibilities conflicts with the demands of a traditional masculine model of employment.

THE DISTRIBUTION OF PARENTS' TIME ACROSS
UN-WAGED WORK

The implications of gender-segregated responsibilities are most strik-ing when we focus on the kind of work which occupies women's and men's time in the home (Figure 9.3). Mothers' time is primarily

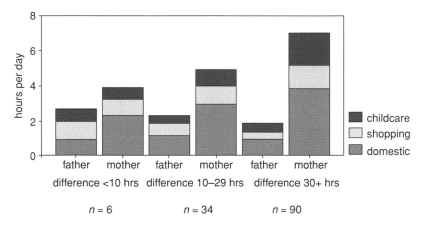

Figure 9.3   Time spent by fathers and mothers on un-waged work, by differences in hours of employment: households with children under 12

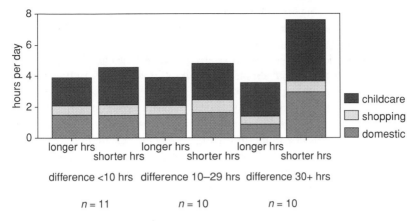

Figure 9.4   Time spent on un-waged work by respondents, by differences in hours of employment: households with children under 17

devoted to domestic work. An important reason for this preoccupation is that men's contribution to the domestic base is so small (in the two dual-earner groups the average time devoted by men to domestic work represents just 28 per cent of the total average household time). The structuring of responsibilities along lines of gender presents women with the burden of domestic work and creates hierarchies that can squeeze out time for the more pleasurable aspects of caring for children, particularly when they are young.[18]

Figure 9.4 shows that for both lesbian parents child-care occupies a far greater amount and proportion of time than seems possible for mothers more generally (compare Figure 9.3);[19] one important reason being their equitable division of domestic labour. (It is worth adding here is that, when they were constructing their 'Household Portraits' in the joint interview, their perceptions of who did what in relation to a wide range of household and child-care tasks and responsibilities bore no relationship to the gender-segregated patterns that shape heterosexual arrangements (see Dunne, 1998a).) In the two dual-earner groups this is close to a 50/50 division, with shorter employment hours not necessarily shifting the balance of domestic inputs. This reflects the idea, often expressed, that the choice to spend more time at home was to engage in child-care (a job in itself), not to take on a greater share of domestic work. The significance of the more equitable and efficient domestic contributions of women parenting together cannot be overstated. Even when both partners are employed full-time, regardless of the age of their children, their combined time spent primarily occupied with child-care is higher than the average in full-time/at home heterosexual contexts (see Dunne, 1997b). This suggests that it is not mothers' employment commitments *per se* that shape the availability of time for children, but gender-segregated responsibilities.

Time allocation data for lesbian parents allow us to see what divisions of labour look like when they are not structured along lines of gender polarization, and the implications are far-reaching. Importantly, my findings undermine justification for the polarization of labour along lines of gender, by showing that they are not only unfair, but inefficient. The practice is unfair to women because they continue to bring up children largely on their own. Further, a strategy which prioritizes men's working lives at the expense of women's confirms and accentuates gender inequalities in earning potential and access to employment opportunities, both on a societal as well as household level. Ironically, a practice that keeps one parent out of the house and burdens the other with domestic work makes little sense if the logic behind gender divisions of labour has anything to do with having relaxed and enjoyable time with children. Ruth, birth mother of a grown-up son and co-parent of a primary-school-aged boy called Greg, describes what must be a common experience for heterosexual mothers:

> When Jack was little I was still with his father, I resented a lot of the things that I now enjoy with Greg. Because his father was like – these are the jobs that you do – it took away a lot of the choice and therefore a lot of the pleasure.

This analysis also illustrates the interrelationship between the organization of waged and un-waged labour, and reveals the artificial and exploitative nature of the masculine model of employment. If, for example, men had to perform their share of subsistence work they would probably find the time demands of employers as difficult to comply with as did the respondents in this study and women more generally. In the absence of widespread transformation in the home, women with children will continue to be disadvantaged in the labour market in relation to men. Likewise, failure to critique the association between work commitment and freedom from the time-demands of home-life means that both male and female employment 'success' may have to increasingly rely on exploiting the labour of others, usually working-class women (see for example Gregson and Lowe, 1995). The very different 'solutions' to the problem of balancing the work, pleasures and responsibilities of the home and formal workplace negotiated by respondents suggest that a powerful engine of change lies in people's approach to their intimate relationships. A widespread social commitment to gender equality in the home would have a major impact upon the organization of employment, and access to opportunities. It would also challenge capitalism in its present form.

I will now conclude by exploring why lesbian partnerships may offer greater possibilities for the negotiation of more balanced, egalitarian domestic arrangements.

DOING GENDER BEYOND HETEROSEXUALITY: 'THEY'RE JUST JOBS FOR US'

What is it about lesbian relationships that appear to turn upside-down many of the assumptions which shape heterosexual practice and maintain the *status quo*? The simple answer is that for women together these assumptions do not make sense and therefore cannot be easily operationalized. Their similarities as women, together with the differences that place them outside conventionality, provide the opportunity for (and almost require) the conscious re-thinking of household arrangements. This is reflected in Dolly's comments. She has been living with her partner, Jo, for the past 19 years:

> I suppose because our relationship doesn't fit into a social norm, there are no pre- set indications about how our relationship should work. We have to work it out for ourselves. We've no role models in terms of how we divide our duties, so we've got to work it out afresh as to what suits us. ... We try very hard to be just to each other and ... not exploit the other person.

Central to understanding lesbian creativity is the interaction between gender (difference) and (hetero)sexuality which shapes practice. Gender, as formulated by West and Zimmerman (1987), and Connell (1987), is something that is continuously achieved in our ongoing everyday interaction with others – we do rather than have gender. We do gender in our mode of dress, through our occupation of and movement in space, in how we manipulate objects, etc. This kind of thinking has been useful for understanding why domestic arrangements negotiated between women and men are so resistant to change (Berk, 1985; Lewis and O'Brien, 1987; Hochschild, 1989; Morris, 1990; Fenstermaker *et al.*, 1991). As Berk (1985) suggests, the home is a 'gender factory'. The domestic division of labour is about linking the musts of work to be done with the shoulds of gender ideals (Berk, 1985; Seymour, 1992a). In this way 'situated human interaction contributes to the reproduction of social structure' (Fenstermaker *et al.*, 1991: 295). Rather than consciously participating in an exploitative process of labour appropriation, women and men are simply doing what women and men do – in the performance/non-performance of household tasks they are affirming their gender difference.

We can develop this line of thinking about gender in a way that is attentive to the significance of sexual identity for shaping practice (see Dunne, 1998b). For example, the idea that gender difference is affirmed through the performance of specific tasks is somewhat dependent on this work being allocated between women and men. The human interaction that is reproducing the social structure in this case is the doing of gender through heterosexuality. When Dolly and Jo approach 'dividing their duties' they are forced to break with the shoulds of gender ideals. This is apparent in this next example from Anet and Mary, who are both biological mothers of primary-school-aged boys and have full-time employment. They reflect upon their completed household portrait:

ANET: We've put a lot of things 50/50, but within that we divide them up, like at different times, and it's like a fluid thing. *Why do you think it's fluid, where does this come from?* We don't have expectations within this set-up on how we should interact. ... In a heterosexual situation ... there's this gender inequality which has come with just the way that you've been brought up.

MARY: It's just jobs to do for us, things that need doing and they don't have a value, a sort of female or male value within our set-up, they are just things that need doing and there's none of that gender thing going on.

By having to 'work it out afresh' as Dolly and Jo did, or by seeing household tasks as 'things that need doing' in the case of Mary and Anet, respondents illustrate an additional gender dimension to the 'doing of gender' – the gender of the person one is doing gender for/with and who does it to us makes a difference. With persistent regularity, respondents spoke of being greatly advantaged by the absence of 'gender scripts' to guide their relationships with women (see also Dunne, 1997a). They contrasted the ease with which domestic arrangements emerged in their partnerships with women with their past heterosexual experience. Mandy, who works half-time and is the co-parent of a two-year-old boy, describes this:

In comparison with heterosexual experience, is there any difference in how you approach and feel about doing housework?

MANDY: Oh yes! Because it is open for negotiation in a much more real sense, and you are not fighting against anything. No matter how New Mannish or not, there is a prevailing subconscious belief that women do housework. And I think a lot of women – I mean, I did – fall into that. I did more than my fair share, or I battled not to. But I didn't negotiate on an equal footing. So yes, I think there is a big difference because it's up for grabs. ... You are not battling against either overt or covert beliefs in who should do what.

What Mandy describes is her earlier experience of being 'up against something' very real (Connell, 1987: 92), in her attempts to resist the 'doing of gender difference'. Despite having been married to an exceptionally egalitarian man, her experience of being a woman in that relationship drew her into a process where her un-waged labour was appropriated.

The advantages of occupying the same position in the gender order were often stressed. In comparing their situation to past experience or that of the heterosexual mothers in their kin/friendship networks, there was a general sense of relief at not having to struggle with the same kind of externally derived inequalities which reinforced gender imbalances. Vicky and June discuss the way their relationship differs from previous heterosexual experience. Vicky is the birth mother of a primary-school-aged girl and has part-time employment which is home-based. June is the birth-mother of two pre-school-aged children, and has a full-time paid job as a technician:

VICKY: I think it is impossible [to get balance in a heterosexual relationship]. I've had to do so much rebellion against the

status I was expected to have in a heterosexual relationship. ... It's just too complicated. I mean it's difficult for
feminists anyway.

What gets in the way?

JUNE: Internalized sex roles and external pressure. ... I was
constantly adding it all up in my head (cooking, cleaning
the bathroom, etc.) and thinking this isn't fair. Sex roles
get in the way of everything. You can't forget it, you can't just
let it go along, which I think we pretty much do really, don't
we?

VICKY: Right. If there's a problem then it's between June and me,
it's not a problem between men and women like the world
over, or history conspiring against us.

Like Vicky, most understood that any relationship – heterosexual or
lesbian – involves differences and power imbalances. However,
the achievement of a 'good' relationship, by definition, requires
imbalances to be worked through to some happier medium. When
explored in interviews, respondents appeared to understand the term
'equality' to mean the balancing of differences so that they had less
overall consequence.

Importantly, respondents' similarities as women enabled greater
transparency in the evaluation of the fairness of contributions. This
contrasts with the situation for men and women in heterosexual relationships where gender difference not only structures contributions
but hinders change by shaping evaluative criteria (Gordon, 1990: 97;
Hochschild, 1989). A mis-match can arise when a man compares his
contributions favourably to other men and finds it hard to understand
why he fails to satisfy his partner. The ability to be in tune with the
rhythm of the household is something that women have learnt. This
capacity to notice and anticipate disadvantages women in heterosexual partnerships because on the whole men do not do it, but it is a
great source of advantage for women managing a home together – in
the individual interviews respondents usually spoke of both themselves and their partners being actively involved in keeping things
ticking over on the domestic front.

If, as I argued at the beginning of the chapter, heterosexual outcomes are assured though the suppression of similarities between
women and men, and gender is an ongoing accomplishment, then we

should not be too surprised to find that, when men and women form heterosexual partnerships, gender difference is being affirmed in the everyday routines of social life. The imperative link and overlap between doing gender difference and doing heterosexuality represents an important, but rarely recognized or discussed, factor in the reproduction of the *status quo*.

CONCLUSION

The exploration of the question, what difference does 'difference' make, reveals as much about the nature of constraints in heterosexual relationships as it does about the possibilities for egalitarianism in women's same-sex partnerships. The creativity that lesbian women can bring to bear on their approach to work is facilitated by their sharing a similar position on the gender hierarchy, and comparable gender ideologies and experience. For two women managing and financing a household together, the logic underpinning specialization in heterosexual relationships cannot automatically make sense. This, together with their positioning outside conventionality, insists upon a degree of reflexivity and that would be unusual in heterosexual partnerships. The alternative 'solutions' to the problem of balancing home-life and employment responsibilities offer practical insights for heterosexual couples seeking to operationalize their egalitarian ideals.

The distance that separates the arrangements of women parenting with women from those dominating heterosexual practice gives some indication of how far we have to journey before we can begin to say that a person's gender is irrelevant for shaping life-chances. All the reasons that can be mobilized to explain why it is difficult for men and women to achieve the balance experienced by women together highlight the extent to which the organization of social life and economic structures is based upon polarization along lines of gender, and thus the immensity of the feminist project.

The important links between (hetero)sexuality and gender (difference) need greater acknowledgement in how we approach the analysis of work and family life. Understandings will remain impartial so long as we ignore the role of heterosexuality in supporting the differentiated life-chances of women and men. It is deeply implicated in the construction and maintenance of dichotomous and hierarchical gender categories and practices. Since much of what makes women and men socially different relates to the structures of power that feminists are challenging we need to recognize our common interests in undermining the institutional dimension to heterosexuality.

ACKNOWLEDGEMENTS

I am extremely grateful to the following for their help and comments, and the lively insightful debates we have had as the ideas in this chapter have emerged: Shirley Prendergast, Ginny Morrow, Andrea Doucet, Kim Perren, Esther Dermott, Jackie Beer and Bob Blackburn. Additionally I am grateful to the Economic and Social Research Council for funding the project (reference number R00023 4649).

NOTES

1. An earlier version of this chapter (Dunne, 1998a) was published in the journal *Work, Employment and Society*.
2. This situation holds for partnerships where we might expect change to be most evident – for example, households where men are unemployed (Morris, 1995) and women are sole earners (Wheelock, 1990), full-time dual-earner couples with children (Brannen and Moss, 1991) and without children (Mansfield and Collard, 1988), where both are in pro-fessional occupations (Gregson and Lowe, 1994) or where the wife has a higher-status job than her husband (McRae, 1986). Even men and women who perceive themselves to be sharing do not necessarily escape the impact of gender-differentiated assumptions shaping their work strategies (Doucet, 1995a).
3. See the critique of Queer Theory and post-modern approaches to gender and sexuality in Jeffreys (1997) and Jackson (1995).
4. See examples of the individualistic and decisive approach to the critique and defence of heterosexuality in a series of commentaries in the journal *Feminism and Psychology* (1993), vol. 3, no. 3 and (1994), vol. 4, no. 2.
5. See, for example, Kitzinger *et al.* (1992).
6. See Dunne (1999) for an outline of the findings and methods.
7. See Dunne (1998d) for a discussion of parenting, donors and kinship arrangements.
8. See Dunne (1997b) for a more detailed analysis of respondents' perceptions of 'who does what'.
9. The Household Portrait was first developed by Andrea Doucet for illuminating the allocation strategies of egalitarian heterosexual couples. This technique involves both partners placing a broad range of task/responsibility tokens (colour-coded by themes such as routine

domestic, household service work, child-care, etc.) onto a board offering a continuum ranging from 100 per cent partner A to 100 per cent partner B. This visual representation encourages respondents to reflect upon and discuss how their household is run and participate in some initial analysis as patterns emerge (Doucet, 1995b).

10. I define higher qualifications as those above A level.

11. The data (and tabulations) used were made available through the ESRC Data Archive. The data were originally collected by the ESRC Research Centre on Micro-Social Change at the University of Essex. Neither the original collectors of the data nor the Archive bear any responsibility for the analysis or interpretations presented here.

12. The general tendency for women in partnerships to hold a more integrated view of the allocation of time between paid work and home-life has been commented upon in other research (see the interesting discussion in Seymour, 1992b). As men's conceptions of time are likely to be different from women's (Seymour 1992b: 190), the very attitudes that support balance in relationships *between* women may also serve to reproduce inequality in relationships between women and men.

13. To maintain confidentiality the names of participants and their children have been changed.

14. In the 15 households with older children (aged five to 16), we find these employment combinations:

	Percentage	Number
Full time/full-time	33	5
Part-time/part-time	20	3
Full-time/part-time	20	3
Part-time/home	13	2
Full-time/home	7	1
Home/home	7	1

15. So that the week reflects some sense of typicality, respondents were asked to avoid a time period which they knew in advance would be unusual, for example, half-term or holidays.

16. To facilitate comparison with other time-use collections, the diaries and coding frame are based upon those used in the large-scale diary collection (SCELI) conducted in 1987 by Jonathan Gershuny, with whom I am collaborating. The main task performed in each 15-minute time slot in the diary is categorized into different sorts of activities, paid work (which includes commuting time), domestic work, child-care, active and passive leisure, and then divided by seven to provide a sense of what an average day looks like. This 'day' represents an average for activities that are contained within a seven-day period (weekdays and weekend). It is, of course, an artificial construct because people's paid work is usually concentrated into weekdays and their leisure and perhaps domestic work into weekends.

17. See Seymour (1992b) for discussion of gender differences in perceptions of appropriate time-use.
18. The more recent 1995 Omnibus Time Use Survey (Office of National Statistics) indicates little has changed since 1987. Full-time employed mothers still have considerably shorter paid working days than employed fathers. Full-time employed mothers divide their time fairly equally between waged and un-waged work and domestic tasks monopolize their time at home. Fathers specialize in paid employment and spend little time on domestic work or child-care.
19. The age of children has a major bearing on time spent on activities within the 'child-care' category. The differences I have noted are particularly striking for households with pre-school children; they hold regardless of the occupational status of parents in the SCELI sample. Social class differences, however, are more relevant for domestic work contributions. Men in professional or managerial occupations devote an average 20 minutes a day more to domestic work than other men; their share of total domestic work performed in partnerships is 30 per cent compared with 21 per cent for other men.

REFERENCES

Berk, S. F. (1985) *The Gender Factory: The Apportionment of Work in American Households* (New York: Plenum).
Blaisure, K. and Allen, K. (1995) 'Feminists and the Ideology and Practice of Marital Equality', *Journal of Marriage and the Family*, 57, pp. 5–19.
Blumstein, P. and Schwartz, P. (1985) *American Couples* (New York: Pocket Books).
Bradley, H. (1989) *Men's Work, Women's Work* (Cambridge: Polity).
Brannen, J. and Moss, P. (1991) *Managing Mothers: Dual Earner Households after Maternity Leave* (London: Unwin Hyman).
Butler, J. (1990) *Gender Trouble: Feminism and the Subversion of Identity* (London: Routledge).
Cappuccini, G. (1996) 'Role Division and Gender Role Attitudes: Couples Adjusting to the Arrival of their First Baby', unpublished Ph.D. thesis, University of Birmingham.
Cappuccini, G. and Cochran, R. (1996) 'Role Division and Gender Role Attitudes: Couples Adjusting to the Arrival of their First Baby', paper presented at the British Psychological Society Annual Conference, the University of Strathclyde, Glasgow, 16–18 September.
Connell, R. W. (1987) *Gender and Power* (Cambridge: Polity).
Dex, S. and Shaw, L. (1986) *British and American Women and Work* (London: Macmillan).
Doucet, A. (1991) 'Striking a Balance: Gender Divisions of Labour in Housework, Childcare and Employment', Working Paper no. 6, Sociological Research Group: University of Cambridge.
Doucet, A. (1995a) 'Gender Equality, Gender Difference and Care', unpublished Ph.D. thesis, Cambridge University.

Doucet, A. (1995b) 'Encouraging Voices: Towards More Creative Methods for Collecting Data on Gender and Household Labour', in L. Morris and S. Lyon (eds), *Gender Relations in the Public and the Private* (London: Macmillan).

Dunne, G. A. (1992) 'Differences at Work: Perceptions of Work from a Non-Heterosexual Point of View', in H. Hinds and J. Stacey (eds), *New Directions in Women's Studies in the 1990s* (London: Falmer Press).

Dunne, G. A. (1997a) *Lesbian Lifestyles: Women's Work and the Politics of Sexuality* (London: Macmillan).

Dunne, G. A. (1997b) 'Why Can't a Man Be More Like a Woman? In Search of Balanced Domestic and Employment Lives', *LSE Gender Institute Discussion Paper Series*, 3.

Dunne, G. A. (1998a) '"Pioneers Behind Our Own Front Doors": Towards New Models in the Organization of Work in Partnerships', *Work, Employment and Society*, 12(2), pp. 273–95.

Dunne, G. A. (1998b) 'A Passion for "Sameness"? Sexuality and Gender Accountability', in E. Silva and C. Smart (eds), *The New Family?* (London: Sage).

Dunne, G. A. (1998c) 'Add Sexuality and Stir: Towards a Broader Understanding of the Gender Dynamics of Work and Family Life', in G. A. Dunne (ed.), *Living 'Difference': Lesbian Experience of Work and Family Life* (New York: Haworth Press).

Dunne, G. A. (1998d) 'Opting into Motherhood: Lesbians blurring the boundaries and re-defining the meaning of parenting', *LSE Gender Institute Discussion Paper*, Issue 13.

Dunne, G. A. (1999) 'Balancing acts: Lesbian experience of work and family life', in L. Sperling and M. Owen (eds), *Women and Work: The Age of Post-Feminism?* (Aldershot: Ashgate).

Faderman, L. (1985) *Surpassing the Love of Men: Romantic Friendship and Love between Women from the Renaissance to the Present* (London: Women's Press).

Fenstermaker, S., West, C. and Zimmerman, D. H. (1991) 'Gender Inequality: New Conceptual Terrain', in R. L. Blumberg (ed.), *Gender, Family and Economy: The Triple Overlap* (London: Sage).

Ferri, E. and Smith, K. (1996) *Parenting in the 1990s* (London: Family Policy Studies Centre).

Gershuny, J. I. and Jones, S. (1987) 'The Changing Work/Leisure Balance in Britain, 1961–84', *Sociological Review Monograph*, 33, pp. 9–50.

Gordon, T. (1990) *Feminist Mothers* (London: Macmillan).

Gregson, N. and Lowe, M. (1994) 'Waged Domestic Labour and the Renegotiation of the Domestic Divisions of Labour within Dual-Career Households', *Sociology*, 28(1), pp. 55–78

Gregson, N. and Lowe, M. (1995) *Servicing the Middle-Classes: Class, Gender and Waged Domestic Labour* (London: Routledge).

Greenberg, D. F. (1988) *The Construction of Homosexuality* (Chicago, IL: University of Chicago Press).

Haas, L. (1990) 'Parental Leave in Sweden', *Journal of Family Studies*, December, pp. 403–23.

Hartmann, H. (1981) 'The Unhappy Marriage of Marxism and Feminism: Towards a More Progressive Union', in L. Sargent (ed.), *Women and*

Revolution: A Discussion of the Unhappy Marriage of Marxism and Feminism (Boston, MA: South End Press).

Hochschild, A. R. (1989) *The Second Shift* (New York: Avon Books).

Jackson, S. (1995) 'Gender and Heterosexuality: a Materialist Feminist Analysis', in M. Maynard and J. Purvis (eds), *(Hetero)Sexual Politics* (Bristol: Taylor & Francis).

Jeffreys, S. (1997) 'The Queer Disappearance of Lesbians', in B. Mintz and E. D. Rothblum (eds), *Lesbians in Academia* (New York: Routledge).

Joshi, H., Dale, A., Ward, C. and Davies, H. (eds), (1995) *Dependence & Independence in the Finances of Women Aged 33* (London: Family Policy Studies Centre).

Kitzinger, C., Wilkinson, S. and Perkins, K. (eds), (1992) 'Heterosexuality: a Special Issue', *Feminism and Psychology*, 3(2).

La Rosa, R. (1998) 'Fatherhood and Social Change', *Family Relations*, 37, pp. 451–7.

Lees, S. (1986) *Losing Out: Sexuality and Adolescent Girls* (London: Hutchinson Education).

Lewis, C. and O'Brien, M. (eds), (1987) *Reassessing Fatherhood: New Observations on Fathers and the Modern Family* (London: Sage).

Mansfield, P. and Collard, J. (1988) *The Beginning of the Rest of Your Life: A Portrait of Newly Wed Marriage* (London: Macmillan).

Maynard, M. and Purvis, J. (eds), (1995) *(Hetero)Sexual Politics* (Bristol: Taylor & Francis).

McRae, S. (1986) *Cross-Class Families: A Study of Wives' Occupational Superiority* (Oxford: Clarendon Press).

Melhuish, E. and Moss, P. (eds), (1991) *Day Care for Young Children: International Perspectives* (London: Routledge & Kegan Paul).

Morris, L. (1990) *The Workings of the Household* (Cambridge: Polity).

Morris, L. (1995) *Social Divisions: Economic Decline and Social Structural Change* (London: UCL Press).

Oerton, S. (1998) 'Reclaiming the "Housewife"? Lesbians and Household Work', in G. A. Dunne (ed.), *Living 'Difference': Lesbian Experience of Work and Family Life* (New York: Haworth Press).

Office of Population Censuses and Surveys (1997) *Social Trends 27* (London: HMSO).

Ortner, S. B. and Whitehead, H. (eds), (1981) *Sexual Meanings: The Cultural Construction of Gender and Sexuality* (Cambridge: Cambridge University Press).

Pateman, C. (1988) *The Sexual Contract* (Cambridge: Polity).

Peace, H. F. (1993) 'The Pretended Family – a Study of the Divisions of Domestic Labour in Lesbian Families', *Leicester University Discussion Papers in Sociology*, no. S93/3.

Peplau, L. A. and Cochran, S. D. (1990) 'A Relationship Perspective in Homosexuality', in D. McWhirter, D. D. Sanders and J. M. Reinisch (eds), *Homosexuality/Heterosexuality: Concepts of Sexuality* (Oxford: Oxford University Press).

Pleck, J. H. (1985) *Working Wives, Working Husbands* (Beverly Hills, CA: Sage).

Rich, A. (1984) 'On Compulsory Heterosexuality and Lesbian Existence', in A. Snitow, C. Stansell and S. Thompson (eds), *Desire: The Politics of Sexuality* (London: Virago).

Rubin, G. (1975) 'The Traffic in Women: Notes on the "Political Economy" of Sex', in R. R. Reiter (ed.), *Towards an Anthropology of Women* (London: Monthly Review Press).

Segal, L. (1994) *Straight Sex: The Politics of Pleasure* (London: Virago).

Seymour, J. (1992a) ' "Not a Manly Thing To Do?" Gender Accountability and the Division of Domestic Labour', in G. A. Dunne, R. M. Blackburn and J. Jarman (eds), *Inequalities in Employment, Inequalities in Home-Life*. Conference Proceedings for Cambridge Social Stratification Seminar, 9–10 September.

Seymour, J. (1992b) ' "No Time to Call My Own": Women's Time as a Household Resource', *Women's Studies International Forum*, 15(2), pp. 187–192.

Shelton, B. (1992) *Women, Men and Time: Gender Differences in Paid Work, Housework and Leisure* (Westport, CT: Greenwood Press).

Steinberg, L., Epstein, D. and Johnson, R. (eds), (1997) *Border Patrols: Policing the Boundaries of Heterosexuality* (London: Cassell).

Tasker, F. and Golombok, S. (1998) 'The Role of Co-Mothers in Planned Lesbian-led Families', in G. A. Dunne (ed.), *Living 'Difference': Lesbian Experience of Work and Family Life* (New York: Haworth Press).

VanEvery, J. (1995) *Heterosexual Women Changing the Family: Refusing to be a 'Wife'!* (London: Taylor & Francis).

Walby, S. (1990) *Theorizing Patriarchy* (Oxford: Basil Blackwell).

Walby, S. (1997) *Gender Transformations* (London : Routledge).

West, C. and Zimmerman, D. (1991) 'Doing Gender', in J. Lorber and S. Farrell (eds), *The Social Construction of Gender* (London: Sage).

Wheelock, J. (1990) *Husbands at Home: The Domestic Economy in a Post-Industrial Society* (London: Routledge).

10 Sex, Money and the Kitchen Sink: Power in Same-Sex Couple Relationships

Brian Heaphy, Catherine Donovan and Jeffrey Weeks

INTRODUCTION

While there has been notable sociological concern with the themes of power, equality and inequality in couple relationships, the focus has almost exclusively been on heterosexual couples. At an empirical level a large body of work has focused on the intimate and domestic lives of men and women, and this suggests that gender relations, particularly within 'the home', continue to be marked and structured by inequalities with regard to labour and status (for discussions of change in this context see VanEvery, 1995; Benjamin and Sullivan, 1996). The limited research available on same-sex relationships emphasizes the *difference* between heterosexual and non-heterosexual relationships in this regard. In brief, it is suggested that members of same-sex couples are allowed to remain free of the traditional 'entrapments' of feminine/masculine stereotypes, and in the absence of conventions and guidelines are faced with the opportunity and possibility of developing more egalitarian relationships (for a review of the literature on same-sex couples see Weeks *et al.*, 1996).

In this chapter we consider this view by drawing on a exploration of interview data from a research project entitled 'Families of Choice: the Structure and Meaning of Non-heterosexual Relationships'.[1] Funded by the Economic and Social Research Council as part of its Population and Household Change programme, the main body of research involved in-depth semi-structured interviews with 96 non-heterosexuals – a term including the broad self-definitions given in interviews such as lesbian, gay, queer and so on (for a discussion of the methodological issues see

Heaphy *et al.*, 1998). We suggest that non-heterosexuals are actively involved in 'everyday experiments' with regard to the creating and maintaining of relationships, and that such experiments appear to be carried out with reference to an 'egalitarian ideal' (Peplau *et al.*, 1996; Dunne, 1997). That our interviewees believe their relationships to offer considerable potential for equality is most clearly evident in the accounts related in the first section of this chapter. These are framed in terms of differences between same-sex relationships and dominant heterosexual forms. In this context the potential offered by same-sex relationships is most widely framed in terms of the extent to which the 'irrelevance' of heterosexual models of relationships allows for the possibility of moving beyond gendered roles. While there are some notable differences in the ways that men and women articulate these possibilities, particularly with regard to the area of domestic labour, an emphasis on emotional expression and affirmation through involvement in democratic, egalitarian relationships appears to be the norm for both non-heterosexual men and women. Indeed, it is in terms of an emphasis on 'emotional equality' that a strong cultural guideline emerges.

It is not, however, that such relationships operate in a power-free zone. Rather, the focus is on 'relative equality' and attempts to achieve an egalitarian ideal. The aim of egalitarian relationships has to be struggled for against other inequalities such as those relating to income, day-to-day commitment, emotional labour, ethnic difference and the like, which present important limits for the operation of equality. It is clear from the data presented in the second section of this chapter that potential sources of inequality do exist in same-sex relationships, particularly in terms of individuals' access to cultural, material and social resources. However, in terms of financial issues, division of labour, and sexual lives, the extent to which relationships are negotiated is emphasized by respondents.

In the third section of this chapter we explore the extent to which the stories told of 'relative equality' and 'potential inequality' are in tension with each other. In doing so we suggest that both can be understood in terms of an emerging ethic.

LOOKING OUT AT HETEROSEXUAL RELATIONSHIPS: 'ROLES', 'INEQUALITY' AND 'ENTRAPMENTS'

so much is somehow assumed in heterosexual relationships, whereas in gay relationships it has to be made somehow more explicit. ... You can't slide through recognised patterns of relationships. You've got to make a more conscious decision about what you want from each other ... same-sex couples are much more obliged to be explicit about or think – scrutinise what they want from a relationship – what they're expecting – think about it.   (M25)

The above extract, from an interview with a gay man, touches on three interrelated themes that emerge from our interviewees' accounts of 'looking out' at heterosexual relationships. These relate to questions of difference, the 'irrelevance' of dominant models of relationships for same-sex relationships, and the extent to which non-heterosexuals must be both explicit and reflexive regarding how they want their relationships to be. Implicit in the above quotation is a notion that informed many of our interviewees' accounts of difference: that same-sex relationships involved fashioning in a way that heterosexual forms did not. Such a notion was expressed with regard to the various forms of relationships that non-heterosexuals might have, from family relationships to couple relationships, as the following extracts illustrate:

it is also about being creative and being pioneering, about not wanting to be defined in, not wanting to conform in terms of what family needs to look like. So it's all about that.   (F44)

speaking from my generation, you know – my age – discovering that I was homosexual meant having to invent myself because there was nothing there that ... there weren't any role models there. It may well be different for gay men coming out now, I don't know. Well, yes, it is. I do know now actually. But there's still that element of self-invention and finding ... defining things how you want them to be. So I don't think heterosexuals do that. They slip into roles that are pre-ordained and it goes along that route. Whereas we don't have any pre-ordained roles so we can actually invent things how we want them.   (M17)

Accounts such as the above are evident in many lesbian and gay coming-out stories (Hall Carpenter Archives, 1989a,b; Porter and Weeks, 1990), and the extent to which self-invention is central to lesbian and gay experience has been widely noted in the literature on lesbian and gay identity (Weston, 1991; Plummer, 1992, 1995; Blasius, 1994; Weeks, 1995). As such it is not surprising that, in interviews concerning the intimate lives of non-heterosexuals, such themes should be extended to stories of the necessity of 'creating' relationships. A similar point has been made in the research on lesbian and gay relationships, where it is argued that, because their relationships lack institutional supports and cultural guidelines, members of same-sex couples are free to fashion their own modes of relating to each other (Harry and DeVall, 1978; Mendola, 1980; McWhirter and Mattison, 1984; Johnson, 1990; also see Peplau *et al.*, 1996; Weeks *et al.*, 1996). As Blasius (1994) notes, it is not only that they are 'free' in this regard but may, in many senses, be obliged to do so:

> The problematization of their own lifestyle (indeed, more broadly, their way of life) has been based upon a conscious imperative among lesbians and gay men to invent the self and ways of relating to others … lesbians and gay men must create a self out of (or despite) the heterosexual self that is culturally given to them…. They must invent ways of relating to each other because there are no ready-made cultural or historical models or formulas for erotic same-sex relationships, as there are for different-sex erotic relationships.
>
> (Blasius, 1994: 191)

There are, of course, similarities here with notions of self-invention out-lined in the theoretical literature that has emphasized the fluid nature of social possibilities, and the extent to which the present era has been marked by a break with the constraints of traditional institutional patterns (e.g., Giddens, 1992; Weeks, 1995). In terms of changing patterns of intimacy, recent work has related the necessity of engaging in experiments with regard to everyday life and relationships to both homo-sexual *and* heterosexual experiences (Giddens, 1992; Bech, 1992; see Weeks *et al.*, this volume). While this work suggests that there may be overlaps between heterosexuals and non-heterosexuals in this regard, as the extract from one respondent (M17) above indicates, amongst many non-heterosexuals there is a sense that the necessity of fashioning oneself and one's relationship is a distinguishing factor of non-heterosexual experience. From our interviews a key perception of difference between same-sex relationships and heterosexual forms emerges in terms of observations that, while some 'changes' may be occurring in the ways that heterosexual relationships operate, they continue to be structured by set patterns, expectations and assumptions:

> I think there's a lot less structure in gay relationships in that hetero-sexual relationships in my eyes follow a pattern. … Whereas a gay

relationship, I don't think there's the same kind of 'career structure' as it were ... there's a lot less 'You do this here, this here and this here'. (M12)

For many respondents the lack of institutional supports and cultural guidelines implies that same-sex relationships allow for 'freer' relationships, in the sense that they are disembedded or cut off from the dominant models, assumptions and conventions that inform heterosexual relationships. Amongst our interviewees such 'freedom' was articulated widely in terms of the opening-up of choices (see also Weston, 1991; Giddens, 1992; Dunne, 1997):

I think straight relationships are unbearably boring, in terms of – there's just so many rules about how they do things and how they don't do things and why they do things and when they do it, that I ... I mean, I like the freedom that you have with lesbian relationships. I think that's a big difference. (F02)

I know it's terrible and you shouldn't say these things, but I think it's actually a better lifestyle. ... Because you have to think about it all the time. So nothing that you do is ever just following the set pattern that someone ... you know, it's not set down ... I mean I know it's all very restrained by the sort of oppressions out there but within a group of lesbians and gay men, you get to choose the way you want to behave and you're not restrained by stupid bloody conventions. (M11)

While there are, of course, many limits placed on freedoms and choices – most often framed by respondents in terms of the extent to which 'homophobia' and 'heterosexism' set important limits on how relationships can be lived – the 'freedoms' available in and through same-sex relationships were often compared with the perceived 'entrapments' of marriage that might work to limit heterosexuals' choices:

I would like to think that people in gay relationships stay together because they actually want to stay together to a greater extent than heterosexual relationships do ... it's possible that the expectations of society and the trappings attached to marriage and all that, put more pressure on heterosexuals to stay together against their will than is the case with gay men and lesbians. (M15)

In addition to the 'creation' of relationships, some respondents also perceived that particular factors relating to the operation of hetero-sexuality and 'homosexuality' might allow for more agency regarding the leaving of relationships. Key factors that were identified in these accounts related to the extent to which the perceived emphasis on independence within same-sex relationships might make it easier for members to leave (cf. Weston, 1991; Dunne, 1997). Other social factors were also identified:

> I don't know – I mean – it seems to me as if relationships between lesbians and gay men are. ... I was going to say less ... less long-standing than heterosexual relationships but I don't actually think that's the truth. I think what probably is the stereotypical judgement is that lesbians and gay men have short-term relationships ... I think that they're just more acknowledging of when relationships have run their course. And I also think there's a certain amount to do with the kind of ... the way that lesbians and gay men socialise, which means that – you know – the possibility of finding new part-ners is more possible for more people than it perhaps is for some heterosexuals.   (F01)

While some theorists have suggested that the power of 'compulsory heterosexuality' is effective in silencing or making invisible 'possible ways of being' for non-heterosexuals (see Blasius, 1994), others have noted that the lack of the structural foundation of heterosexuality (grounded, as it is, in gender difference and resulting in inequality) can be located by lesbians (Dunne, 1997: 181; Weston, 1991: 149) and gay men (Weston, 1991: 149) as making the task of creating more equal relationships easier in same-sex relationships. From our inter-views the extent to which our respondents believed that same-sex couple relationships offer unique possibilities for the construction of 'more' egalitarian relationships is striking. The potential offered by same-sex relationships is most widely framed in terms of the extent to which the 'irrelevance' of heterosexual models of relationships allows for the possibility of moving beyond gendered roles. In this sense the lack of cultural or historical models of same-sex relationships may be experienced as being a negative factor with potentially positive effects:

> In a way, not having had any role models, any of us as we grew up – in certain ways that's still very damaging, I think, for lesbians and gay men – but in certain ways it at least means we haven't had so

much to throw out. You know – whereas I do think that heterosexual friends who are trying to create more equal relationships are
having to be very conscious about it all the time.   (F21)

I think they're different because they – I think they're more equal
than heterosexual relationships. I think they're more equal because
I think there is less of a male/female role ... being able to negotiate,
being on an equal level to be able to negotiate in the first place.
And I think that's what makes them different.   (M04)

From respondents' accounts it is clear the creation and maintenance of
'more equal' relationships necessitates a considerable amount of
labour. Such labour, primarily spoken about in terms of the need
for discussion and negotiation, was, however, overwhelmingly compared favourably to the labour that was perceived to be involved in
challenging the assumptions and set patterns that informed heterosexual relationships. While the work in and on their own relationships
tended to be perceived as having potential rewards in terms of 'more
equality', the need to engage in challenges and contests to facilitate
change in relationships between men and women was often seen as
having less potential. Women particularly emphasized this point:

With lesbian relationships everything has to be – well, the lesbian
relationships I've had – there are no assumptions about how you
will relate, what you will do, who does what. Everything has to be
discussed, everything is negotiable. With relationships with straight
men, certain things seem to be assumed and then you have to fight
to get something else. That has been my experience.   (F29)

I think certainly I'm aware that heterosexual friends who are feminists
have to work much harder at creating equal relationships than we do,
because they're fighting the rest of the world.   (F21)

The 'Entrapments' of Female/Male Roles

In 'looking out' at heterosexual relationships, the accounts of our
female respondents are consistent with those provided in Dunne's
(1997) research. Dunne (1997: 181–2) suggests that her interviews
highlight two main aspects of heterosexual relationships which were
understood to pre-empt an egalitarian outcome. The first of these concerns structural inequalities, which relate to the different material

resources available to men and women. In our own research this was most often articulated in the terms of there being 'an essential power imbalance' (F34) between women and men. The second feature concerns gendered assumptions and expectations that impact on the operation of heterosexual relationships. Many of the women we interviewed placed a strong emphasis on the unequal expectations and assumptions about the labour women perform in heterosexual relationships and family forms:

> when I look at other people's relationships [heterosexuals], yeah, there's differences. I think they're much more role-defined, although they would like to think that they've moved on a lot from where they were, I don't see it very often. It may be hidden, but it's still very role-defined. I still see the women doing the majority of the housework and looking after the children and the men going out doing their leisure time. (F36)

> I just found the family and heterosexuality really oppressive. I constantly, constantly had battles about my rights to any sort of equal status in terms of cleaning, cooking, washing, childcare, going out to work, having friends, having a life of my own. I think from beginning to end it was a struggle and a battle and I hadn't realised that they were battles and struggles. (F28)

Importantly, in some of the women's accounts it was not only individuals who were located as being implicated in the operation of 'unequal' relationships, but rather that heterosexuality itself was perceived to be bound up with the disempowerment of women. As is evident in the extract above (F28), for some women with experience of heterosexual relationships, heterosexuality was experienced and talked about as producing pressures to conform to hegemonic notions of 'appropriate' gender behaviour, but also constraining impulses in terms of 'possibilities of being'. In this sense the perception that heterosexuality was central to the construction of ways of being for women that are in line with what has been termed an 'emphasized femininity' (Connell, 1987) was espoused:

> I think, my heterosexual relationships and my bisexual relationships with men, I think I had bigger expectations. I think I expected them to do more work in the relationship. If things went wrong I would have felt guilty and thought it was me, but I would have

expected them to do something about it.... Much more sort of help-less, weak ... I think that's one of the things heterosexuality does to women.   (F30)

for me, they're [lesbian relationships] based on trying to kind of – find some equality between two people and they're based on freedom and they're based on not owning a person and not dictating to the person what they can do and what they can't do ... [in heterosexual relationships] there is a role that is ascribed to the man and a role that is ascribed to the woman. And I don't mean roles as in housework and breadwinner – I mean roles as in – you know – game-playing, manipulation, being passive, being victimy – whatever.   (F03)

In developing her account, the respondent (F03) above also points to another perception of the difference between her present relationship and the types of relationships that were possible to have with men: those with women were seen to offer much more potential for emotional fulfilment. As with many other women, this respondent emphasizes 'trust' and 'honesty', particularly with regard to questions of love and sex:

[It is about] a complete level of honesty and trust that I've never experienced – and I don't – in a heterosexual relationship, and I really don't see how women can experience that level of trust and honesty in a heterosexual relationship.

[In the present relationship] it's fine not to feel sexual, not to want sex at particular points in time. I think when we were starting our relationship I think it was quite difficult for me because I'd come from not having relationships ... only having relationships with men. So my experiences and my framework that I'd been operating in were the heterosexual one, which was: you had to give men sex all the time. If you didn't give them sex then they would leave you or they would stop loving you or whatever.   (F03)

In many of the accounts provided by women regarding their under-standings of the operation of heterosexual relationships the influence of feminist analyses of power is evident (cf. Dunne, 1997). From women's responses it was clear that feminist discourses – or what Benjamin and Sullivan (1996: 229) term 'the feminist value system' – were often employed as a personal resource in making sense of 'power' in interpersonal relationships. On the surface this could be said to be the case for some of the men interviewed, such as M04 earlier. The extract below, from an interview with a male respondent, brings together many of the themes addressed above and focuses explicitly on the relationship between heterosexuality, gender roles and hegemonic forms of masculinity and femininity:

> I suppose I would have to relate it to my experience of having been in a heterosexual relationship, really. And I mean, it's something to do with how I think we're socialised as men and the way that we think we can be. ... I think there is less a sense of possession, or property, in same-sex relationships, and more emphasis on ... emotional bonding ... that's not quite what I mean, but they're less ritualised really. ... I think that kind of creates a necessity for ... same-sex relationships to find their own identity – whereas I think that heterosexual relationships, they can ... coast more ... there is more kind of ascribed roles. ... You know, I think the kind of macho male bit is very destructive and you know – there's an awful lot of it about really. As there is the stereotype of the kind of passive, the passive female. But I mean, those are kind of stereotypes, but you can see them being acted out.   (M39)

While many male respondents talked of the potential that same-sex relationships offered in going 'beyond' gendered roles, such potential did not, in the main, refer to the *structural* differences between men and women or address questions of unequal labour that women undertake. Rather, the tendency was to emphasize the 'entrapments' of the male role as they related to the pressure to conform to hegemonic notions of masculinity (Connell, 1987, 1995). While women focused on the material and the emotional, in men's accounts the primary focus is the extent to which heterosexuality and heterosexual relationships are bound up with particular notions of masculinity – and particularly the 'possibilities of being' in terms of their emotional lives. In this sense responses were often framed in terms of the extent that homosexuality and same-sex relationships provided ways of imagining being men that did not have to conform to notions of 'hegemonic masculinity'. The above extract (M39) points to a key common factor that was identified by both male and female respondents in terms of the emphasis on emotional bonding. Related terms that reoccur in the men's accounts are 'honesty' and 'openness':

I think partners in a gay relationship are much more honest and open about what they feel for each other; what they want from a relationship; I think they're much more honest about expressing feelings of like or dislike or whatever and I just think there's much more forum for discussion.   (M23)

The emotional rewards of same-sex relationships were echoed in other respondents' accounts. For many men, heterosexual relationships were productive of pressures to conform to hegemonic notions of masculinity – primarily in terms of emotional lives and worlds. Some respondents' stories of what heterosexual relationships looked like were bound up with stories of 'unemotional' and 'uncommunicative' men:

I think it's much easier to have equal relationships if you're the same-sex. I'm not at all sure how heterosexual men of my age get emotional support. I think a lot of them don't. That's a tragedy for them … I mean, to be a heterosexual former public schoolboy. I mean can you imagine how they cope with life? I mean, I just don't think they know who they are or who anybody else is ever. I don't think they get beyond a certain level of knowledge of people.   (M03)

One of the defining elements of hegemonic masculinity, and the entrapments of male roles, that emerges from accounts such as the above is heterosexual men's perceived inability to communicate on an emotional level, and an inability to 'know' others (cf. Duncombe and Marsden, 1993). In these accounts it was not women who were located as problematic, but rather the extent to which heterosexual models were implicated in the reproduction of particular 'types' of masculinity. In this construction, heterosexual men's perceived inability to access emotional support is located in terms of the lack of mutuality. The perception of heterosexual men's inability to 'know themselves' and 'know others' (both are understood to be inter-dependent), are seen as traits of hegemonic masculinity that are undesirable. Equality, in accounts such as these, is located in reciprocal emotional relationships.

While there are differences between men and women in terms of *how* same-sex relationships are experienced and articulated as being more equal, there are also commonalities. Where non-heterosexual women are likely to place a notable emphasis on the unequal divisions of labour within heterosexual relationships, both non-heterosexual men and women emphasize the 'emotional' possibilities opened up in same-sex relationships. While there are differences in terms of how it is articulated, and what is focused on, what emerges is the notion of an 'egalitarian ideal' (Peplau *et al.*, 1996; Dunne, 1997), where 'equality' is given a central place in narratives of the potentials offered by same-sex relationships. This ideal concerns the desire to exist within, and actively construct, democratic, egalitarian relationships.

LOOKING IN AT SAME-SEX RELATIONSHIPS: 'POWER', 'INEQUALITY' AND 'NEGOTIATION'

The notion of an egalitarian ideal is also present in respondents' accounts of 'looking in' at their own relationships. This is particularly evident in the emphasis placed on the negotiation of domestic, emotional and sexual lives. Almost all respondents, however, identified factors that had the *potential* to cause inequality. While the percentages have varied dramatically across studies, some early North American work has suggested that up to 59 per cent of lesbians (Peplau and Cochran, 1980, cited in Peplau *et al.*, 1996) and 60 per cent of gay men (Harry and DeVall, 1978) describe their relationships as being 'equal'. While most of our respondents felt that their relationships were equal 'in the main', none of them presented their relationships as a 'power-free' zone. Whereas respondents located 'gender' power in heterosexual relationships, they located other forms of power in their own relationships. As one woman put it:

> I think – the way I think about power, is that it's one of those things that we all have and it's part of us and it's kind of like everything else. And, I don't think it's a big scary thing – I think it's something that you live with and you have to deal with.   (F02)

There were a broad set of factors identified that could influence, or impact negatively on, the operation of the egalitarian ideal that respondents espoused. The aim of egalitarian relations has to be constantly struggled for against inequalities of income, unequal emotional and physical labour, ethnic and class differences, and so on. Peplau *et al.* (1996: 255–6) note that much of the work on same-sex relationships identifies that greater relationship-defining power can accrue to the partner who has greater personal resources. While this has usually been framed in terms of financial resources and education, we suggest that a broader focus on capital is more apt. Such a focus can allow us to take into account cultural, economic and *social* resources. Our interviews suggest that one important potential source of differential 'relationship-defining power' that has tended to be overlooked is unequal access to *social* capital (see Wan, 1995; Weeks, 1996). In terms of being lesbian or gay, social capital can relate to questions of 'outness' and the ability to access local or 'lesbian and gay community' knowledge and supports. In this way we can understand comments such as the following, from a gay man who felt that he belonged to strong network of lesbian and gay friends who were a part of a local lesbian and gay community:

> There are a lot of things that potentially make it very imbalanced in terms of power because I'm more experienced in gay life and I'm more comfortable in it than he is. I'm much more secure in my sort of – friendship networks than he is and I have a lot of people to talk about my relationship with James and he doesn't have those people. (M11)

As was noted earlier, a key issue in accounts of the potential for equality was the extent to which dichotomous gender scripts and 'roles' were not at play in same-sex relationships. When 'looking in' at their own relationships, the notion that couples might organize their own domestic lives in accordance with male/female (or 'butch/femme') roles, or that they might be perceived by others as doing so, was sometimes seen as shocking and almost always refuted by respondents. In the few cases in which respondents themselves suggested that their household division of labour could 'appear' to match such roles, the notion of choice was emphasized:

> I occasionally look and think 'My God! We're a 1950s butch/femme couple' with 'who is doing with round the house', sort of thing. Uhm there are aspects of that. I'm reasonably comfortable with that – so it's OK. I would worry – in some ways it feels less of a problem in a lesbian relationship than it would in a heterosexual relationship where one would be working harder at getting rid of gendered roles … as I've got older I've got easier about the fact that actually I do like cooking and I really don't like hammering nails into fences … I'm less bothered because I don't … because the fact that two adults of the same gender choose to do different things within the house,

doesn't give kids a message that says 'Men are only supposed to do this one' or 'Women are only supposed to do that one'.   (F21)

While our interviewees highlighted that assumptions about the domestic division of labour could not be made in terms of gender difference, some respondents' accounts pointed to the possibility of assumptions being informed by other factors. The extract from one respondent below, who is retired and lives with a male partner who is over 20 years younger, highlights that tensions around domestic labour may arise when both members of a relationship are not in paid employment:

> we very rarely get angry with each other. He still complains I don't do enough housework. … Well, we didn't have a row, we had a discussion the other day and I said 'Alright look'. He was busy and he couldn't clean the bathroom for a fortnight and because he hadn't done it he thought that I should have done it. 'Right, we'll sit down and we'll make a list of the jobs that need doing and we'll write a list of who is going to do what and then we're not going to have these misunderstandings' … because in a way I feel that I'm … this is my retirement when I should have leisure and the time to do things and what not … well I feel as if I don't really benefit very much from being retired … and he's got a very exacting job.   (M44)

From the account of the respondent above it is clear that factors such as employment status (and age) can cause conflict in terms of expectations regarding domestic work. While this respondent stressed the negotiated nature of the relationship when first discussing household labour – it is clear from the above that such dilemmas also necessitate ongoing reassessment. This example highlights the extent to which power relations within same-sex relationships are not static and stable. Material inequality, for instance, can be influential in informing the extent to which it is felt that the relationship is equal, but does not necessarily remain constant. The extract below, from a woman who is temporarily unemployed and who lives with a partner who is in paid employment, highlights both points:

> I think until I'm working and earning the same amount of money that she is, it can never be equal. In, in certain ways and yet it can be. In other ways. But I think as individuals we probably make it difficult to be equal because there's, even if she was perfectly fine,

and said, even if we had a joint bank account and, which we don't at the present time, and I could take any of her money whenever I wanted it, or whatever, I wouldn't feel equal. Because I wouldn't feel that I was making an equal contribution. So, I would make myself feel unequal.   (F43)

Beyond differences related to division of labour and economic resources, other stories respondents told about power, inequality, and equality also highlighted the complexity of 'flows of power'. Consider the following extract from a couple interview:

A: Well, I would say I think we're both equally [powerful] – but knowing Sean would say no. Go on.

S: [It is] I mean, from my point of view, quite deep or quite involved ... the fact that Arthur's older and black, he didn't have much formal education but that's just how he was brought up in [country]. The fact that I'm younger and white and got a degree but I had the opportunity to do that. I mean, externally that would be viewed in a certain way. I think that it gets internalised and almost reversed. ... I suppose it's difficult finding the right terminology for all these things, but because of our actual social backgrounds and how we'd be perceived, I would be the one that would be seen as being socially – if you want to use the word 'powerful', which is ... it would be true, externally, but I think within the relationship, in a sense that it's maybe been turned around, for different reasons ... I would say I don't like to speak on your behalf – but Arthur would see those perceptions but would try to overcome them by not allowing – giving me any space to kind of exert those perceived – that perceived status. And I think I mean, I would again acquiesce to that, comply with that. Try and deal with it in some way – negotiate it. So I would say, for a long time, I mean, we went through ups and downs and sticky patches and had a lot of difficulty. And I think that was at the bottom of it. I think it took a long time to kind of fathom it out and kind of work it out and gradually get an understanding of it.

(M37/38)

From the interview data it is clear that there are many factors that can be in tension with the operation of an egalitarian ideal. However, the emphasis, with regard to issues such as those in the extracts cited, is on the possibilities offered by negotiation and the potential for 'working out' these issues. Indeed, the *more* respondents identified potential power imbalances in their relationship, the more the necessity to 'talk' and 'negotiate' was emphasized. This resonates with the findings in Finch and Mason's (1993) work, where less discussion was equated with a more 'traditional' allocation of caring tasks. For some respondents the ability to negotiate issues to do with power was identified as particularly important:

S: … because we have an S/M relationship, power is a very important feature, and it's something that … sexually we negotiate – almost every time we have sex.

J: Mm

S: sort of, who has the power to do what or how much emotional power is one of us prepared to hand over, and is that a permanent thing or is it a temporary thing, and is it something that we're playing with, or is it something that's real. And so the power bounds within our domestic arrangements is completely separate to sexual power … it's very important to us that we don't abuse power – because it's so easy to do … with that very temporary relationship I had … I abused my power there. That was not an S/M relationship, but there was an S/M aspect to it – which was probably why I didn't find it fulfilling. And emotionally I had all the power, which I was really uncomfortable with. I didn't like it at all. And even when I used to say to the girl 'Look, you know – this isn't working – it's really unbalanced', she'd just say 'Well I love you and I want to continue'. So there's sort of a … guilt trip there of, you know, 'I've got all this power and I can't hurt her', but at the end of the day having that imbalance was really bad for me, and that's why I finished it.   (F14/15)

The latter respondent indicates that there are, of course, limits to negotiation. These were emphasized in situations where there was a lack of reciprocity and mutual commitment to the relationship, or when the grounds on which the commitment was based were radically altered. While some respondents had successfully negotiated the shifting from monogamy to non-monogamy, or even the shift from a sexual relationship to a non-sexual one, such negotiations were perceived to be possible only where the changed relationship was *mutually* desired:

he said 'I don't ... I don't want us to have sex any longer', and I said 'Erm ... that's not so easy for me, because I do see sex as a very important part of our relationship'. And he didn't want to stop seeing me but he didn't want to have sex with me and I didn't want to necessarily see him if it wasn't going to be that kind of relationship. ... I wrote him a really angry letter which he'd never received one like that before from me. And I think it had quite shocked him ... I think he was more frightened than angry and realised that ... we had to negotiate around this somehow, but at the same time I was seeing this as fairly untenable because you can't kind of say to someone 'I don't care if you don't want to have sex with me – you've got to have sex with me. ...' You know, you can't do that.   (M25)

Similarly, negotiations could take place only where the emotional commitment in the relationship was not threatened, unlike in the following case:

It's a downward spiral, because my response to feeling threatened by her loving someone else more than me, is to behave in a way which makes her feel controlled and ... so therefore she doesn't love me as much – or can't express her love so much. And I know it's a vicious circle. You know, the only way out for me is to let go ... It doesn't feel equal because I think there's a level on which I need her more than she needs me and I don't like that.   (F29)

It is clear from the accounts of non-heterosexual women and men that same-sex relationships do not dissolve 'power'. Indeed, one of the striking issues to emerge from respondents' accounts of both heterosexual *and* their own relationships, is the *extent* to which non-heterosexuals appear to have stories about power to tell. As the extracts outlined in this section highlight, among our respondents there would appear to be an acute awareness of potential imbalances within their relationships. This is particularly so with regard to differential access to material, cultural and social resources. While the accounts of 'looking out' at heterosexual relationships stress the extent to which assumptions regarding roles and positions within relationships cannot be made in terms of gender, in accounts of 'looking in' at same-sex relationships there is an emphasis on the need for negotiation of the potential inequalities that are influenced by *other* dynamics. Such negotiation is seen to be key to the construction and operation of egalitarian relationships.

POSSIBILITIES OF BEING: ROMANTIC STORIES OR AN
EMERGING ETHIC?

A key question arises in relation to how we make sense of the 'egalitarian ideal' that has been outlined above. Previous attempts to
address the 'equality' of lesbian and gay male relationships suggest
that they can be understood to be structured around 'best-friend'
models of relating (Harry and DeVall, 1978; Peplau, 1981; Harry,
1984; Kehoe, 1988). The 'friendship model', as it is generally
employed, includes the notion of more egalitarian couple relationships than is deemed possible in heterosexual relationships. As Peplau
et al. (1996) suggest:

> A friendship script typically fosters equality in relationships. In con-
> trast to marriage, the norms of friendship assume that partners are
> relatively equal in status and power. Friends also tend to be similar in
> interests, resources, and skills. Available evidence suggest that most
> American lesbians and gay men have a relationship that most closely
> approximates best friendship.   (Peplau *et al.*, 1996: 403)

Friendship scripts also imply a substantial degree of autonomy for
each partner. While the friendship model is not universally employed
to explain same-sex forms of relating, there is broad agreement that
friendship has a significant role to play in the structuring of these.
Indeed, Blumstein and Schwartz (1983), in their study of same-sex and
heterosexual couples, have argued that lesbians and gay men appear
to combine the need for friendship and romantic love in one person to
a greater extent than do heterosexuals. From our own research it is
clear that for many non-heterosexuals friendship is seen as central to
the operation of 'successful' couple relationships:

> I'm back again on my friendship kick, I'm afraid, I think that under-
> pinned everything ... I'm stuck in the groove on that ... I think that,
> as they say, was the sort of rock, the underpinning, whatever you
> want to call it.   (F47)

The notion of friendship has also been employed with regard to same-
sex relationships in other ways that are worth noting here. In terms of
the emotional lives of lesbians the term 'intimate friendships' is
used by Dunne (1997) to denote the reciprocal nature of lesbians'
emotional relationships. This is in contrast to the notion of 'intimate

strangers' that is employed by Mansfield and Collard (1988) to refer to the different emotional goals that husbands and wives may have in marriage. Blasius (1994) also focuses on friendship, though in his scheme it is termed 'erotic friendship' which is 'characterised by reciprocal *independence* (not interdependence based upon complementarity)' (219–20; original emphasis). The key to equality in erotic friendships, Blasius suggests, is that these are relationships based on the *reciprocal* giving and receiving of pleasure. Echoing some of our interviewees' accounts as outlined earlier, he argues that the power to shape the other in such relationships is limited by the freedom of that other to remain in or leave the relationship.

An interesting question arises: Is what we are seeing in both the data and the literature the emergence of a romantic love/friendship story? As Weston (1991) notes in her discussion of the extent to which some of her own respondents located equality as a distinguishing feature of relations within lesbian and gay couples:

> The portrayal of lovers as a union of equals rather than a relation of subjugation has clear ties to romantic ideologies of heterosexual marriage.   (Weston, 1991: 149)

Also, it has been suggested by some theorists of heterosexual relationships that 'even private testimonies given in research interviews are themselves publicly-scripted' (Burgoyne and Clark, cited in Duncombe and Marsden, 1996: 150). Duncombe and Marsden (1993, 1996) note a key influence in heterosexual couples' stories may be the desire to conform to the model of the happy companionate relationship:

> A key part of emotion work where the couple relationship is old or shaky may be the couple's management of their image to outsiders – including interviewers – so as to present a picture of companionate love.   (Duncombe and Marsden, 1993: 237)

Elements of 'romantic' and 'companionate' love stories do exist in our respondents' accounts. Yet these narratives are also in keeping with what Giddens (1992) describes as 'confluent love'. While particularly apt for discussion of our data, this notion has been developed in an attempt to conceptualize broader transformations in patterns of intimacy that are cutting across the homosexual/heterosexual dichotomy:

Confluent love is active, contingent love, and therefore jars with the 'for-ever', 'one-and-only' qualities of the romantic love complex [i.e., less the 'special person' that counts and more the 'special relationship'].... Romantic love has long had an egalitarian strain.... *De facto*, however, romantic love is skewed in terms of power. For women dreams of romantic love have all too often led to grim domestic subjection. Confluent love presumes equality in emotional give and take, the more so the more any particular love tie approximates closely to the prototype of the pure relationship. Love here only develops to the degree to which intimacy does, to the degree to which each partner is prepared to reveal concerns and needs to the other and to be vulnerable to that other.   (Giddens, 1992: 61–2)

There are strong similarities between the themes discussed in the extract above and the themes that have emerged from our data. There is, however, another way of making sense of what are, in effect, research stories. It is in this context that we can suggest that, far from an *absence* of cultural guidelines for same-sex relationships, the narratives of power in relationships outlined in the previous sections suggest the existence or emergence of strong 'local' or 'community' guidelines – that emphasize the egalitarian ideal. The literature and respondents' accounts overwhelmingly emphasize the *lack* of cultural guidelines and models for the construction of same-sex relationships. Yet one crucial and central set of 'local' guidelines or knowledges concerning 'possibilities of being' in same-sex relationships emerges that has marked similarities with what Giddens (1992: 58) terms the 'pure relationship': relationships of sexual and emotional equality that are sought and entered into as long as they are mutually fulfilling.

What also emerges is a sense of what Blasius (1994: 206) calls a lesbian and gay ethic: a type of existence that is the consequence of coming out, and which is bound up with a set of knowledges about the possibilities of living as lesbians and gay men. Such knowledges are potentially accessed through 'coming out' of the heterosexual selves that are allocated to individuals, and 'coming into' non-heterosexual 'communities'. Coming out necessitates re-evaluation and relearning with regard to *how it is possible to live and relate* in the world as lesbians and gay men (cf. Davies, 1992). As such it can facilitate an engagement with community knowledges that are informed by various analyses of power – including those influenced by 'feminist value systems' and lesbian and gay politics. From Blasius' account we can locate some of possible resources that might be accessed in this re-evaluation and relearning:

A way of life produces knowledge needed in order to exist in the world at a particular historical moment. This ethos necessitates the production of knowledge, understood not just as theory, but including practical guides to and reflections upon living – such as self help manuals (concerning medicine, the law, relationships, etc.), fiction, autobiography and scientific research.

(Blasius, 1994: 212)

Other important resources are what Plummer (1995) refers to as 'sexual stories'. Such stories circulate in and through developing interpretive communities. In this sense private testimonies, such as those of our respondents, *are,* in part, publicly scripted. It is not that these testimonies simply reproduce particular stories (of equality) – but rather that the stories are themselves *reflexively* produced (Plummer, 1995), as are the analyses of power that are central to them. As noted in the previous section, it is not that the 'egalitarian ideal' dissolves power in same-sex relationships, but that the self-reflexivity that is necessary for the creation and maintenance of same-sex relationships might make 'power' an issue for more *explicit* consideration and negotiation within the relationships themselves. Indeed, our data would suggest that this is the case.

CONCLUSION

Our discussion of power in same-sex relationships has been based on non-heterosexuals' 'stories' of the potential offered for equality, reciprocity, and negotiation in same-sex couples. We would like to conclude with a brief consideration of what these stories reveal about the 'reality' of power in same-sex relationships. In this regard we take seriously Duncombe and Marsden's (1996: 150) point that it is necessary to account for a connection between the narrative of living that is constructed in the interview and 'the life as lived by the subject' (see Heaphy *et al.*, 1998, for a discussion of research stories in relation to questions of validity). In making sense of our respondents' accounts we have found it useful to consider these in terms of the consequences of telling a particular story under specific circumstances. By doing so, the concern is with what can be said, why it is said now and not at other times, and the effects of telling a particular story in a particular way. In this way, Plummer (1995) suggests, stories can be examined for the roles they play in lives, in contexts, in social order. Hence, the concern is with the role a certain kind of story plays in the life of a person or society (Plummer, 1995: 172).

It is not possible to claim that the accounts of non-heterosexuals outlined in this chapter reveal the essential truth about the nature and operation of same-sex relationships. Rather, we suggest that the accounts about couple relationships and power tell us something important about the ways in which these social actors see relationships in both the non-heterosexual and heterosexual worlds, and shape their lives accordingly. These narratives are, in part, publicly scripted, and they bear a striking resemblance to broader narratives (including some of those produced by academics and researchers) of the possibilities offered in same-sex relationships. They are reflexively constructed – as are the relationships they are concerned with. In the end it is not *simply* stories of equality that are at stake, but stories that significantly shape the ways in which non-heterosexuals conceive of the possibilities of existing in couple relationships.

NOTE

1.   This chapter is based on research conducted for a project funded by the Economic and Social Research Council, entitled 'Families of Choice: the Structure and Meanings of Non-Heterosexual Relationships' (ref: L315253030). The director of the project was Jeffrey Weeks, with Catherine Donovan and Brian Heaphy as research fellows. The core of the research involved in-depth interviews with 48 men and 48 women who broadly identified as non-heterosexual (gay, lesbian, queer, bisexual and so on). All female interviews are denoted by 'F', male interviews by 'M'.

REFERENCES

Bech, H. (1992) 'Report from a Rotten State: "Marriage" and "Homosexuality", in "Denmark"', in K. Plummer (ed.), *Modern Homosexualities: Fragments of Lesbian and Gay Experience* (London: Routledge).

Benjamin, O. and Sullivan, O. (1996) 'The Importance of Difference: Conceptualising Increased Flexibility in Gender Relations at Home', *Sociological Review* 44(2), pp. 225–51.

Blasius, M. (1994) *Gay and Lesbian Politics: Sexuality and the Emergence of a New Ethic* (Philadelphia, PA: Temple University Press).

Blumstein, P. and Schwartz, P. (1983) *American Couples* (New York: William Morrow).

Connell, R. W. (1987) *Gender and Power* (Cambridge: Polity).

Connell, R. W. (1995) *Masculinities* (Cambridge: Polity).

Davies, P. (1992) 'The Role of Disclosure in Coming Out Among Gay Men', in K. Plummer (ed.), *Modern Homosexualities: Fragments of Lesbian and Gay Experience* (London: Routledge).

Dunne, G. A. (1997) *Lesbian Lifestyles: Women's Work and the Politics of Sexuality* (London: Macmillan).

Duncombe, J. and Marsden, D. (1993) 'Love and Intimacy: the Gender Division of Emotion and Emotion Work', *Sociology* 27(2), pp. 221–41.

Duncombe, J. and Marsden, D. (1996) 'Can we Research the Private Sphere? Methodological and Ethical Problems in the Study of the Role of Intimate Emotion in Personal Relationships', in L. Morris and S. Lyons (eds), *Gender Relations in Public and Private: Research Perspectives* (London: Macmillan).

Finch, J. and Mason, J. (1993) *Negotiating Family Responsibilities* (London: Routledge).

Giddens, A. (1992) *The Transformation of Intimacy: Sexuality, Love and Eroticism in Modern Societies* (Cambridge: Polity).

Hall Carpenter Archives (1989a) *Inventing Ourselves: Lesbian Life Stories* (London: Routledge).

Hall Carpenter Archives (1989b) *Walking After Midnight: Gay Men's Lifestories* (London: Routledge).

Harry, J. (1984) *Gay Couples* (New York: Praeger).

Harry, J. and DeVall, W. B. (1978) *The Social Organisation of Gay Males* (New York: Praeger).

Heaphy, B., Donovan, C. and Weeks, J. (1998) '"That's like my life": Researching Stories of Non-Heterosexual Relationships', *Sexualities*, 1(4), pp. 453–70.

Kehoe, M. (1988) 'Lesbians over 60 Speak for Themselves', *Journal of Homosexuality*, 16(3/4), pp. 1–111.

Johnson, S. E. (1990) *Staying Power: Long Term Lesbian Couples* (Tallahassee, FL: Naiad Press).

Mansfield, P. and Collard, J. (1988) *The Beginning of the Rest of Your Life? A Portrait of Newly-wed Marriage* (London: Macmillan).

McWhirter, D. and Mattison, A. M. (1984) *The Male Couple: How Relationships Develop* (Englewood Cliffs, NJ: Prentice Hall).

Mendola, M. (1980) *The Mendola Report: A New Look at Gay Couples in America* (New York: Crown).

Peplau, L. A. (1981) 'What Homosexuals Want in Relationships', *Psychology Today*, March, pp. 28–38.

Peplau, L. A., Venigas, R. C. and Miller Campbell, S. (1996) 'Gay and Lesbian Relationships', in R. C. Savin-Williams and K. M. Cohen (eds), *The Lives of Lesbians, Gays, and Bisexuals* (New York: Harcourt Brace College).

Plummer, K. (ed.) (1992) *Modern Homosexualities. Fragments of Lesbian and Gay Experience* (London: Routledge).

Plummer, K. (1995) *Telling Sexual Stories: Power, Change and Social Worlds* (London: Routledge).

Porter, K. and Weeks, J. (1990) *Between the Acts: Lives of Homosexual Men 1895–1967* (London: Routledge).

VanEvery, J. (1995) *Heterosexual Women Changing the Family: Refusing to be a 'Wife'* (London: Taylor & Francis).

Wan, M. (1995) *Building Social Capital: Self Help in the 21st Century Welfare State* (London: IPPR).

Weeks, J. (1995) *Invented Moralities: Sexual Values in an Age of Uncertainty* (Cambridge: Polity).

Weeks, J. (1996) 'The Idea of a Sexual Community', *Soundings*, 2, pp. 71–83.

Weeks, J., Donovan, C. and Heaphy, B. (1996) *Families of Choice: Patterns of Non-Heterosexual Relationships. A Literature Review*, Social Science Research Papers No. 2 (London: South Bank University).

Weston, K. (1991) *Families We Choose: Lesbians, Gays, Kinship* (New York: Columbia University Press).

11 'I Won't Let Her in my Room': Sibling Strategies of Power and Resistance around Computer and Video Games

Sara McNamee

Space is fundamental in any form of communal life; space is fundamental in any exercise of power.

(Foucault, in Rabinow, 1984: 252)

INTRODUCTION

This chapter examines issues of power and resistance around the ownership and use of computer and video games in domestic space. In particular I want to discuss the way in which domestic space has become contested space when both boys and girls are using the home as a leisure site. Domestic space has been considered the province of girls and women. From the adolescent 'bedroom culture' to the housewife watching soaps, women's leisure has traditionally been seen as taking place within the home. However, my work is beginning to show that the leisure of boys and young men is increasingly based around the home rather than out on the streets and, more particularly, is located in the bedroom and around the computer (see also Wheelock, 1992). The question arises, therefore, what happens to those whose space that traditionally is? How does this shift in the siting of boys' leisure affect the traditional site of girls' leisure? An examination of the activities and regulation of children and young people in domestic space has been missing from the literature around the sociology of the family, the sociology of leisure, and from studies of childhood and youth. Such work is useful when looking at what McRobbie (1994) has called the 'dignity of the specific' – that is to say, the micropractices of power in everyday life.

THE STUDY

The fieldwork on which this chapter draws took place between 1994 and 1995 in the East Riding of Yorkshire. A questionnaire survey was carried out with children aged between 8 and 18 ($n = 1600$) in one primary and two secondary schools. In the primary school all the children ($n = 50$) aged between 8 and 11 completed a questionnaire, and at the secondary schools all pupils present on a particular day were given a questionnaire to complete. In addition to this, around 60 in-depth interviews were carried out with groups of children aged between five and sixteen. Some parents were also interviewed although, due to the low response rate from parents, it should be noted that the material gathered from these interviews cannot be generalized. Rather, the value of this material lies in the insights this material provides.

In the main, the material on which I draw in this chapter was gathered from children aged between 11 and 18 in two secondary schools, one of which was in a leafy middle-class area of a city, the other in a rural, mainly working-class, area. What I want to do is first to draw out some of the survey results in order to illustrate the general patterns of gendered ownership and use of computer and video games, and then to discuss these in relation to the interview material and the existing literature. Drawing on questionnaire and interview material I argue that the examination of a particular leisure activity – in this case the playing of computer and video games – can illuminate wider issues of parental and sibling control of children and young people's leisure in the home. More specifically, it allows us to see the ways in which the leisure time and space of girls and young women is subject to ever-increasing control.

GENDERED OWNERSHIP AND USE OF COMPUTERS AND VIDEO GAMES

This study found that there was little difference between girls and boys in liking to play video games – 95 per cent of girls and 98 per cent of boys said that they liked to play. Differences appear when the children and young people in the study are asked how frequently they play – boys reported playing every day or most days 35 per cent more than girls. Such gender differences in the extent of playing computer and video games has often been noted in the literature (see, for example, Kubey and Larson, 1990), but reasons as to why this might be have not so far been fully examined, although some writers have attributed this gender difference to the content of the games themselves (Provenzo, 1991). I intend to show that there are several, often intermingled, reasons why girls do not play as much as boys. The first reason I want to discuss is that boys own more machines than girls do.

We can see from Table 11.1 that while half of the computers and video game machines in the homes of those who took part in the survey are either owned by other family members or are shared with the respondent and a family member, over 35 per cent are owned exclusively by boys compared with only 14.9 per cent owned by girls. Kath and Bill, parents of one boy and two girls aged between 10 and 14, seem to be in disagreement about who the computer in their house was for:

S.M.:   And who did you buy it for – was it for all of them or was it
          ...
KATH: We bought it for Paul. It was more ... he came with us to
          buy it ...
BILL: [*talking over Kath*] ... it was a joint present, but the girls
          have argued that it was for Paul.

Kath's description of the computer being more for their son because 'he came with us to buy it' is illuminating when considered alongside

Table 11.1 'Who owns the machines in your house?' (whole sample: girls $n = 725$, boys $n = 825$)

Other family members/shared machines	49.9%
Boys own outright	35.2%
Girls own outright	14.9%
Total	100%
Total number of machines owned	2802

the following extract from an interview with 7-year-old Alan and Julia. I asked them who played the video game machines in their house:

ALAN: My sister isn't allowed, only my brother is.

S.M.:   Why?

ALAN: Cos she was asleep when we went out shopping with my mum and bought the Sega.

S.M.:   So she's not allowed to play? Who says she can't play? Do you say she can't play?

ALAN: Yeah.

S.M.:   And what does your mum say?

ALAN: 'She is!'

S.M.:   [*laughing*] and you still won't let her?

ALAN: No!

S.M.:   Well! [*Alan giggles*]

S.M.:   And does she want to play it as well? [*Alan nods*] Does she get upset?

ALAN: Yeah.

JULIA: I bet!

S.M.:   But you still won't let her? [*Alan shakes head, smiling*]

'Being there' when the computer is bought seems to be used here as a strategy for excluding siblings – often sisters. At 7 years old, Alan is confident that he can justify excluding his sister from playing with the computer game. That computers tend to be bought for sons rather than daughters has been discussed previously. Gailey informs us that in her study, and in others she had reviewed, 'almost all the parents claimed to have bought the Nintendo sets for their children, particularly their sons' (1993: 85–6; see also Wajcman, 1991: 153; Wheelock, 1992). What is more, as the following discussion of the survey material illustrates, girls are also subject to more control as to when and where they can play computer and video games than are boys.

VIDEO GAMES IN FAMILIES

Those taking part in the survey were asked 'Who decides when and where you play computer and video games?' In the main, both boys and girls report that they decide when and where they play computer and video games. However, girls report being controlled in their

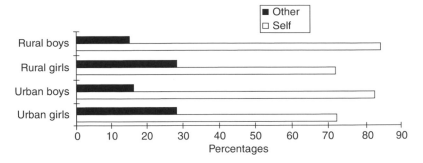

Figure 11.1 'Who decides when and where you can play computer and video games?' (variables recoded into 'self' and 'other'). All secondary school pupils. (Whole sample: boys n = 825, girls n = 725. Rural children: boys n = 386, girls n = 310; urban children: boys n = 405, girls n = 349)

access to the games and machines 12 per cent more overall than boys are – this relates to around 100 of those girls who filled in a questionnaire. This is demonstrated in Figure 11.1.

To some extent, then, both boys and girls are controlled in their access to computer and video games. I turn now to a discussion of this notion of control and elaborate it by taking into account family composition. Tables 11.2, 11.3, 11.4 and 11.5 examine four

Table 11.2   'Who decides when and where you can play?': by family with mixed siblings, sex and location

	Mixed siblings			
	Rural children		Urban children	
Who decides?	*Girls (%)*	*Boys (%)*	*Girls (%)*	*Boys (%)*
I do	71.6	78.8	73.4	77.6
Parents	17.9	14.1	14.1	20.4
Sibling(s)	4.5	6.1	7.8	2.0
Someone else/multiple	6.0	1.0	4.7	0
Totals	100	100	100	100
	(n = 67)	(n = 99)	(n = 64)	(n = 98)

family types – those in which the respondent has both brothers and sisters (mixed siblings); those with brothers only, sisters only or with no siblings – and shows the relationships between family type, who decides when and where the child can play computer and video games, geographic location and sex of respondent.

While between 70 and 80 per cent of children with both brothers and sisters report that they decide for themselves when and where to play video games, there are still many children who have someone else decide for them. Where there are both brothers and sisters in the household, control over access to computer and video games is largely carried out by parents, especially for rural girls and urban boys. Sibling control is exercised most over rural boys and urban girls. This contrasts with Table 11.3, which shows what happens where there are no siblings.

In families in which the respondents have no siblings we have the highest rates of autonomy – especially for boys. Urban children, and especially urban girls, are controlled by their parents more than the rural children, but without siblings, both boys and girls are more able to decide for themselves when and where they can play. In families made up of girl children only, the results shown in Table 11.4 are found:

Table 11.3 'Who decides when and where you can play?': by family with no siblings, sex and location

	No siblings			
	Rural children		*Urban children*	
Who decides?	*Girls (%)*	*Boys (%)*	*Girls (%)*	*Boys (%)*
I do	87.2	93.6	80.0	91.2
Parents	7.7	2.1	14.3	8.8
Sibling(s)	0	0	0	0
Someone else/multiple	2.6	4.2	5.7	0
Totals	100	100	100	100
	(*n* = 39)	(*n* = 47)	(*n* = 35)	(*n* = 34)

Table 11.4   'Who decides when and where you can play?': by family with sisters only, sex and location

Who decides?	Sisters only			
	Rural children		Urban children	
	Girls (%)	Boys (%)	Girls (%)	Boys (%)
I do	73.7	86.9	74.8	89.1
Parents	19.7	11.1	18.9	8.8
Sibling(s)	2.6	0	2.7	1.5
Someone else/multiple	3.9	2.0	3.6	0.7
Totals	100	100	100	100
	(n = 76)	(n = 99)	(n = 111)	(n = 137)

Where there are sisters only, there is little sibling control. Girls with sisters are controlled more by parents than boys with sisters. There is little control by sisters for either girls or boys. Finally, Table 11.5 shows the data from families in which there are brothers only.

Where there are brothers only, girls have the least autonomy in their access to computers and video games, and are controlled heavily

Table 11.5   'Who decides when and where you can play?': by family with brothers only, sex and location

Who decides?	Brothers only			
	Rural children		Urban children	
	Girls (%)	Boys (%)	Girls (%)	Boys (%)
I do	65.6	84.1	67.7	80.6
Parents	16.4	12.1	17.7	14.7
Sibling(s)	15.6	2.3	13.1	0.8
Someone else/multiple	2.4	1.5	1.5	3.9
Totals	100	100	100	100
	(n = 122)	(n = 132)	(n = 130)	(n = 129)

by their brothers. Between 13 per cent and 15 per cent of girls state that their brothers decide when and where they can play, compared with only 0.8 per cent of urban boys and 2.3 per cent of rural boys who have brothers only.

Taking all four tables into account, parents do the least controlling when there are no siblings (Table 11.3). They are more involved in controlling girls, but not boys, when there are sisters only (Table 11.4). Girls are most controlled when there are brothers only (Table 11.4) and are most autonomous when there are no siblings (Table 11.3). This analysis shows that girls' access to computers and video games is controlled more than that of boys, and that much of this control is exerted by their brothers. This kind of control has also been noted by Wheelock, who informs us that: 'daughters are squeezed out of using the computer by their brothers, sometimes aided by their parents' (1992: 110).

GENDERED DOMESTIC SPACE

In an interview with parents in the urban area I asked Sue, a middle-class mother of three teenagers, who uses the computer most:

SUE: It tends to go in cycles ... and it tends to depend on where it is in the house. The first year we had it in the front room because I was doing my [unclear] and I had lots of work to do on the word processor, etc. My eldest son was doing his GCSEs and had coursework to do on it. The other two used it occasionally for word processing but they – the three children – mainly used it for video games. Since ... we've sort of re-vamped the front room and moved the desk out, and the table that the computer was on, it's now gone up into the loft which is our middle son's bedroom ... accessible to all of them ... the use of the games has gone down significantly since it's been up there ... So it's out of the way ... it's almost like out of sight, out of mind.

Sue might be right – it may be a case of 'out of sight, out of mind' but although she seems convinced that all the children can have free access to the computer, which is now in one of the boys' bedrooms, it might be more likely that this son controls his space efficiently, which may explain why the use of the computer for playing games has gone down in this family.

During the interview with Sue and her husband it became clear that, unless she was using the computer for her work, when she had priority use, her middle son used it the most, and her daughter used it the least. Mitchell discusses relations between family members based around the video game and informs us that:

> Videogame consoles were usually considered property to be shared by all members of the family. However, in families with sons, possession by the boys was considered appropriate; and sisters had to request permission for access to the games. When the games were located in a bedroom, instead of the living room or family room, it was always the boy's bedroom even though he may have been the younger of the siblings.   (1985: 129)

Sue also remarked that when the computer was downstairs, there were a lot of arguments over use:

S.M.:   Have there ever been any arguments about using it, between the kids?

SUE: Lots. Especially when it was down here. More so if they had friends in ... you know, 'well me and Julie want to play on it' or 'me and Ben' ...

Moving the machine has resolved the arguments, but it also means that use is mainly going to be decided by the son in whose bedroom it is situated. The following excerpt from Bill and Kath, two parents from the rural area, shows the ways in which consideration is sometimes given to the siting of computer and games machines in the home:

BILL: Well, Paul sometimes ... he gets the preferential in some respects 'cause ... I don't know, you tend to, it's the old fashioned ideas, innit, he's the only lad, and lads play with computers, girls play with dolls ... but ... it in't like that now. [pause] That's why, in a way ... originally it was going to go in the attic room, which was going to be Fiona's room and a shared room, in the other half of it, but that never worked out. Fiona dominated that room, so ... no way was the computer going up there.

It seems in this case that through negotiation the computer was sited in the shared space of the living room because of the potential for conflict if it had gone in Fiona's room as originally intended. Bill suggests that putting the computer into one of the girls' bedrooms would have meant that Paul would not get the 'preferential treatment' in terms of access to the machine to which, as 'the only lad', his parents believe he is entitled. These parents were keen throughout the interview to present their daughters as not being interested in using the computer, and I argue that their traditional notions of gender-appropriate behaviour might be one explanation. Table 11.6 draws on my questionnaire data to examine this gendered use of space in the home, for as Foucault stated; 'space is fundamental in any form of communal life; space is fundamental in any exercise of power' (1984: 252).

Table 11.6 shows the relationship between ownership of machine, sex of child and location of machine within the home. We can see that where the machine is owned by all the family, both boys and girls say that it is more likely to be kept in a family room. Conversely, when the young person her/himself owns the machine, it is more likely to be kept in a bedroom. In both these cases there is little difference between girls and boys, although girls are slightly more likely to say that their machines are kept in family rooms. When the machine is shared with a brother, however, we can see that, for girls, this has an effect on where the machine is kept: almost 20 per cent more girls than boys who share a machine with their brother say that the shared machine is kept in a family room, while girls who share a machine with a brother keep it in their own bedrooms 25 per cent less than boys who share a machine with a brother. This can also be seen in the last column of Table 11.6, which shows that, when a machine is shared with a sister, boys sharing the machine with a sister are more likely to keep it in their own bedroom while girls who share with a sister keep their machine in a family room.

Where machines are located in a family room, use of them is automatically subject to more control. Because many games consoles need to be connected to a TV set, play can take place only with agreement from other family members using the room. For example, one 11-year-old girl explained that she could not use her computer (which was located in the living room) to play games at the weekend because her mother used that room at that time for ironing the weekly wash. In addition, many games contain repetitive music:

Table 11.6 Ownership of machine by sex and siting of machine in the home (figures are percentages and do not add to 100)

	Who owns it?										
	All the family		'I own it'		Shared with brother		Shared with sister	
	Girls (n = 188)	Boys (n = 185)	Girls (n = 409)	Boys (n = 966)	Girls (n = 61)	Boys (n = 118)	Girls (n = 44)	Boys (n = 34)
Where is it?								
Family room	62.7	54.6	19.0	14.2	37.8	16.8	34.2	25.5
Unspecified bedroom	22.8	27.5	41.8	43.2	44.2	43.2	34.1	38.3
My bedroom	10.6	12.4	36.7	40.1	8.2	33.9	18.2	29.4

MARY: If we feel that he's using them over much then he's told to come off. He isn't allowed to play. He isn't allowed to play with the hand held game gear particularly when we're around because it irritates us.

S.M.: The noise?

MARY: Yes. Extremely irritating.

STRATEGIES OF POWER AND RESISTANCE BETWEEN SIBLINGS

The quotation used in the title of this chapter is from Phil, a 14-year-old from the urban school and who has a younger sister with whom he shares a Nintendo games machine. Phil's description of what happens in his house around computer and video games demonstrates the effect on his sister of keeping a shared machine in his room:

S.M.: You've got a sister, Phil. You said that your Nintendo was shared with her – do you ever fight about going on it?

PHIL: Well, it's always kept in my room and there's a lot of arguments because I won't let her on it because it's in my room. I won't let her in my room.

S.M.: Did you say your sister was older or younger?

PHIL: Younger.

S.M.: How much younger?

PHIL: Ermm, she's 11.

S.M.: So you won't let her in your room, you won't let her play on it?

PHIL: She likes different types of games to me so if I let her, she ... like ... she [unclear].

S.M.: [...]Does she ever complain to your mum about it?

PHIL: Yeah. She starts getting real annoyed and that and starts saying 'Oh well, that's it now. Next time I'm gonna trash your room' and all this lot.

S.M.: What does your mum say?

Phil: She tells us both to pack it in. She usually blames it on me sister.

S.M.: Does she? Does she ever threaten to take it off you?

PHIL: Yeah. She has done a couple of times.

S.M.: Why? For fighting?

PHIL: She says it causes nothing but problems.

It is not only, as Mitchell (1985) suggests, that the machines are always located in a boy's bedroom, although Table 11.6 shows clearly that boys are more likely to have these items in their rooms, but that for girls computers and video games are more likely to be located in shared space – in family rooms rather than their bedrooms. Girls' use of these items in shared space means that they have to negotiate use of that space with other family members, as discussed above. The issue of space is important for an understanding of gender relations, as Massey (1994) points out. She says:

> space and place, spaces and places, and our senses of them ... are gendered through and through. Moreover they are gendered in a myriad different ways, which vary between the cultures and over time. And this gendering of space and place both reflects *and has effects back on* the ways in which gender is constructed and understood in the societies in which we live.   (1994: 186; emphasis in original)

In an interview with a group of teenage girls at the urban school, 14-year-old Jenny revealed that her 8-year-old brother has the power to prevent her from playing with their shared machine:

S.M.:   Do you have brothers and sisters?
ALL: Yeah.
S.M.:   And do you have to share your machines usually?
JENNY: Yeah, you can't get him off it.
S.M.:   Is that your brother?
JENNY: He brings all his friends round and they get it set up [unclear] you can't get in.
S.M.:   How old is he?
JENNY: 8.
S.M.:   If he's on it and if you ever want to go on it will he let you go on?
JENNY: No.
S.M.:   Do you ever fight?
JENNY: Yeah. [*laughter*]

Although she is the eldest in the family, Jenny has to use physical force to gain access to the machine in her home. Nick, a 15-year-old from the rural school, has two younger sisters. I asked him if they ever wanted to play on his video game machine:

NICK: Sometimes they want to …
S.M.: Do you let them?
NICK: Yeah.
S.M.: You don't ever fight then?
NICK: Depends. Depends whether I want a go.
S.M.: So if you want to use it, you come first?
NICK: Yeah.

During the interviews with children and parents, many examples of such conflict were reported to me (for further discussion see McNamee, 1997). Disputes ranged from damaging each others' property to physical violence and verbal abuse. Often parents (and especially mothers) were called upon to resolve disputes. Power and resistance can been seen in action in disputes over access to computer and video games.

CONCLUDING THOUGHTS: POWER/RESISTANCE IN GENDERED LEISURE

In this chapter I have suggested that boys tend to personally own computers and video game consoles more than do girls, and boys tend to play on these machines more often than girls. Even when computers and video games are shared between brothers and sisters they are located in particular spaces within the home where they become appropriated by the boys in the family, or where girls cannot freely have access to them. I have shown that boys' use of leisure space in the home is less constrained than that of girls' and that this constraint on girls' use of the home for this particular leisure activity is compounded in that their brothers are controlling their access to leisure in the form of computer and video games. I argued in the introduction to this chapter that an examination of the activities and regulation of girls and boys in domestic space allows us to see the micropractices of power in everyday life: 'Foucault enables us to understand power very broadly, and yet very finely, as anchored in the multiplicity of what he calls "micropractices", the social practices that constitute everyday life in modern societies' (Fraser, 1989: 18). This chapter, then, shows the ways in which the power to control girls' leisure activities and space in the home is exercised, contested and resisted.

REFERENCES

Foucault, M. (1984) 'Space, Knowledge and Power', in P. Rabinow (ed.), *The Foucault Reader* (London: Penguin).

Fraser, N. (1989) *Unruly Practices: Power, Discourse and Gender in Contemporary Social Theory* (Cambridge: Polity).

Gailey, C. W. (1993) 'Mediated Messages: Gender, Class and Cosmos in Home Video Games', *Journal of Popular Culture*, 27(1), pp. 81–97.

Kubey, R. and Larson, R. (1990) 'The Use and Experience of the New Video Media among Children and Young Adolescents', *Communication Research*, 17(1), pp. 107–10.

Massey, D. (1994) *Space, Place and Gender* (Cambridge: Polity).

McNamee, S. (1997) 'Youth Gender and Video Games: Power and Control in the Home', in G. Valentine and T. Skelton (eds), *Cool Places: Geographies of Youth Cultures* (London: Routledge).

McRobbie, A. (1994) *Postmodernism and Popular Culture* (London: Routledge).

Mitchell, E. (1985) 'The Dynamics of Family Interaction around Home Videogames', *Marriage and Family Review*, 8(1/2), (special issue, *Personal Computers and the Family*, pp. 121–35).

Provenzo, E. F. (1991) *Video Kids: Making Sense of Nintendo* (Cambridge, MA: Harvard University Press).

Wacjman, J. (1991) *Feminism Confronts Technology* (Cambridge: Polity).

Wheelock, J. (1992) 'Personal Computers, Gender and an Institutional Model of the Household', in R. Silverstone and E. Hirsch (eds), *Consuming Technologies: Media and Information in Domestic Spaces* (London: Routledge).

12 Prostitutes, Ponces and Poncing: Making Sense of Violence

Jo Phoenix

INTRODUCTION

This chapter examines the contradictory ways in which women engaged in prostitution make sense of 'poncing' relationships (i.e. intimate relationships between men and prostitute-women within which the practice of financial exploitation (often) via threat of violence occurs). It is divided into five sections. In the first section I address the way in which previous academic work on ponces, poncing and prostitutes has made sense of the phenomena with particular attention paid to the conceptual framework within which the issues are debated. The second section outlines some of the empirical realities of poncing, the effects of these upon the women who experience them and the ways that individual prostitute-women have talked about the men who financially exploited and abused them. In the third section I briefly describe the protocols for analysis that I adopted when analysing the empirical data collected. The fourth section explores and explains the contradictory and multiple ways in which prostitute-women have made sense of their exploitative and abusive intimate relationships. By way of conclusion I offer a few thoughts on the implications of the arguments contained in this chapter – especially in terms of the question of resistance.

Relationships between prostitutes and men who financially exploit and abuse them have been stereotyped as relationships between sadistic abusers and young and vulnerable women; as relationships between prostitutes and their boyfriends; and as business relationships between prostitutes and their managers. The British legal framework, via Sections 22(1) and 30(1) of the Sexual Offences Act 1956 which criminalize male procurers and men living off 'immoral earnings', construct the prostitute/ponce relationship as, first and foremost, a coercive relationship (cf. Rook and Ward, 1997). Ponces and poncing are contested issues within research on prostitution in that researchers have argued that they are: manifestations of men's ability to control women (Barry, 1979), legal fictions by which the State can further harass and criminalize prostitutes (cf. Pheterson, 1993) and/or ordinary relationships which are perceived to be different because they occur within the context of prostitution (Hoigard and Finstad, 1992).

There are two arguments in this chapter. The first argument is specific to prostitution-related debates and in particular to how we understand and conceptualize poncing (i.e. the practice of financial exploitation of prostitutes which occurs within specific, sometimes intimate relationships and is often, but not necessarily, accompanied by threats, violence and intimidation), ponces (i.e. the men who practise poncing) and prostitutes' relationships with them. The argument contained herein is that neither the men nor the practice is 'simply' known and identified via specifying and defining particular forms of behaviour (i.e., taking prostitutes' money, physically or sexually assaulting prostitutes, controlling, dominating or brutalizing prostitutes and so on) as poncing. Rather, ponces and poncing are known and constructed at the symbolic level. Therefore, the same set of behaviours (for example punching a woman and taking her money) are understood in multiple, diverse and contradictory ways, as are the men who abuse and exploit prostitutes. Hence, as will be demonstrated below, the behaviour of a man to a prostitute with whom he has an intimate relationship (i.e. punching her and taking all or some of her money) is understood as both a business practice *and* victimization. The men who do these actions are understood as business partners, abusers *and* boyfriends. In short, the same actions are made sense of differently. The men and their behaviours signify nothing in themselves; they become meaningful only within specific contexts and underpinned by particular sets of meanings.

The second argument of this chapter is a more general argument relating to how we conceptualize violence. Following the logic outlined above, if specified forms of behaviour or actions come to be understood as exploitation and abuse by those who experience them only within specific symbolic landscapes, then there is nothing self-evident about violence either. Violence, like poncing, is not entirely identifiable as an action (or actions) which are easily objectively known. Such an argument is not new. Early feminist work concerning domestic violence demonstrated how the same actions of men (i.e. punching someone) carried out in different contexts (i.e. in the home or on the streets) come to take on fundamentally different meanings (cf. Dunhill, 1988). I will return to the implications of arguing that there are no single, uniform or even clear meanings of violence, at the end of this chapter, for it has a profound impact on how we begin to think about resistance.

This chapter draws on work that was conducted for a wider research project that sought to understand the conditions in which women are sustained within prostitution. Questions were asked about how it was possible for prostitutes to make sense of their involvement in prostitution given that they experienced that involvement in contradictory ways, and given that the stories they elaborated, which were put forward as justificatory explanations, were paradoxical. Overall, it was an ethnography of how some women, who existed within tremendously adverse economic and social conditions, were able to accommodate the contradictions of their lives and survive their poverty. It argued that engagement in prostitution became meaningful via the construction of a prostitute-identity which was underpinned by two specific but shifting sets of meanings for 'men', 'money' and 'violence' (Phoenix, 1997). This chapter uses the empirical data collected for that project. Twenty-one life historical interviews were conducted in MidCity during 1994 with prostitute-women. The women who were interviewed were either currently working as prostitutes when the interviews took place, or had been working in the 18 months preceding the date of interview. They worked primarily from the streets, in their own homes and in saunas, parlours and brothels. Twenty were white women and one was of mixed parentage. The respondents' ages ranged between 18 and 44 years old and they had been involved in prostitution between 9 months and 27 years. The women were contacted through the use of two gate-keepers (one from a sexual health outreach project and one from a probation-ran drop-in centre run specifically for women involved in prostitution, although used by other offending women as well).

In general, prior to their engagement in prostitution these women's lives were shattered and fractured by the aggregate consequences of poverty, unemployment, living on social security benefits, being single parents, growing up in Local Authority Care, physical and sexual abuse by their carers (i.e. parents, foster-carers, etc.) and/or their partners, and homelessness and housing difficulties. Since being engaged in prostitution the respondents had had extensive experience of financial exploitation, continuous arrest, prostitution-structured and prostitution-enforced poverty, violence and housing problems. Indeed, for these women, involvement in prostitution produced contradictory effects because, although engaging in prostitution provided them with a means to attain some degree of economic and social stability, it also threatened their material existence and at times their very lives (Phoenix, 1999).

PONCES, PONCING AND PROSTITUTES

Earlier prostitution-related research which was interested in ponces (or pimps)[1] and poncing tended to focus on the extent to which individual prostitutes are or are not ponced. Thus, Barry (1979) contended that 90 per cent of all American street-working prostitutes were being pimped, whereas others argued that such a figure represented a gross over-estimation (cf. Alexander (1988), who claimed that the 'true' figure was in the region of 30–40 per cent). Others still argued that such crude quantification falsely grouped together the managers or partners of prostitutes, hotel managers renting rooms to prostitutes, parents who may receive money from prostitutes, grown-up children still dependent on their prostitute-mothers with the men who coerce women into being or staying involved in prostitution in order to exploit the earnings they make (cf. Pheterson, 1993). In the late 1990s, however, it is largely agreed that trying to quantify, accurately, the phenomenon of poncing (and ponces) is an impossible task for a variety of (mainly methodological) reasons, not least of which is the hidden nature of poncing (Faugier and Sargeant, 1997).

Even though the goal of quantification has been abandoned, the debate it engendered opened up a very important theoretical space which permitted writers, academics and campaigners to discuss what was meant by the terms ponce and poncing in ways which were not based in and upon strictly legal definitions (i.e. of men living off 'immoral earnings'; cf. Rook and Ward, 1997). It is this debate, and in particular the manner in which it has produced polarized ways of thinking, that forms the wider context of this chapter.

There are two conceptions that frame current research and writing about ponces and poncing. Firstly, there is a theoretical demarcation that various writers have invoked between boyfriends and ponces. The assumption is that boyfriends are not ponces and ponces are not boyfriends, because a boyfriend (or partner) is not, by definition, an exploitative abuser, whereas ponces are. Thus, McKeganey and Barnard (1996) asserted that the men who were present in the red-light area of Glasgow when they did their ethnography of prostitution and who would 'often take ... money [from prostitutes] as it was earned to reduce the potential for a woman to be mugged and lose the money' (McKeganey and Barnard, 1996: 18) were partners and *thus* were not ponces. Similarly, Hoigard and Finstad (1992), in their research into prostitution in Oslo, argued that the extent of pimping is greatly exaggerated in Norwegian public debate precisely because the pimp is a stereotype. For the most part, they opined: 'He is not a pimp. He is a boyfriend' (Hoigard and Finstad, 1992: 159). Within the English context, O'Neill (1996, 1997) argued that ponces are not usually partners or grown-up children, despite the manner in which the law does not distinguish between different categories of individuals who economically gain from the income of prostitutes, but rather criminalizes them equally (O'Neill, 1997: 20).

Ponces and poncing have also been conceptualized in terms of a continuum from the 'heavy ponce' (i.e. the prototypical villain who coerces vulnerable women into prostitution and subsequently uses violence (and drugs) to control and exploit them) through to the individual boyfriend/partner of a prostitute woman, or 'passive ponce' (cf. McLeod (1982), who discussed passive ponces as partners who do not work and so literally live off the earnings of their prostitute girl-friends or wives, but who also exercise no control over them, are not violent, do not intimidate them and so on) (see also Scambler and Scambler, 1997; Scambler, 1997). Faugier and Sargeant (1997) note that, in an earlier ethnography of street prostitutes, Eleanor Miller (1995), for example, distinguished between ordinary men and ponces according to the number of prostitutes they have. Thus a ponce is a man who is involved with a number of prostitutes, and is not loyal or monogamous with just one.

Drawing a line of demarcation between ponces and boyfriends opened a very interesting theoretical space in which it became possible for various writers to pursue the question of difference in a more detailed fashion. To wit, if ponces are, by definition, not boyfriends, then the question arises as to what are the differences between these two categories of men, and what are the differences between the relationships of prostitutes and ponces and the relationships of prosti-tutes and boyfriends. Unfortunately, the theoretical space that opens as a result of conceptualizing ponces as different from boyfriends has ultimately been foreclosed by analyses which have conflated the indivi-dual men (i.e. ponces) with the practices of poncing. To put it more simply, the question of difference has been answered by various writers within the past two decades, but only in terms of what it is that ponces *do* that is different from what it is that boyfriends/partners do (i.e. ponces exploit, control, dominate and abuse prostitutes). Within such a conceptual framework, examination of the phenomenon is focused upon the actions and behaviours that are apparent in any particular relationship. Analysis of ponces, poncing and prostitutes is thereby limited to investigating the 'quality' and 'type' of relationship that exists between the women and their ponces. And, in a polarized manner, researchers have argued that the relationship that exists between prostitutes and their ponces is either a 'false' intimate relationship characterized by abuse and exploitation or a 'true' intimate relationship. In short, the ponce/prostitute relationship is seen as being a manifestation of men's ability to control women and epiphenomenal to wider patriarchal social structures (McLeod, 1982; O'Neill, 1996), *or* as being an intimate relationship whose everyday realities correspond to those of other non-prostitution-related relationships (Hoigard and Finstad, 1992).

The understanding of the prostitute/ponce relationship as a manifestation of male sexual violence and men's ability to control women can be seen in Barry's (1979, 1995) work wherein she described in detail the strategies by which potential ponces give the impression of care and love for the women they ponce. For her, the poncing relationship is constituted by, and within, the sexual exploitation of the individual prostitutes. Barry (1995) invited an analysis which placed the type and quality of the relationship between individual men and prostitutes in the foreground. She argued that the real question when analysing a relationship is whether or not, and to what extent, the relationship is characterized by the sexual commodification and exploitation of the prostitute – regardless of how the individuals make sense of their relationships. Within such a theoretical framework, Barry (1979) showed how the care that a ponce displays is merely a ploy to entrap an otherwise lonely and vulnerable woman into prostitution. In a similar vein, Faugier and Sargeant (1997) argued firstly that ponces range from men who 'merely' exploit women to men who keep women in a state of 'female sexual slavery'. Secondly, they argued that within the contemporary British context of an institution of prostitution which increasingly feels the impact of crack cocaine addiction, individual ponces are becoming rarer. Instead, the drug men who sell prostitutes crack cocaine have become the new ponces. Faugier and Sargeant (1997) were clear, however, that while the individualized nature of the poncing relationship may have changed – specifically, the control of prostitutes is no longer achieved via a one-to-one relationship, but via the highly gendered relations of illicit drug culture – prostitute/ponce relationships are relationships in which individual women are controlled and exploited by men. They wrote: 'the development of the drug as pimp has provided men with a new means of status attainment through the sexual degradation of women' (Faugier and Sargeant, 1997: 126). In other words the relationship that exists between ponces and prostitutes is, in type, an exploitative, degrading relationship in which prostitute-women are controlled and dominated by their drug men. For both Barry (1979, 1995) and for Faugier and Sargeant (1997), the focus of analysis is the objectively known behaviour of ponces (i.e. do they assault, abuse or otherwise subordinate the women?).

In a similar way, conceptualizations of the prostitute/ponce relationship as an intimate relationship which corresponds in all important respects to other, non-prostitution-related intimate relationships are also based upon the conflation of individual men (i.e. ponces) and the practice of poncing. Hoigard and Finstad (1992) provide the clearest example. In their study they devoted an entire chapter (entitled *'Whatever Happened to the Pimp?'*) to understanding poncing, ponces, prostitutes and the relationships between them. The majority of the chapter is a simple description of all the different types of intimate relationships that prostitutes have with men. The categorizations are based on the behaviour and actions of the men. Hoigard and Finstad (1992) described the relationships with (i) non-violent boyfriend–pimps which they defined as characterized by joint economic decision-making; (ii) violent boyfriend–pimps which Hoigard and Finstad (1992) asserted were relationships that loosely resemble all other relationships that are marked by men's violence and abuse; (iii) sex pimps, which they see as being relationships characterized by a brief sexual attraction that exists between pimp and prostitute; (iv) stable pimps, which Hoigard and Finstad (1992) asserted are rare relationships that closely mirror those of the stereotypical prostitute/ponce relationship wherein ponces use violence to completely dominate prostitute-women; and (v) sex-club pimps, which they claimed are even rarer relationships in which several women work for one man simultaneously (Hoigard and Finstad, 1992: 141–60). After a close and detailed examination of each of the relationships in terms of what behaviours the men engage in, Hoigard and Finstad concluded that the majority of intimate relationships that prostitutes have with men, which are also marked by a degree of economic exchange, are not necessarily poncing relationships because the quality of such relationships is the same as any ordinary love relationship. It is worth quoting them at length to demonstrate the manner in which, within their analysis, they maintain a line of demarcation between pimps and boyfriends whilst simultaneously conflating the behaviours of individual pimps with the category pimp.

> We have shown that the women we interviewed do not see their partner as a pimp. He is a boyfriend or a husband. And that is something totally different. Being a couple – that is, literally, sharing a common fate. What is more natural than for two lovers to help each other? ... A love relationship is a *real* relationship. ... But relationships based on love don't have to be perfect; not among 'normal' people either. ... In a male-dominated society such as ours, the woman in a relationship will often be subject to oppression from her male partner. Relationships among those working in prostitution are similar to other love relationships. For better or worse. Prostitutes can be oppressed by their men too – not because they are prostitutes, but because they are women.   (Hoigard and Finstad, 1992: 169)

Thus, Hoigard and Finstad (1992) erased most pimping relationships by saying that the specified set of behaviours traditionally associated with pimping and pimps are also present in a normal relationship.

However, Hoigard and Finstad (1992) did not argue that no pimps exist. They simply deployed a different set of specified behaviours from which it is possible to delineate the pimp. Instead of identifying pimps as men who are merely violent and/or sexually exploitative, for Hoigard and Finstad pimps are men who use violence *for the purpose of wielding power* in a fashion that makes a women's choice about her involvement in prostitution an anathema. In arguing accordingly, Hoigard and Finstad (1992) did not displace the conceptual framework of most work on ponces, poncing and prostitutes, but they did add a new complexity to the level of analysis of prostitutes' intimate relationships. They contended that relationships of the same 'quality' (i.e. violent and marked by exploitation) might not be of the same 'type' (i.e. they might be poncing relationships or ordinary love relationships within a patriarchal context). The line of demarcation is drawn not simply in terms of specific actions men engage in, but is also drawn in relation to the *purpose* and *intention* of such violence or exploitation.

My argument with contemporary research on poncing is not whether or not the findings of various projects are correct or incorrect, or whether or not the relationships that are identified by the researchers are, in fact, poncing relationships. Rather, current ways of thinking about ponces, poncing and prostitutes, while arising from some very interesting lines of questions, remain locked within an either/or analysis resulting from: (i) the conflation of the category ponce with the practices of poncing and (ii) conceiving of ponces as, by definition, not partners. The logic of current writing is that either ponces are ponces, *or* they are boyfriends. A man is either a ponce *or* not, according to whether or not he engages in specific actions such as violence, exploitation, completely dominating a woman and so on. The result of invoking an either/or analysis of the phenomenon is that the space to make visible, much less explain, the complex and contra-dictory ways that the women, themselves, talk about ponces and the practices of poncing is eclipsed. However, by maintaining a line of demarcation between ponces (as a category of men) and poncing (as a specific set of practices within prostitution wherein prostitutes are financially exploited and often abused) and by collapsing the demarca- tion between partners and ponces, the space is opened in which an understanding of ponces as exploitative abusers, business partners *and* loving partners can be achieved.

THE EMPIRICAL REALITIES OF PONCES, PONCING AND PROSTITUTES

One of the most striking features to arise from the empirical investiga-tion (and regardless of how the empirical realities were made sense of by the interviewees) was the extent to which the respondents were, in reality, financially exploited by men with whom they had had relation-ships and who used violence, threats, intimidation and coercion to secure such exploitation. Indeed, all but two of the 21 respondents recounted that at some point during their engagement in prostitution they had had persistent experiences of the practice of poncing.

For the women who took part in my research, the empirical reality of the practice of poncing was that these women often gave up (or had taken from them) most of their money, which had the effect of dramatically increasing the women's already-existing poverty. Lois' and Ruthie's experiences were typical.

I never seen a penny of the money I earned. I was only given two pound fifty a day. He even took my social money off me as well. ... Two pound fifty and it's hard when you're out there from 10: 00 in the morning till any time up to about 9: 00 at night. You've got two pound fifty and you've gotta decide which is more important, cigarettes, condoms or food?   (Lois, aged 21)

When I started working every penny went to him. Every penny! I was given a fiver, like, for a packet of Durex and 20 fags or something. Sometimes he bought things for me from the money he had off me – I was thinking 'Oh, all these nice new clothes.' But he was spending my money on clothes to make me look nicer. When I look back now, I think I was fucking stupid.   (Ruthie, aged 25)

Part of the practice of poncing was the threats, violence and intimidation that was used as a strategy by the men to achieve the exploitation of their prostitute-women partners. All of the 19 women who talked about being ponced also talked about violence. They told desperate tales of being forced to work until they earned enough money to satisfy the demands of their ponces, of having their money taken from them under threat of violence and of being continuously and regularly beaten, hit, kicked, slapped or punched (or, at the very least, threatened with being hit, slapped, kicked or punched). Indeed, six women recounted that they had been sadistically beaten (which occasionally left them hospitalized), raped (not just by the individual boyfriend, but also by his friends), held captive and/or threatened or assaulted with weapons such as knives and guns.

Counter-intuitively, the women did not necessarily constitute the men who did these things to them as ponces, even though these men and the nature of the relationships the women had with them may have greatly resembled the stereotype of ponces and being ponced. And while the respondents did occasionally speak of ponces, and of their poncing relationships, they also spoke of these men as boyfriends, partners, lovers, and their relationships as intimate relationships. Importantly (and contrary to the theoretical framework outlined earlier in this chapter) what the interviewees did *not* do was distinguish between ponces and boyfriends in terms of the practice of financial exploitation or violence. Such demarcations as were made, were made at a symbolic level. Thus, ponces were constituted by, and within, a complex web of meanings that enables the construction of the practices of financial exploitation achieved via the threat of violence as poncing and the individuals that engage in such actions as being ponces. An examination of the manner in which the interviewees used the term ponce will be both illustrative of this point and help to contextualize the ensuing analysis.

The interviewees used the term ponce in two distinct (but ultimately inter-related) ways. First, they used the term ponce to signify the men with whom they were involved, who financially exploited them and who may have used violence, coercion and intimidation and/or love and charm in order to achieve such exploitation. But the term was more often used in an imaginary, symbolic fashion to represent the dangers of engagement in prostitution. In this respect ponces occupied a pivotal position in the respondents' symbolic landscape, for the image of the ponce contained all of the assumed (and actual) threats to the women's survival. In short, ponces were discussed as though they were sadistically violent men who would kidnap and entrap the women, take all of their money, treat (and trade) prostitute-women like chattel property, and from whom there was no sanctuary, escape or evasion.

A ponce makes a girl stand out there and if she hasn't raised the money he wants, he beats her up and sends her back. They don't live with the girls and they've got about eight or nine girls all over the streets and one's for his petrol and the other's for his food and the other's for his clothes and that's the way it goes.

(Helena, aged 35)

A ponce is someone that beats up a woman and takes every penny she earns – her and a half a dozen others. That's how he gets his money. (Janet, aged 37)

This imaginary, notional construction of ponces was made possible by the women's implicit deployment of particular discourses of (i) masculine criminality and (ii) masculine violence which constitute certain men in terms of being 'tough' and 'alien' and which conjoin in the expression being 'bad' (cf. Katz, 1988: 80–113). These discourses position ponces as 'not only not here for others, but native to some morally alien world' (Katz, 1988: 113) and as outsiders to ordinary morality. Ponces, accordingly, are constituted as being interested only in what they can get for themselves.

Ponces don't give a shit about you – they only care about what they can get for themselves, how much money you'll earn them.

(Sammy, aged 18)

Ponces are not like other men. They ain't got no heart – they only ever want money. Like once there was this young girl, she had a ponce and he used to beat her up all the time, man! There was one time she hurt her leg really, really badly and we told him to take her to the hospital. He wouldn't. He shoved her back on the street and she fell, running for a punter, and she couldn't get up, her leg was that bad. All he could say was 'Oh leave her! She's gotta earn money.' Now that's a ponce, a big bad man who doesn't give a shit.   (Helena, aged 35)

In addition to accepting and deploying these discourses, the women also accepted discourses which essentialize male violence through constituting men as though they are always and already (at least potentially) violent, and violence as always masculine (cf. Segal, 1990; Kersten, 1996). Deploying both sets of discourses permitted the women to talk about the imaginary ponces as *essentially* violent and predatory individuals, preying on the women's money through financial exploitation and violence.

What you gotta understand is that he was a PONCE. I mean, if I didn't make enough, he'd send me back out. He was the proper order ponce. He wanted – I got, and if I didn't he'd kill me.
                                                        (Ingrid, aged 44)

After I killed my ponce I realised that it weren't really his fault that he was like that. [*Like what?*] Well, beating up on me, raping me, making me have sex with dogs and shit, taking all my money. Some men are just like that – I think it's in their nature. The one thing I've learned through all this is that you gotta steer clear of ponces. It's just too dangerous to get involved with them.   (Anna, aged 36)

PROTOCOLS FOR ANALYSIS – SUSPENDING AUTOBIOGRAPHICAL REALISM

To prise open the complex web of meanings that underpin how these interviewees made sense of their relationships with men who abused and financially exploited them requires adopting analytical protocols which permit analysis not simply of what the women say, but of how their stories become plausible, subjectively meaningful accounts. It requires calling into question the realism of the women's narratives. This is made possible by recent theoretical developments within the study of autobiography. Of especial importance is the critique of two traditional assumptions of autobiography: namely, that auto-biographies are simple representational mirrors of life-as-lived (Denzin, 1989) and that autobiographical description is a clear and translucent process wherein a central author (or self) has access to the unmediated, social reality of her or his life and has the ability to re-present that reality in a text (either written or spoken) which is, itself, a direct reflection of the selfhood of the author (Roos, 1994). As a result of these two critiques, autobiographies are not conceived of being more or less accurate presentations of an individual's life, but rather as 'illusions' generated by silent sets of meanings underpinning (cf. Derrida, 1972; Stanley, 1994) the individuals' explicit accounts of their lives. Treating the women's talk about their relationships with financially exploitative and abusive men as autobiographical events, subsequently, opens the theoretical space in which the analytical focus is not so much on the explicit details recounted by the interviewees, but rather on the sets of meanings implicit within their tales of poverty and violence that enable the explicit story to be plausible. Put more simply, suspending the notion that the women's stories directly reflect the 'pure' social reality of their lives shifts the analytical efforts away from distilling, from the stories, objective facts about the interviewees' relationships with men who take advantage of them towards inter-preting the web of meanings within which the story that they tell comes to be an understandable, coherent, rational account of staying involved with often violent, exploitative men. Thus, suspending the assumption of realism permits an examination which probes behind the explicit account (i.e. 'He's my boyfriend even though he takes my money and abuses me') and exposes the sets of meanings which allowed these women to *not* distinguish between ponces and boyfriends according to specific forms of behaviour.

The rest of this chapter is concerned with examining how it is that women talked about their relationships with men who took advantage of them, took their money and were often physically and sexually abusive towards them. There were three main ways in which the women made sense of their poncing relationships: (i) as business relationships; (ii) as loving relationships; and (iii) as victimizing relationships. It is important to note that the three characterizations that the interviewees invoked were not mutually exclusive. The women did not describe their relationships in 'either/or' terms. All 19 of the 21 women who talked about these types of relationships invoked at least two of the three descriptions, sometimes referring to different relationships, and occasionally referring to the same relationship.

Two articulations of the meanings for 'men', 'money' and 'violence' underpinned these three characterizations by providing the complex symbolic structure in which the same actions and behaviours take on different and contradictory meanings. First, there is a symbolic conflation of the meanings for men and money whereby involvement with men is defined as necessarily incurring a cost. In this instance, and as will be demonstrated below, involvement with men was understood by the respondents as incurring 'opportunity costs' (or a form of expense or payment that was paid in order that something else could be obtained, such as protection) and 'hidden costs' (or a form of expense or payment that was unknown at the time that cost-calculation was made). Secondly, there is an articulation of the meanings for men and money wherein involvement with men was understood by the interviewees as being risky because men were seen as predators preying on the women's ability to earn cash. In what follows, each of three characterizations is described and examined.

'YOU GOTTA HAVE SOME MAN TO WATCH YOU': PONCING AS A BUSINESS RELATIONSHIP

Approximately half of the women who experienced financial exploitation within their intimate relationships talked about such relationships as business arrangements. This construction was made possible, in part, by the contextualization of such relationships in relation to the dangers of working as a prostitute, especially the dangers related to street work. Of primary importance to this context was the reality of, and the women's beliefs about, the ever-present risks of punter violence, harassment and intimidation from potential ponces, hassle from street vigilante organizations and robbery or assault from other people inhabiting the same city streets that the women worked. Within such a context these women were able to use their involvement with men who financially exploited them to signify that they were working 'the right way' and that such relationships were simply 'good business sense'. Hence, Anna (aged 36) and Sammy (aged 18) remarked:

> The street's a dangerous place. If you're gonna be smart you have to have a man to protect ya and make sure no one kidnaps you or drives off with you – so what if you have to give him some money.
>
> (Anna, aged 36)

It's the done thing where I work. Every working girl has an old man – she needs one if she's going to do it properly. Ya need someone to watch out for ya 'coz there are too many creeps out there.

(Sammy, aged 18)

For these respondents the financial exploitation and violence they experienced within their intimate relationships was symbolically erased and transformed into a representation of their success as business-women. The following statements were typical.

I have worked with a ponce for most of the time I've worked, but there is girls that work without ponces. But the majority of them that don't – it's because they're that heavy on drugs that a ponce wouldn't touch them, because they wouldn't be getting anything if they did! (Andrea, aged 27)

You want your ponce to look good, man. You want them to dress good, get nice cars and wicked gold. You give them your money so they can look good. I look at it as good advertising, you know what I mean? [*Not really.*] Well, it's like this, if I were some stupid crackhead or something, I couldn't be earning the money I earn to make my man look good. (Katrina, aged 20)

Underpinning and making possible the interviewees' inscriptions of such relationships as business arrangements was a symbolic landscape in which there was a complete conflation between the meanings for men and money whereby involvement with men represented incurring 'opportunity costs' (i.e. payments made for the purpose of achieving something else). Involvement with men who ponced them was understood by the respondents as providing them with protection, but for a cost. The respondents talked about the necessity to make calculations about the type and quality of protection that these men could offer them in exchange for the financial exploitation (and possible violence) that they would have to submit themselves to.

After nearly four weeks of working in Greenvale, I got beat up really badly by a punter. I mean, when I walked in the house, me own kids didn't even recognize me and that's when I got a ponce. I started paying Carmichael. He would drive around checking on me – making sure I was all right, checking on me in the car.

(Helena, aged 35)

I'm not so frightened of him now [i.e. her previous ponce]. I got this new ponce to stand up for me and he has told him to fuck off and leave me alone. I have to pay him though.   (Diane, aged 37)

After Dagger got arrested for poncing me I paid Germaine. Germaine was somebody that was friends with Dagger but I paid him to watch us girls while we was out for a little extra protection like.   (Gail, aged 28)

The construction of involvement with financially exploitative men as generating costs was most clearly seen in the respondents' discussion of 'bad' ponces – i.e. men who had reputations for being 'nutters', 'psychos' and 'hard cases'. During these discussions the women emphasized that the opportunity costs were extremely high. In addition to subjecting themselves to financial exploitation the women also ran the risks of ponce-related violence and abuse. However, they constructed such 'opportunity costs' as worthwhile because they believed that the protection these men could offer them was, simply, the best protection money could buy. Hence, Barbara remarked:

There's a thing around here. Once they know who you're working for and what status he's got in Greenvale – like who's the baddest, who's the hardest, who's got the gun and who hasn't [pause]. You only have to mention 'X' [i.e. her ponce] and that was that. People would leave you alone. The other ponces and other girls would just leave you be. They wouldn't meddle. We had a whole street to ourselves [*Why?*] He's notorious! He's psychotic! He's one very sick, twisted individual. People are afraid of him.   (Barbara, aged 24)

Of course, the irony of these relationships was that, although the women inscribed their involvement with financially exploitative men as a form of 'opportunity cost', providing them with protection from the dangers of street prostitution, in reality these men provided them with little protection and in fact exposed them to further violence (and certainly further financial exploitation). Sammy (aged 18) remarked that the man she was involved with was never there when she 'was doing the business with punters' and so could not intervene in the case of trouble. Katrina (aged 20), later in her interview, went on to discuss the brutal violence that she experienced at the hands of the man she was involved with. Gail (aged 28) talked about how Germaine told Dagger (her ex-ponce who was after her for reporting him to the police) where she was, which resulted in Gail being brutally beaten, shot with an air rifle and stabbed. Hence, although the women inscribed involvement with these men as incurring 'opportunity costs' in their endeavours to protect themselves against prostitution-related violence, such protection was seldom a reality.

'I'M HELPING HIM OUT': PONCING AS A LOVING RELATIONSHIP

Fifteen of the 19 respondents who spoke of financially exploitative and abusive relationships also characterized and described them as loving relationships. Such a construction occurred in relation to the women's descriptions of themselves as 'loving women' making choices and taking courses of action based on the love they felt for the men with whom they were involved. However, unlike the previous representation of financially exploitative relationships as business arrangements, the representation of them as loving relationships was made possible only through denuding such relationships of their prostitution-related context.

Drawing on discourses in which intimate and romantic love as experienced by women is constituted as a sublimation of the women's desires (Person, 1988) and a concomitant centralizing of men's desires (Sayers, 1986), these prostitute-women talked about their willingness to sacrifice everything for their partner regardless of how they were treated by them. So, for example, when the interviewees who had been violently ponced were asked why they did not report these men to the police for the assaults they suffered, over half of them remarked 'because I loved him' (cf. Wilson, 1983: 92). Andrea (aged 27) recounted her experiences with Cain – a man who violently abused her for five years, forced her to work seven nights a week and allowed her to keep the money she earned from only one of those seven nights. Reflecting on this time in her life, Andrea (aged 27) commented.

> I don't suppose he really was a ponce. ... I think he's the only person I ever really loved. Even now I sometimes get upset over it, 'coz I did love him. I was willing to give him everything I'd got – body, soul, EVERYTHING! (Andrea, aged 27)

Structuring the women's description of financially exploitative relationships as loving relationships was a blurring of the symbolic meanings for 'love' and 'money'. Giving money to a particular man signified loving him. Ingrid (aged 44), Andrea (aged 27) and Georgie's (aged 35) comment on their relationships to illustrate this:

> He used to kill me. I mean I stayed for nine years and he was always beating on me, took all my money, but I stuck it out. [*Why?*] You do don't you. I think it's because you wanna be loved. [*What do you mean?*] Well, it's hard to put. Cutter made me feel good. I loved him and so I gave him my money.   (Ingrid, aged 44)

> I stayed with him but I had a right dog's life. [*Why?*] He was a very bad alcoholic and was a very bad heroin addict and I used to get battered. I worked because of him – I was keeping his drink habit and his cars and you know [pause]. I worked harder for him than anyone else I've been with. I was under more pressure then than all the fifteen years I've worked. I had to earn one hundred an fifty pounds every day for his habit. But I loved him, so I did it.   (Andrea, aged 27)

> You meet someone and they're the type of people that you like. ... You know, they talk very very nice to you and make you feel special, then before you know it, you fall for them, you work for them and you give them all your money because you've fallen for them.
>   (Georgie, aged 35)

Underpinning and sustaining the women's descriptions of their relationships with financially exploitative and abusive men as loving relationships was a further symbolic conflation of the meanings for men and money. Here, as before, involvement with men is understood to incur expense, but instead of incurring 'opportunity costs', involvement with men is understood as incurring 'hidden costs'. Or, to be more precise, involvement with men as partners was made sense of as having a cost attached which was unknown at the time of calculation (i.e. at the beginning of the relationships) but became clear as the relationships progressed. Two of the 21 respondents represented being involved and having intimate relationships with men as incurring the 'hidden cost' of *initial* entrance into prostitution – this cost was hidden because it emerged only after their relationships were established. Witness Margie, who claimed that she became involved with a man who 'asked her to do him a favour' and become a prostitute so that she could earn, and then give him the money she earned so that he could buy a new car. When reflecting on this, and on why she eventually agreed, Margie made the following comments.

He was a lot stronger in character than me and to be totally truthful out of anybody I'd ever seen, he was the only person I really did love and find attractive and fancy. I did it because I wanted to be with him. (Margie, aged 32)

In a similar fashion, Ruthie concisely summarized her initial engagement with prostitution as being a result of 'having the knickers charmed off' her. She met a man who later convinced her that he needed money.

I started going out with this guy – I fell for him ... but I suppose I fell for the wrong one. He put me on the game. [*What do you mean?*] Well, he charmed the knickers off me if you want the truth. He kept saying it was real easy and how I would really help him out 'coz he needed money for this, that and the other. I really liked him and the time we spent together. I wanted to stay with him and thought it would be no big deal to help him out for a while.
(Ruthie, aged 25)

In common with Ruthie's and Margie's characterization of their initial involvement in prostitution and their subsequent financial exploitation as being the 'hidden cost' of keeping their relationships, most of the other interviewees constructed the 'hidden costs' of their intimate relationships as being *continued* engagement in prostitution. Witness Anna:

There's a lot of pressure. You have to do it [i.e. prostitute] 'coz you need the money yourself. Then you get mixed up with someone and you have to do it again to help him, to keep a hold of him and because you love him. (Anna, aged 36)

It is very tempting to flatten these narratives, at this point, and treat the interviewees' talk about the 'hidden costs' of intimate relationships as though the women somehow 'misrecognized' the practices of financial exploitation that occurred within their relationships. In other words, it is tempting to reconstruct the women's narratives and *impose* an understanding of these relationships as being nothing less and nothing more than instances of financial exploitation and abuse. But the interviewees did not constitute these relationships as merely and only poncing relationships. These relationships, while marked by the practice of financial exploitation, were also constructed as intimate, loving relationships (cf. Hoigard and Finstad, 1992). As Andrea explains:

> A ponce is somebody that beats up a girl and says get on the corner and make the money. But I suppose that's not true. You meet a man. ... You're working and first of all you give them a tenner or whatever 'coz they're skint. And then you think 'Oh I love you' and you give fifty or a hundred pounds. And eventually ... you're having to raise a certain amount and you're keeping maybe five or ten pounds for yourself.   (Andrea, aged 27)

The following extract provides indications of how this simultaneous construction occurs, and in which intimate involvement with men becomes encoded as incurring 'hidden costs'.

> Roger – I classed him as my boyfriend. I mean he had all his clothes at mine and he had a jewellery shop so he was doing his own thing. But he still used to have a hundred pounds off me a day like. But I had strong feelings for him, although they weren't good enough really, 'coz no matter how hard I worked, or how much money I gave him, he still left me.   (Christine, aged 23)

This extract indicates that, within the context of an intimate relationship, the interviewees reconstructed the practice of financial exploitation and deployed it to signify the value that they placed on their relationships. To put it more clearly, the women believed that giving their partners the money they earned through prostitution demonstrated the depth of their feelings for these men, and the esteem and value they assigned to these relationships.

'I COULDN'T DO ANYTHING, I WAS HIS VICTIM':
PONCING AS A VICTIMIZING RELATIONSHIP

In this construction of the respondents' financially exploitative relationships, the women's inscription of the men they were involved with as both partners *and* ponces is most apparent. Fourteen women characterized their financially exploitative relationships as victimizing and abusive relationships, which can be seen in the ways in which: first, the respondents believed that their financially exploitative ponces were able to determine everything about the their lives and, secondly, where the prostitute-women implicitly situated themselves as passive agents who quiescently accepted the injurious and harmful actions of others.

> [After a particularly heated argument with her boyfriend] Minnie said to me 'Oh he's mad, he's gonna kill you.' And he come back and kicked in the door. He was going mad. And then he went and took Minnie home. He came back about 1:00 a.m. ... He was being all friendly and all of a sudden, he just clicked and battered me. My nose was all cracked and bleeding and I had two black eyes. I left for a few days and he took me telly, me jewellery, the video [*Why?*] Thought he owned it. Suppose I left him and so all my assets were his. (Christine, aged 23)

> At that point I'd had enough. I went to him and he said 'You're going back on the streets.' I said 'No.' He said 'You will if I tell you to. If I want, you know you gotta go.' I said 'Well I'll report you.' And that was that, that was the final straw. He just started slapping, slap, slap, slap on me head and me earrings shot out. He stormed off and I went back to the streets to get his money. (Margie, aged 32)

> I ain't got no personal life. My life is COMPLETELY ruled by Fabulous. (Katrina, aged 21)

Indeed, the belief in the ability of their financially exploitative partners to control their lives was so strong that six women commented that they were completely unable to change the nature of their relationships, or even leave them.

> At the end of the day we're all gonna get thrown away with nothing. We're gonna be disrespected. Nobody's gonna want us. But we got no choice. (Katrina, aged 21)

> When I had a ponce – I had no choice about what I did, I was completely controlled by him. [*Did you report him to the police?*] No. [*Why not?*] I couldn't. I was completely controlled by him. (Anna, aged 36)

It was mentioned in the previous section on poncing as loving that many women claimed that the reason they did not report their financially exploitative and abusive partners to the police was because 'they loved them' – a rationale made possible through the conflation of meanings for love and money. But within the construction of their poncing relationships as victimizing/abusive relationships, eight women (and in four cases the same women who inscribed their relationships as loving relationships) asserted that they did not report their partner-ponces to the police because of fear.

[*Why didn't you just stop giving him the money and stop seeing him?*] 'Coz he'd kill me. He'd beat the hell out of me. I know that. You just know it at the back of your mind. It's easier to just do what he wants.   (Margie, aged 32)

He put me on the game. [*Why didn't you say no?*] Well, it's not just him. He's got a BIG family. When I say BIG – you mess with one and you mess with a lot of them. I'd have ended up dead and I'm not into that!   (Katrina, aged 21)

[*Why didn't you go to the police about him?*] 'Coz I've felt his punches. Anyway, it doesn't matter if I did, 'coz wherever I go he'd hunt me down.   (Sammy, aged 18)

So strong was these women's fear of reprisal that many of them spoke about their fear of being murdered by the men they were involved with.

I've told friends and it been like 'Well, why on earth don't you run?' It's easier said than done when you've got a gun in your head and you do as you're told. I mean, I didn't know at the time that it had got a blocked barrel. You just do as you're told, otherwise you're dead.   (Barbara, aged 23)

He [i.e. her ponce] kept me for a while. Then he said I had to work seven days a week. ... The final straw was when he decided he could get more money by getting me to do anal sex on the street. I thought 'There's no way!' but I couldn't do anything. I just kept thinking 'He's going to kill me' and then I couldn't do anything.   (Lois, aged 21)

It is not surprising that these respondents feared reprisals from their ponces given that the prostitute-women also recounted numerous episodes of brutality, violence, sexual assault, etc. However, it is my contention that, in addition to describing some of the realities of their everyday existence with violent men, in these statements the respondents are constituting those relationships as victimizing brutal relationships, through locating themselves as passive victims, unable to effectively resist their partners' violence or financial exploitation.

Making possible the construction of their financially exploitative relationships as abusive and victimizing relationships was a particular articulation of meanings for men and money in which men represented risk and danger and money signified the object conditioning women's vulnerability to men's dangerousness. Once again, men are defined in relation to money. However, rather than as in the previous conflation of men with expense (in the form of 'opportunity costs' or 'hidden costs'), in this categorization men are constituted as dangerous predators of women's money. Hence, men are defined as posing specific threats to the respondents' material and social security by preying on the women in order to achieve their own financial security through using tactics such as violence and intimidation to achieve such exploitation.

Interestingly, the articulation of meanings wherein involvement with men signified riskiness and danger, because men were defined as preying upon prostitute women's money, is best seen in the women's discussions of their partners. Examining how the women talked about their partners also demonstrates the way in which these women were able to symbolically transform their intimate relationships into, specifically, poncing, abusive and victimizing relationships and their partners into being, also, ponces.

Partners were encoded by the interviewees as suspect men who could not be trusted in that they were constituted as men who might become ponces. This particular construction occurred in relation to the prevalence of financial exploitation within the institutional setting that the respondents worked in (i.e. from the streets, saunas, parlours and their own homes) and, more importantly, in relation to joint economies and modalities of living in which women help to economically support their partners. Hence, more than half of the women spoke about boyfriends with uncertainty. Witness the following:

> You gotta watch having boyfriends 'coz they'll ponce ya if you're not careful. In the end you think, boyfriend, ponce, boyfriend, ponce, what's the difference? If they aren't one to start, they'll be one in the end. (Barbara, aged 24)

I didn't mind giving him money. I mean we were together, but then he started expecting it off me. That's when I knew it, that when I knew he'd become a ponce.   (Christine, aged 23)

If you had a boyfriend and he found out about you working, he'd start taking your money off you, because they start off very sly without you even realising it.   (Georgie, aged 35)

In contrast to the essentialized inscription of imaginary ponces (as outlined at the beginning of this chapter), the respondents believed that boyfriends became ponces because of the women's engagement in prostitution. More precisely, many of the women (particularly those with extensive experience of financially exploitative relationships) believed that they turned their boyfriends into ponces by being willing to share their money.

The father of my second child was good – oh I loved him. But I know it sounds crazy, but I turned him into a ponce. [*How did that happen?*] 'Coz when I was with him, I started spoiling him 'coz I had all this money and we were getting on great and, um, he only had to mention that he wanted this or that and he got it. 'Coz I had the money he got it. But then he got lazy and that's when the beatings started. He'd become a ponce and it was my fault.
                    (Ruthie, aged 25)

Well, to tell you the truth, it was my fault that he turned into my ponce. I'd give him money. I mean, he started to get violent 'coz he started to want more and he was spending all my money on drink and drugs. I completely changed him.   (Michelle, aged 33)

Everyone's really down on ponces, but you know, all they are is a greedy boyfriend. Women make men into ponces – it's not the opposite way round! You start giving your boyfriend money and eventually, there's never actually any say so, eventually you're having to raise a certain amount and you're keeping less and less for yourself.   (Andrea, aged 23)

These extracts have two interesting features. First, they are informed by discourses of femininity in which women are placed as being ultimately responsible for the ways in which their intimate relationships develop and progress. In this respect the women situated themselves as being responsible for the transformation of their intimate relationships into poncing relationships and the change of their boyfriends into their ponces.

Secondly, there is an implicit (and fluid) line of demarcation between boyfriends and ponces that the women drew in their talk about 'boyfriends-as-suspect'. Boyfriends became ponces, the women indicated, when they 'got greedy'. To put it another way, for the interviewees the difference between boyfriends and ponces did not reside in the economic nature of the relationship, because the women inscribed all intimate relationships as being marked by the exchange of money (and not necessarily an egalitarian sharing of the total economic resources of the couple). Instead, the difference was whether or not the men were believed by the respondents to be taking more money from the women than they felt the men were due. This is seen in Janet's statement.

> I met Freddy and he was all right. He was supposed to be some bad ponce, but he was my boyfriend really. 'Coz, see, I didn't mind giving him my money. He weren't greedy or nothing. He'd take me out to restaurants, he'd bring me out to work and he'd dress me. He always made sure I had a few bob in my pocket. I felt for all that he did, he was due some money. So he was my boyfriend and not my ponce. (Janet, aged 37)

Janet deployed a characterization of Freddy as not being 'greedy' in order to demonstrate that he was her boyfriend and not her ponce. Hence, and in consequence, boyfriends were defined as suspect and not to be trusted in relation to the already-existing economic exchanges marking the women's intimate relationships.

Having argued that the interviewees drew a line of demarcation between partners and ponces, it must be noted that this line was ultimately collapsed. The symbolic landscape wherein involvement with men was understood as being risky, because men were seen as being dangerous, constituted partners as suspect and untrustworthy because they might become ponces. Thus, if all men the women had relationships with (i.e. partners) are constructed as being also (potentially) ponces, then there is no line of demarcation between partners and ponces. To be even more specific, unlike previous academic constructions wherein there was a line of demarcation drawn between ponces and partners and/or where one category was collapsed into the other (see above), the respondents were able to recognize their intimate relationships as *also* abusive, victimizing, exploitative poncing relationships because, at the symbolic level, there was no distinction between ponces and partners. Ponces were also partners; partners were also ponces. Hence, on one level, involvement in prostitution was signified by these women as a trap from which they could not escape. A trap constituted by both (i) the reality and the risk of the ponce's physical, often brutal retaliations and the poverty that was the result of being ponced, and (ii) the belief that poncing was inevitable and inescapable because all partners were also ponces.

CONCLUDING THOUGHTS: EXPLOITATION, VIOLENCE AND RESISTANCE

The main argument of this chapter was outlined at the beginning, and for that reason I will not be summarizing it here, beyond noting that, by deconstructing prostitute-women's talk about their financially exploitative and occasionally violent relationships, it can be seen that the line of demarcation that may exist between ponces, poncing and boyfriends and intimate relationships was drawn not in terms of whether these men extorted money under threat of violence, but rather at the symbolic level. Hence, the symbolic landscape which constituted involvement with men as being an expense (in the form of 'opportunity costs') permitted these women to describe their financially exploitative relationships as business relationships. Moreover, a structure of meaning whereby involvement with men is understood to incur 'hidden costs', and where there exists a symbolic conflation between the meanings for love and money, permitted the respondents to describe and encode the practices of financial exploitation as being a demonstration of love, in that giving up their money, and not reporting the violences they suffered, signified the value they placed on their intimate relationship. Similarly, a symbolic landscape in which men are defined as dangerous predators permitted the women to describe and encode the practices of poncing as acts of abuse and victimization.

What also becomes apparent is that the practice of financial exploitation accompanied by threats, violence, intimidation and coercion has no single, clear, translucent meaning. Rather, it becomes meaningful in different, and occasionally contradictory, ways. This, in turn, calls into question the notion that violence (and indeed exploitation) can be conceptualized and defined in terms of specified forms of behaviour. Hence, it is asserted that there is nothing self-evident about ponces, poncing or violence.

One of the implications of such an argument is that just as violence, exploitation, ponces and poncing are all constructed and made possible within unique and specific articulations of meanings, so too is resistance. Put simply, the way in which the realities of financial exploitation and violence are made sense of and constructed by those who experience them directly impacts upon their consequent actions. If prostitute-women make sense of the reality of violence and financial exploitation in a manner in which such reality is symbolically transformed into examples of their love and devotion for their partners, or their business success, then the notion of resistance to that reality is, at best, incongruent and problematic and, at worst, irrelevant. If, however, the same sets of behaviours are made sense of in terms of being part of an abusive relationship in which the women locate themselves as victims, then a space is opened in which the women can locate themselves, oppositionally, as survivors and resist the victimization they suffer. For these reasons alone I have not discussed the women's resistance within these relationships. Each construction presupposes an entirely separate and distinct set of responses, resistances and reactions. It is my contention that, before resistance can be examined, it is necessary to analyse violence and exploitation in terms of how they become meaningful and are made sense of by the individuals who experience them.

ACKNOWLEDGEMENTS

I acknowledge the research studentship grant given by the Economic and Social Research Council that provided the monies for me to undertake the wider research project that this chapter draws on. Most especially I thank Pat Carlen, whose advice and comments have always been insightful, inspirational and helpful.

NOTE

1.   The terms 'ponce', 'poncing' and 'pimp', 'pimping' are often used interchangeably. The interviewees in this study used the term 'ponce' and, thus, that is the term I have adopted. However, when discussing other people's work I use the term that they adopt.

REFERENCES

Alexander, P. (1988) 'Prostitution: a Difficult Issue for Feminists', in F. Delacosta and P. Alexander (eds), *Sex Work* (London: Virago).

Barry, K. (1979) *Female Sexual Slavery* (London: New York University Press).

Barry, K. (1995) *Prostitution of Sexuality* (London: New York University Press).

Denzin, N. (1989) *Interpretive Biography: Qualitative Research Methods*, vol. 17 (London: Sage).

Derrida, J. (1972) *Positions* (London: Athlone Press).

Dunhill, C. (ed.) (1988) *The Boys in Blue: Women's Challenge to the Police* (London: Virago).

Faugier, J. and Sargeant, M. (1997) 'Boyfriends, 'Pimps' and Clients', in G. Scambler and A. Scambler (eds), *Rethinking Prostitution: Purchasing Sex in the 1990s* (London: Routledge).

Hoigard, C. and Finstad, L. (1992) *Backstreets: Prostitution, Money and Love* (Cambridge: Polity).

Katz, J. (1988) *The Seductions of Crime: Moral and Sensual Attraction of Doing Evil* (New York: Basic Books).

Kersten, J. (1996) 'Culture, Masculinities and Violence Against Women', *British Journal of Criminology*, 36(3), pp. 381–95.

McKeganey, N. and Barnard, M. (1996) *Sex Work on the Streets* (Milton Keynes: Open University Press).

McLeod, E. (1982) *Women Working: Prostitution Now* (Beckenham: Croom-Helm).

O'Neill, M. (1996) 'Researching Prostitution and Violence: Towards a Feminist Praxis', in M. Hester, L. Kelly and J. Radford (eds), *Women, Violence and Male Power* (Buckingham: Open University Press).

O'Neill, M. (1997) 'Prostitute Women Now', in G. Scambler and A. Scambler (eds), *Rethinking Prostitution: Purchasing Sex in the 1990s* (London: Routledge).

Person, E. (1988) *Dreams of Love and Fateful Encounters: The Power of Romantic Passion* (New York: Norton).

Pheterson, G. (1993) 'The Whore Stigma: Female Dishonour and Male Unworthiness', *Social Text*, No. 37.

Phoenix, J. (1995) 'Prostitution: Problematizing the Definition', in M. Maynard and J. Purvis (eds), *(Hetero)Sexual Politics* (London: Taylor & Francis).

Phoenix, J. (1999) *Making Sense of Prostitution* (Basingstoke: Macmillan).

Rook, P. and Ward, R. (1997) *On Sexual Offences: Criminal Law Library* (London: Sweet & Maxwell).

Roos, J. (1994) 'The True Life Revisited: Autobiography and Referentiality after the "Posts"', *Auto/Biography*, 3(1/2).

Sayers, J. (1986) *Sexual Contradictions: Psychology, Psychoanalysis and Feminism* (London: Tavistock).

Scambler, G. (1997) 'Conspicuous and Inconspicuous Sex Work: the Neglect of the Ordinary and Mundane', in G. Scambler and A. Scambler (eds), *Rethinking Prostitution: Purchasing Sex in the 1990s* (London: Routledge).

Scambler, G. and Scambler, A. (eds) (1997) *Rethinking Prostitution: Purchasing Sex in the 1990s* (London: Routledge).

Segal, L. (1990) *Slow Motion: Changing Masculinities, Changing Men* (London: Virago).

Stanley, L. (1994) 'Introduction: Lives and Works and Auto/biographical Occasions', *Auto/Biography*, 3(1/2).

Wilson, E. (1983) *What is to be Done about Violence Against Women?* (Harmondsworth: Penguin).

Index